KNOWING CHRIST IN THE CHALLENGE OF HERESY

A Christology of the Cults
A Christology of the Bible

Steven Tsoukalas

University Press of America,® Inc.
Lanham • New York • Oxford

Copyright © 1999 by
University Press of America,® Inc.
4720 Boston Way
Lanham, Maryland 20706

12 Hid's Copse Rd.
Cumnor Hill, Oxford OX2 9JJ

Library of Congress Cataloging-in-Publication Data

Tsoukalas, Steven
Knowing Christ in the challenge of heresy : a christology of the
cults, a christology of the Bible / Steven Tsoukalas.
p.   cm.
Includes bibliographical references and indexes.
l. Jesus Christ—Divinity—Biblical teaching. 2. Heresies,
Christian—History. 3. Bible. N.T.—Theology. I. Title.
BT216.T76 1999   232—dc21   98-53447 CIP

ISBN 0-7618-1331-4 (pbk: alk. ppr.)

∞™ The paper used in this publication meets the minimum
requirements of American National Standard for Information
Sciences—Permanence of Paper for Printed Library Materials,
ANSI Z39.48—1984

In loving memory of my mother, Olga Tsoukalas,
and for His glory.

Contents

Preface

This book and its theme did not arise out of a vacuum. I stand on the shoulders of competent scholars whose contribution to my learning has been enormous. Two in particular stand out, Robert L. Reymond and Harold O. J. Brown. Professor Reymond's *Jesus, Divine Messiah* is a solid exegetical work on the person of Christ. Professor Brown's *Heresies* examines the Church's struggle with christological heresies throughout the centuries, and its answers to these challenges. Both books contributed to the sharpening of my Christology, making me aware of the minute, yet eternally important, details of exegetical and historical christological study.

Neither book, however, focuses on the christological challenges of modern-day cults. As a result, their exegetical and christological conclusions do not specifically address the heresies of modern-day cults. This book does.

In each section the first occurrence of a Greek and Hebrew word or phrase will be spelled in Greek and Hebrew *and* transliterated. If repeated, only transliteration will be given. For the most part, when reference is made to a specific text, Greek and Hebrew words will be accented as they appear in the text, not lexically. Greek and Hebrew is transliterated according to the system used in *The New American Standard Exhaustive Concordance of the Bible: Hebrew-Aramaic and Greek Dictionaries* (Nashville, Tenn.: Holman, 1981). Sanskrit is transliterated according to the guide found in Stephen Schuhmacher and Gert Woerner, eds., *The Encyclopedia of Eastern Philosophy and Religion* (Boston, Mass.: Shambala Publications, Inc., 1989), xiii. Arabic is transliterated according to the entries contained in Cyril Glassé, *The Concise Encyclopedia of Islam* (New York: HarperCollins, 1989), with the exception of "Allah," which is transliterated as it appears here.

All Scripture quotations, unless otherwise noted, are taken from the *New American Standard Bible,* The Lockman Foundation, La Habra, CA, 1975.

I wish to thank University Press of America for publishing this work. I thank as well all those who support my ministry. Without them I would not have had the time to accomplish this project. Finally, I thank Paul Parisi for his time and effort toward the setting and printing of this manuscript.

Those desiring to contact me may write to Sound Doctrine Ministries, P.O. Box 1962, Exeter, NH 03833, USA.

Introduction

"Error, indeed, is never set forth in its naked deformity, lest, being thus exposed, it should at once be detected. But it is craftily decked out in an attractive dress, so as, by its outward form, to make it appear to the inexperienced (ridiculous as the expression may seem) more true than the truth itself."—Irenaeus, Against Heresies

God uses heresy. At first glance this is a frightening statement. What could this possibly mean? Simply that in the history of His Church, God has always allowed heresy to challenge the Church. As a result of these challenges, the Church was forced to better understand its faith, and to put this understanding in writing. This is evident in the historic creeds of orthodoxy. For example, the councils of Nicaea (325) and Chalcedon (451) were convened in part to settle issues concerning the deity of Christ and the relationship of the two natures of Christ, respectively. Going back further in time, Irenaeus, the disciple of Polycarp (who was a disciple of the apostle John), wrote his famous *Against Heresies* toward the end of the second century. In it he countered the theologies of various gnostic sects, showing them to be theologically incompatible with the teachings of the apostles, and philosophically flawed. And although these creeds and Irenaeus' work were written *primarily* to correct the heresies of their ages, history has proven that the Christian Church has been blessed and matured as a result of these works.

The situation can be the same today, and it is the theme of this book. Because of the challenges of modern heresies, God's people can come to know better the Scriptures and Him to whom they testify. To this end I have documented the errors of certain groups regarding the person and work of Christ, and answer these errors with a biblical, exegetical treatise on the person and work of Christ.

Orthodoxy And Heresy

To pronounce something as heresy is to presuppose some sort of absolute standard, orthodoxy. As Harold O. J. Brown points out, heresy presupposes orthodoxy.[1] In other words, without orthodoxy we cannot know what heresy is.

What Do These Words Mean?

Orthodoxy comes from the Greek words *orthōs* (ὀρθῶς, "upright," "straight," fig. "correct," "true"[2]) and *doxa* (δόξα, "honor," "glory"). It means *giving right honor to God*.[3] Thus, orthodoxy refers to Christian teaching that gives right honor to God.

Heresy comes from the Greek word *hairesis* (αἵρεσις). The meaning of this term varies significantly according to time period and context.[4] In the time during which the New Testament was written, it came to mean *false teaching*.

---

[1]Harold O. J. Brown, *Heresies: The Image of Christ in the Mirror of Heresy from the Apostles to the Present* (Grand Rapids, Mich.: Baker Book House, 1984), 4.

[2]See Walter Bauer, William Arndt and F. Wilbur Gingrich, *A Greek-English Lexicon of the New Testament and Other Early Christian Literature* (Chicago and London: The University of Chicago Press, 1979), 580.

[3]See Brown, *Heresies,* 1.

[4]These meanings vary from "seizure," "choice," "effort directed to a goal" (classical Greek), to "party" or "sect" ("the heresy [sect] of the Essenes," as Josephus relates in *Antiquities,* XIII.5.9). In the book of Acts we read of "the heresy [sect] of the Sadducees" (5:17) and "the heresy [sect] of the Pharisees" (15:5). The term was also used in the context of disfavor. The apostle Paul apparently took objection to the term when he stated, "according to the Way which they call a sect I do serve the God of our fathers" (Acts 24:14). Paul also uses the word in connection with factions or schisms that arose in the church at Corinth (1 Cor. 11:19). See G. W. Bromiley in *The International Standard*

Peter, Paul, John, and Heresy

The apostle Peter uses the term in its most serious tone when he states, "But false prophets also arose among the people, just as there will also be false teachers among you, who will secretly introduce destructive heresies, even denying the Master who bought them, bringing swift destruction upon themselves" (2 Pet. 2:1). Obviously the heresies Peter mentions have the capability of destroying the exclusive claims of the Gospel, and thus the very identity of the Christian Church.

Paul battled the false teaching of the Judaizers. Though he did not use the term "heresy" in his letter to the Galatians, he warned them that if anyone were to preach another gospel that was contrary to the one that was preached to the Galatians, that one was accursed (1:8, 9). Paul referred to the Judaizers as "false brothers" (2:4). Likewise the Jewish/Greek false teaching that plagued the church at Colossae moved Paul to write his apologetic[5] letter to the Colossians, who could be infected by the "empty deception" (Col. 2:8) of false teachers. And John, in his first and second epistles, was most likely contesting incipient Gnosticism.[6]

Bible Encyclopedia, 4 vols. (Grand Rapids, Mich.: Wm. B. Eerdmans Publishing Co., 1982), 2:684-86.

[5]By apologetic I mean defense. Christian apologetics is the science of the systematic defense of the Christian Faith in response to attacks. The word comes from the Greek noun *apologia* (ἀπολογία, "defense") and the Greek verb *apologeomai* (ἀπολογέομαι, "I defend myself; I make a defense"). The noun is used in 1 Peter 3:15 and Philippians 1:16.

[6]See chap. 1, n. 23, for a definition of Gnosticism. Some gnostic sects believed in the real separation of Jesus and the Christ. Jesus was simply a man, and the Christ was a heavenly aeon that either rested upon or dwelt in the man Jesus. Further, disdain of the material world was characteristic of Gnosticism. John's statements in 1 John 2:22 ("who is the liar but the one who denies that Jesus is the Christ") and 4:2 ("every spirit that confesses that Jesus Christ has come in the flesh is from God") lend favor to the view that the "most likely" reason he wrote his first two epistles was to combat incipient Gnosticism. I use the term "incipient" here because there is no evidence that *full-blown* Gnosticism was flourishing in the first century. Several theological ingredients that make up the well developed Gnosticism of the second century and on are missing in the first century. For defense that there is no evidence for fully developed Gnosticism in the first century (challenging the conclusion that

He as well did not use the term "heresy" in his epistles, but his intent is clear, using such labels as "liar" and "antichrist" (1 John 2:22).[7] Peter, Paul and John took seriously their Lord's words in Matthew 7:15: "Beware of the false prophets, who come to you in sheep's clothing, but inwardly are ravenous wolves."

Heresy and The Early Church

Moving on to some of the early Church theologians, Ignatius of Antioch (ca. 110) uses the term "heresy": "I therefore, yet not I, but the love of Jesus Christ, entreat you that ye use Christian nourishment only, and abstain from herbage of a different kind; I mean heresy."[8] In his *Epistle to the Ephesians,* Ignatius encourages Christians to continue in their good walk with God, that no heresy would have any dwelling place among them.[9] Moving up one century we find Hippolytus (170-236), a disciple of Irenaeus, who wrote *The Refutation of All Heresies.*[10] In it he states, "After we have, not with violence, burst through the labyrinth of heresies, but have unraveled (their intricacies)...by the force of truth, we approach the demonstration of truth *itself*."[11]

Christianity developed out of Gnosticism, and that Jesus' death was merely *another* expression of the gnostic Redeemer myth), see E. M. Yamauchi, *Pre-Christian Gnosticism* (Grand Rapids, Mich.: Wm. B. Eerdmans Publishing Co., 1973). Also, see Yamauchi's articles, "Some Alleged Evidences for Pre-Christian Gnosticism," *New Dimensions in New Testament Study,* ed. R. N. Longenecker and M. C. Tenney (Grand Rapids, Mich.: Zondervan, 1974), 46-70, and "Pre-Christian Gnosticism in the Nag-Hammadi Texts?" *Church History* 48 (1979): 129-41.

[7]The Bible sternly warns against false teaching. See, for example, Lev. 19:31; 20:6; Deut. 13:1-5; 18:9-14; Isa. 8:19-20; Matt. 23; 2 Cor. 11:3, 4, 13-15; Gal. 1:6-8; Col. 1:15-20; 2:9; 2 Thess. 1:8-9; 1 Tim. 1:6-7, 19-20; 2 Tim. 2:17-18; 2 Pet. 2:1; 1 John 2:22; 4:1-3.

[8]*To the Trallians,* 6:1. See Alexander Roberts and James Donaldson, eds., *The Ante-Nicene Fathers,* 9 vols. (Grand Rapids, Mich.: Wm. B. Eerdmans, reprinted, August 1977), 1:68.

[9]6:7. See *The Ante-Nicene Fathers,* 1:52.

[10]It is disputed whether Hippolytus wrote this treatise. See *The Ante-Nicene Fathers,* 5:3-7, and p. 9, n. 1.

[11]*The Refutation of All Heresies,* X.1.1. See *The Ante-Nicene Fathers,* 5:140, parenthetical insertion and emphasis original. More titles of works from

Then there is the traditional story of the apostle John, who, going to bathe at a public bath-house in Ephesus and noticing that the heretic Cerinthus was there, "rushed out of the bath-house without bathing, exclaiming, 'Let us fly, lest even the bath-house fall down, because Cerinthus, the enemy of the truth, is within.'"[12] And Polycarp, the disciple of John, when meeting the heretic Marcion, was asked by Marcion if he knew him. Polycarp replied, "I do know thee, the first-born of Satan."[13] Irenaeus, who relates both these stories to us, follows these accounts with the statement, "Such was the horror which the apostles and their disciples had against holding even verbal communication with any corrupters of the truth."[14]

What Heresy Can Do

Earlier I mentioned a positive side to heresy: God moves His Church to better understand the Scriptures. But there is a negative side to heresy. Two examples shall suffice. I know of a professing Christian church that consistently allows to preach and teach in its pulpit one who denies that Christ is the only way of salvation. Leadership of the church has assured the congregation that this is not false doctrine. This

---

early Church theologians evidence the ongoing battle with heresy. Irenaeus' *Against Heresies* (ca. 180), Tertullian's *Against Marcion* (207), *Against the Valentinians* (no earlier than 207), and *Against Hermogenes* (ibid.), are just a few works testifying that the Church took heresy seriously, and fought against corruption of the truth.

[12]Irenaeus, *Against Heresies*, III.3.4. See *The Ante-Nicene Fathers*, 1:416. Irenaeus was a disciple of Polycarp, the disciple of John. Irenaeus received this story from Polycarp. Cerinthus separated the man Jesus from what he called the heavenly Christ. Consequently for Cerinthus, Jesus was not the Christ. Jesus was merely a man upon whom the heavenly Christ rested when He was baptized; when He was crucified the Christ left Him. This led John to write, "Who is the liar but the one who denies that Jesus is the Christ? This is the antichrist, the one who denies the Father and the Son" (1 John 2:22). Also, "This is the one who came by water and blood, Jesus Christ; not with the water only, but with the water and the blood" (1 John 5:6).

[13]Ibid. Marcion adhered to Gnosticism and is best remembered for his teaching that the God of Abraham was not the true and living God, but a demiurge (an inferior deity) who was responsible for the creation of this world, which is base and defiled.

[14]Ibid.

of course calls into question the leadership's view of the essential nature of the uniqueness of Christ. And not many years ago I visited a church one Sunday evening because it rented out its sanctuary to a Spiritualist church. I witnessed firsthand a medium, in the pulpit of this church, contacting the spirit world through the occult practices of clairvoyance and clairaudience.[15] The negative implications of these examples are serious. In both cases people in the two host churches were led to believe that error is truth. Further, those teaching false doctrine were not challenged with the truth of orthodoxy.

Another negative side to heresy is that it has the potential to take away the very life of the Church and to threaten its unity. Indeed, this is exactly what happened with the first church mentioned above. In its desire to have unity with heresy, it ended up in disunity; some members left because the uniqueness of Christ was compromised. Here the issue involved Christology (the study of the person and work of Christ). Christianity's very identity rests upon Jesus Christ, His teachings, and the teachings of the apostles regarding Him. Indeed, the very event of His incarnation (see later in this introduction for a definition of "incarnate") provides for Christianity the basis for its exclusive claims. Jesus is called God's unique Son (John 1:14[16]), and thus God's *only* way of salvation for all humanity (John 14:6). If He is God's unique Son, then He provides the self-disclosure of God in a unique way that cannot be duplicated by any other figure in history. But what if someone were to come along and teach that there are other paths to God, and that Jesus is only one of them? If this heresy is held by the Church, it not only denies the claims of Christ Himself, but in its denial ceases to be Christian!

The claim that Christ is the only way for the salvation of humanity springs from His person. He is fully God and fully human. Because of His deity He is able to save all who call upon Him, and because of His humanity He is able to provide the sacrifice that the justice and holiness of God require for humanity.[17] This doctrine of Christ as fully God and

---

[15]Meaning "clear seeing" and "clear hearing," respectively. Through the practices of clairvoyance and clairaudience the medium is able to see and hear spirits, and then to relay these spirits' messages to the congregation.

[16]More on John 1:14 in chap. 4.

[17]Harold O. J. Brown writes "that for Christian theology, the great promise of salvation depends on both the deity and humanity of Christ. Unless he is God, he cannot be capable of redeeming humanity, but unless he is also man,

fully man, if denied, undercuts the very heart of the Gospel. No person and no individual church can be Christ's if this denial is held.

Why Is Christology So Important?

Does it really matter what a person thinks of Christ? Must we concern ourselves with the matter of *who* and *what* Jesus is? The witness of Scripture leaves no other option but to say yes.

In John 8:58 Jesus makes the claim, "before Abraham was born, I AM." Several observations arise from this verse. First is the striking use of the Greek phrase *egō eimi* (ἐγὼ εἰμί, "I AM") in the Greek text. Here Jesus claims for Himself that which only Yahweh (the LORD) rightly claimed for Himself. For this reason Jesus' audience immediately picked up stones to stone Him to death (v. 59), for they interpreted His statement as blasphemy of "the Name" (Lev. 24:16).

Second, John intends that his readers *understand* this reaction of the Jews. Levitical law requires death for those who blaspheme "the Name," and John stresses that *egō eimi* would prompt such a reaction. Simply put, Jesus is claiming identity with "the Name." John is employing the LXX[18] usage of *egō eimi* regarding God, making clear to his readers that Christ indeed claimed to be God the Son. For example, Deuteronomy 32:39a translates in the LXX: "Behold! Behold that I am [*egō eimi*; Heb. *ani hu*, אֲנִי הוּא], and before Me there is no God."[19] Likewise Isaiah 43:10 translates: "You are my witnesses, and I am a witness, says the Lord God; and my servant whom I have chosen, in order that you may know, and may believe, and may understand that I am [*egō eimi*; Heb. *ani hu*]. Before Me no other God came into existence, and after Me there will be none."[20] Other Old Testament

---

there is no reason why the merit of his work should be applied to humanity" (*Heresies,* 188).

[18] Also known as the Septuagint. This is the translation of the Hebrew Old Testament into Greek. In the third century B. C., Greek-speaking Jews (the conquest of Alexander the Great was the direct cause of this) were in need of an Old Testament translation in their language. Thus, as tradition has it, seventy (LXX) scholars began in the third century a translation of the Old Testament into Greek.

[19] My translation.

[20] Ibid.

citations may be given,[21] but these shall suffice in the meantime to show that Christ was claiming to be God.

Third, in John 8:58 Jesus is making a distinction between His *eternal* existence and Abraham's (and consequently the rest of humanity's) *finite* existence. Just as John opened his Gospel with the declaration of the Word (Gr. *logos*) always existing as God (John 1:1c), and contrasting that with the created order which *came into being* (John 1:3), Jesus does the same in John 8:58. Before Abraham *came into existence,* Jesus *always was existing.*[22] All the above present the full force of the "I AM" statement in John 8:58, and set the stage for the final part of the answer to the question, "Does it really matter what a person thinks of Christ?"

In John 8:24b Jesus states, "unless you believe *that I am* [Gr. *hoti egō eimi,* ὅτι ἐγώ εἰμι], you will die in your sins."[23] The phrase "that I am" comes directly from the two LXX passages mentioned above, Deuteronomy 32:39 and Isaiah 43:10. In these two passages the LORD is warning Israel not to follow the idols that their sinful natures concoct. Prior to the song of Moses (which comprises all of Deut. 32), Moses states that Israel will turn from the LORD (Deut. 31:29). By stating "Behold! Behold *that I am* [*hoti egō eimi*]," Yahweh is calling what will be a corrupt people to repentance. In Isaiah 43:10 the nation of Israel has already fallen into deep corruption by turning to empty idols. It is in this context that Yahweh states through Isaiah, "know *that I am* [*hoti egō eimi*]."

In John 8:24, Jesus is confronting the very descendants of that nation of Israel who were long ago addressed by Moses and Isaiah. He, now being Yahweh in the flesh, states the same warning He gave through His prophets long ago. Now the warning is direct, coming from the LORD who now stands in their presence: "unless you believe that I am, you will die in your sins." The context of this warning comes to descendants of Israel, namely the Pharisees, who were in the process of denying who Christ was. This denial was outright, as they witnessed His marvelous deeds and heard firsthand His claims.

---

[21] I shall examine John 8:58 in chap. 2, where other *egō eimi* statements in the LXX will be listed.

[22] The force of the present tense (*egō eimi,* "I am"). The present tense signals continuous action. Jesus always, continuously, existed in the past.

[23] My translation.

Moving to an application of this passage to our current situation, anyone *knowingly* denying who Christ claimed to be will die in their sins if they do not repent. Jesus also tells us by implication that faith in Him is to involve content, and that content *must* be biblical. One must have a correct definition of who Jesus is. Paul implies the same as he warns the Christians at Corinth: "For if one comes and preaches another Jesus whom we have not preached... you bear *this* beautifully" (2 Cor. 11:4). Paul was aware that there were counterfeit Christs.

Likewise, today there are counterfeit Christs. Modern heresies as they are expressed by pseudo-Christian cults (soon to be defined) bring to us non-biblical views of Christ. They bring to us "another Jesus" that the apostles never preached. The challenges they present to the Christian Church are damnable, as we have seen. They also have the potential to threaten the very existence of Christianity. Since I will be using the word "cult" from here on, I shall now define the term.

What Is a Cult?

The word *cult* means *a group* of people. In this sense it becomes a neutral term, and there is nothing negative or positive about it. From a Christian theological perspective (there are other perspectives from which to define the word, such as the psychological and the social) we now want to find out what a group (cult) of people teaches and believes regarding four essential areas: God,[24] humanity, sin and salvation.[25] If

---

[24]Involved here is, of course, the person and work of Christ.

[25]Perhaps the reader can think of some cults that are orthodox in some of these areas, and heretical in others. Here I suggest that the most important area is who God is. Reasons for this have been given in the preceding pages. Also, we must watch for the *implications* of theological statements that affect *other* areas of essential Christian doctrine. For example, the Roman Catholic opinion of Mary as "co-mediator" with Christ has heretical implications. First, there is *one* mediator between God and humanity, the man Christ Jesus (1 Tim. 2:5). Further, Paul immediately follows this statement with the identification of the work of this one mediator, stating, "who gave himself as a ransom for all..." (v. 6). The point here is that there is an inextricable link between Christ's mediatorship and His work on the cross. The two go hand in hand; He is mediator because He gave Himself, and He gave Himself *as* the mediator. It is heretical (if not blasphemous), therefore, that Mary (no doubt the greatest of all women) be given this title. Second, Jesus our great high priest (mediator) is just that because of *who* He is. In Hebrews, where He is given this title (see chaps.

the group's teaching in these four areas strays from Christian orthodoxy and is heretical, that group may either be *pseudo*-Christian or *non*-Christian. A cult is pseudo-Christian if it claims to be Christian,[26] and non-Christian if it does not claim to be Christian.[27] The modifiers

---

3, 5, 7), He as God the Son (1: 3, 8) is alone worthy to bear it (see 7:24, and the *result* of His priesthood in 7:25). True, Roman Catholicism affirms this, so it ascribes the above title to Mary with the understanding (as dogma) that Mary, *under* Jesus, is said to be both "mediatrix" (Austin Flannery, gen. ed., *Vatican Council II*, 2 vols. [Northport, N.Y.: Costello Publishing Co., revised 1988], 1:419) and "the mediatrix of graces" (Ronald Lawler, Donald W. Wuerl and Thomas Comerford Lawler, eds., *The Teaching of Christ: A Catholic Catechism for Adults* [Huntington, Ind.: Our Sunday Visitor, Inc., 2nd edition, 1983], 229). Therefore, Roman Catholic's say, Mary in no way competes with the centrality of Christ as the one mediator between God and humanity. I would argue, however, (1) that such teaching is not found in the Bible, and (2) that the titles "mediatrix" and "co-mediatrix" should not be used in any way, given the inextricable link between Christ's work and the title of mediator. Moreover, though the Roman Catholic Church emphasizes on the one hand that Mary's mediatorial role in no way competes with that of Christ's, on the other hand we find such statements as, "She who took part in His redeeming labors as His mother and as sharer of His sorrows participates as mediatrix in His will to bestow salvation upon all" (ibid., 227), and, "But while in the most Blessed Virgin the Church has already reached that perfection whereby she exists without spot or wrinkle (cf. Eph. 5:27), the faithful still strive to conquer sin and increase in holiness. And so they turn their eyes to Mary who shines forth to the whole community of the elect as the model of virtues.... and when she is the subject of preaching and worship she prompts the faithful to come to her Son..." (Flannery, *Vatican Council II*, 1:420). When we add to this the teaching that Mary has been bestowed the title of "Queen over all things" (ibid., 1:418), we must come to the conclusion that Mary is seen as *much more* than simply a mediator "in the sense that all Christians are" when asked to pray for someone.

[26]Such as Jehovah's Witnesses, The Church of Jesus Christ of Latter-day Saints (Mormons), Christian Science, The Unity School of Christianity, Religious Science, The Way International, The Unification Church (Moonies, though they dislike this term), and some New Age cults.

[27]Such as Scientology, Baha'i Faith, Freemasonry, Hinduism, Islam, Judaism, Buddhism, Wicca, Satanism, and some New Age cults. Here a few comments are necessary. First, the reader may wonder about the use of the terms "cult" and "occult." Occult is a practice, and a cult is a group. Thus, Satanism and Wicca are non-Christian cults that practice the occult. Second, some make a distinction between a cult and a world religion, and may take issue with my placing Hinduism, Judaism, Islam and Buddhism in the category

pseudo and *non* are the distinguishing marks, not the term *cult*, as it simply means *group*. In this book I shall use the term "cult" in reference to either Pseudo- or non-Christian groups.[28]

A final note: More often than not, one's doctrine of God affects one's doctrine of sin, humanity, and salvation. For example, if one holds the New Age Movement teaching that all is God (pantheism), the remaining three areas follow in heresy. If all is God, humanity is therefore God. If all is God and humanity is God, how could humanity be sinful in the biblical sense of the term? If all is God, and humanity is God and not sinful, why would there be a need for salvation in the biblical sense of that term?

A biblical concept of God is mandatory if we are to understand who we really are and what we really need. Moreover, knowing who God truly is must involve knowing who Christ is, since Christ is God the Son, second person of the Godhead.[29]

Christological Heresies and the Cults

As mentioned earlier, the apostle Paul warns of another Jesus (2 Cor. 11:4). The Lord Jesus Christ also warns His disciples to watch out for false prophets, who come to them in sheep's clothing, but inwardly

---

of non-Christian cults. But given that "cult" means "group" and that these religions are in fact *non*-Christian, my categorization is logical. Further, I have found that the distinction between cults and world religions is confusing. If by "world religion" one means that adherents are all over the world, are not the Jehovah's Witnesses and the Mormons all over the world? If, for example, a world religion is so labeled because of its ancient origin, *why* is this so? And why, then, is it called a *world* religion?

[28]Technically we have a third type of cult (group), and that is the *Christian* cult. This comprises the group of people all over the world who trust in the biblical Christ for their salvation, and who hold to the other essential areas of the Christian faith, i.e., the Trinity, the virgin birth, the bodily resurrection of Christ, salvation by grace through faith, Christ as the only way of salvation, etc. As was mentioned above, the term *cult* is not the core of the issue, as it simply means *group*. The core of the issue is the *modifier* placed before the term.

[29]It is theologically fallacious to believe that those who reject the biblical Christ and call God by some other designation are worshipping the God of the Bible, the true and living God. God is Father, Son, and Holy Spirit. Thus any person's definition of God that excludes the Son (and the Spirit) as God in the biblical sense results in that person's denial of the true and living God.

they are savage wolves (Matt. 7:15). Christ then states that His
disciples shall know the false prophets by their fruits (Matt. 7:16). Later
in the Gospel of Matthew He further warns, "many will come in My
name, saying, 'I am the Christ,' and will mislead many" (24:5).

We gather implicitly from these verses that false teachers and false
Christs often use the same language Christians use; they use the same
terminology (see Matt. 7:21-23[30]).[31] Keep in mind, however, that the
definitions are different. Take, for example, the following confessional
testimony: "I believe in God the eternal Father, in Jesus Christ His Son
and my Savior, and in the Holy Ghost. I believe in the doctrine of the
Trinity. I believe Jesus shed His blood for my sins. I have been born
again through faith in Jesus Christ, and I am a missionary for the
Gospel of Jesus Christ." That was a testimony of a Mormon! As we
shall see later, though this testimony *sounds* like the testimony of a
Christian, it most certainly is not *once the terms are defined.*

All of the pseudo-Christian cults confess Christ to some degree.
They affirm belief in Jesus Christ.[32] Some pseudo-Christian cults even
utilize the terms "Jesus Christ," "Christ," "Christian," and
"Christianity" in the name of their organizations. Cults like "The First
Church of Christ, Scientist" (Christian Science), "The Church of Jesus
Christ of Latter-day Saints" (Mormons), and the "Unity School of
Christianity" are a few examples. Yet, every pseudo- and non-Christian
group in the world always ends up denying explicitly or implicitly[33] the

---

[30]"Not everyone who says to Me, 'Lord, Lord,' will enter the kingdom of
heaven; but he who does the will of My Father who is in Heaven. Many will
say to Me on that day, 'Lord, Lord, did we not prophesy in Your name, and in
Your name cast out demons, and in Your name perform many miracles?' And
then I will declare to them, 'I never knew you; Depart from Me, you who
practice lawlessness.'"

[31]Interesting is Irenaeus' observation of the heretics in his *Against
Heresies.* Speaking of the heretics, he states that "their language resembles
ours" (I.1.2; see *The Ante-Nicene Fathers,* 1:315). Compare this with Christ's
warning in Matt. 7:15.

[32]They may also affirm the virgin birth, the resurrection of Jesus, and the
Trinity.

[33]Keep in mind that cults can also be identified as heretical not so much by
what they state, but by what they do not state. A hypothetical example is, "We
believe Jesus Christ is fully human." Such a statement is identical with
Christian orthodoxy, but is only half the picture. The statement does not affirm
Christ's deity.

eternal, unique deity of Jesus Christ. The only group that affirms Christ's deity both explicitly and implicitly is the Christian group.

Why do I use the phrase, "the eternal, unique deity of Jesus Christ"? Use *only* the phrase "deity of Jesus Christ," and ask a New Age adherent, "Do you believe in the deity of Jesus?" The reply would be positive. The new ager believes that Jesus was God. *But,* he also believes *he* (the new ager) is God. Thus the New Age Jesus is not unique. If we ask the Mormon the same question, she will reply in the same manner: "Yes, Jesus is God." For the Mormon, however, Jesus is God only for *this* world, *and* His deity is not eternal in the sense of *always* being God the Son from the eternal past to the eternal future. His deity is eternal only in the sense of His *becoming* a god at a certain time in the past, and *since then* He has and will continue eternally as a god.

In using the phrase "eternal, unique deity of Jesus Christ," we are biblical[34] and careful.[35] Jesus Christ is the *unique* Son of God, and God the Son (John 1:1, 14). This therefore excludes all others from their claim that they are Christs, that they are god-men (as Jesus prophesied would occur; see Matt. 24:5, 24). Jesus is the only one in human history that is truly God's Son.[36] Jesus is *eternally* God as well, as John 1:1 and 8:58 teach.

Before concluding this introduction, definitions of three key words are in order.

Incarnate

"Incarnate" comes from the Latin *in* (in) and *caro* (flesh). The event of the incarnation of Christ, therefore, refers to the time when the

---

[34]By the unique deity of Jesus Christ I do not mean to exclude the Father and the Spirit from rank as God. I am simply distinguishing Christ from all self-proclaimed god-men. This will become clear as I proceed in the body of the text above.

[35]Employing the phrase, "the unique, eternal deity of Jesus Christ," is an example of how a statement is biblical, but not found in the Bible in its exact wording. I have developed the phrase because it guards against heresy. This same practice is seen in the historic creeds, especially those of Nicaea (325) and Chalcedon (451).

[36]I shall examine John 1:14 and the Greek word *monogenēs* ("only begotten," "unique") in chap. 4.

eternal *logos* as fully God united with Himself a full human nature in the womb of the Virgin Mary by the direct agency of the Holy Spirit (see John 1:1, 14; Matt. 1:18, 20). As a result of the incarnation, Christian orthodoxy speaks of the *two natures* of Christ (deity and humanity, and each nature is possessed by Christ in its fullness) in the *one person* of Christ.

Ontological and Functional

"Ontological" comes from the Greek word *ontōs* (ὄντως, "really," "being") and *logos* ("discourse"). For our purpose the term indicates *having to do with the nature or essence of someone or something.* "Functional" simply *has to do with the function of someone or something.* "Billy is a human being" is an ontological statement, for it describes the *nature* of someone named Billy. "Billy drove his car to the market and purchased groceries" is a functional statement, for it describes two *functions* of Billy.

These terms will be used in reference to Christ's person and work.[37] In John 1:1, for example, the phrase "the Word was God" is an ontological statement; it expresses something about the *nature* or *essence* of Christ.[38] It expresses that the Son shares in "ontological oneness" with the Father, that they are of the same nature. Yet, with John 14:28 ("the Father is *greater* than I") the word "greater" does not

---

[37]Robert L. Reymond, in his *Jesus, Divine Messiah: The New Testament Witness* (Phillipsburg, N. J.: Presbyterian and Reformed Publishing Co., 1990), 11-12, states that Cullmann (and others) objects to the ontological and functional categories in classical Christology. Such categories, Cullmann argues, find no warrant in Scripture. He states that the New Testament was concerned with Christ in functional terms, i.e., what He *does,* rather than in ontological language, i.e., who He *is* (See Oscar Cullmann, *The Christology of the New Testament,* trans. Shirley C. Guthrie and Charles A. M. Hall [London: SCM Press, 1959], 3-4). Reymond objects to this, stating that the charge of blasphemy by the Jews against Jesus was on *ontological* grounds (see John 5:17-18; 8:58-59; 10:33; 19:7). I agree with Reymond.

[38]This is not to say that the phrase is *completely* void of all functional connotation, for *being* God implies *functioning* as God as well (and vice versa). In John 1:1 I would say that the *thrust* of the phrase is to indicate nature or essence.

lessen Christ's very nature as God (it is not an ontological statement), but has to do with function.[39]

I shall also argue throughout that what Christ *does* (functionally) implies who He *is* (ontologically),[40] just as what Billy did (drove to the market to buy groceries) implies who he is (a human being). For example, in Mark 2:5-7 Jesus forgives sin, which is obviously a divine prerogative. He forgives sin, and since only God can forgive sin, Christ's function of forgiving implies that He is ontologically, intrinsically, deity. If you have never explored in the Gospels Christ's words and actions in order to see in them claims to deity, you will be astonished at your discovery! It was the Son of God, the Son of Man, who made statements only Yahweh could make. It was the Son of God, the Son of Man, who did only what Yahweh could do.

---

[39]The Jehovah's Witnesses and other cults completely miss this distinction, assuming that the *functional* implications of Jesus' statement in John 14:28 therefore have negative *ontological* ramifications regarding the claim that He is God. They assume that Jesus cannot be equal with the Father because Jesus says that the Father is greater than He is. They fail to see the distinction between nature and function. To use an analogy, a supervisor and an employee are ontologically equal because they are both *human.* Yet, the supervisor is greater than the employee *by virtue of function.* The Gospel of John supports this distinction, for the Father and the Son can be equal in nature (as John 1:1 and 5:18 teach), and at the same time the Son can state that the Father is greater than He is (John 14:28).

The Jehovah's Witnesses also cite 1 Cor. 15:28, where the Son will be "subject" to the Father at the consummation of the ages. They, again, see Christ's subjection to the Father as having negative ontological implications. But the above holds true here as well. Moreover, if being subject to someone means that one is not the same in nature (ontologically different) as that someone (as the Jehovah's Witnesses claim for 1 Cor. 15:28), then Jesus was not a human being, for Luke 2:51 states that Jesus went home with His parents and continued to be subject to them. Jehovah's Witnesses, however, would never admit that!

[40]There is no contradiction here with my observations regarding John 14:28 in the previous note. That is to say, because Jesus says that "the Father is greater than I," this does not mean that Jesus is therefore not God the Son. Is a human son *not* human because his human father is greater than he is? No, because a function of this *human* son is obedience to his *human* Father. Jesus states that "the Father is greater than I" (functionally) because a function of God the Son is to be obedient to God the Father. In this case the functional implies the ontological as well!

Conclusion

When we enter into dialogue with people involved in cults, we must first be well grounded in what we believe as Christians, and *why* we believe it. Then we must strive to understand the theology and arguments of the cultist. As God by His grace trains us for this task, we will without doubt be better equipped to forge the apologetic of a biblical Christology against the heresies of modern cults. As we go through this process in this book, I hope that the reader may know Christ better, as was the case with myself. I was challenged by heresy to formulate my understanding of Christ. As I searched the Scriptures to answer attacks, something much more than mere refutation occurred. I worshipped Him more adoringly. I grew to love Him more as I read about Him and studied the biblical passages. In the Scriptures we find the riches of the depths of Christ and His mercy. May God grant us the privilege of knowing Christ in the challenge of heresy.

Chapter 1

Heresy and the Pre-existent Deity of Christ

"Jesus was a created spirit being.... Neither the angels nor Jesus had existed before their creation."—Jehovah's Witnesses, Should You Believe in the Trinity?

"If Christ in the beginning created the heavens and the earth, he must be from eternity; for then he is before the beginning, by which must be meant, the beginning of time."—Jonathan Edwards, Concerning the Deity of Christ

This chapter documents heresies pertaining to a specific area of christological study, the deity of Christ *before* the incarnation. We begin first, though, with a brief Christian affirmation of the doctrine.

Christian Doctrine Explained

Christian orthodoxy affirms that Christ existed from all eternity as the *logos* (the Word, see John 1:1), and that the *logos*, Himself the second person of the Godhead, eternally was with the Father (and the Holy Spirit) in perfect unity. The *logos* is by nature deity, as He shares in the same nature as the Father.[1] The phrase "pre-existence" has as its reference point the incarnation. That is to say, the pre-existence of Christ means that He existed prior to the incarnation. Likewise, the phrase "pre-existent deity of Christ" means he existed eternally as God the Son prior to the incarnation. Denials of the orthodox position now follow.

Jehovah's Witnesses

Jehovah's Witnesses are in some sense the modern successors of an ancient heretic known as Arius of Alexandria. Early in the fourth century, Arius, a theologian from Alexandria, Egypt, challenged the doctrine of the deity of Christ. He "taught that Christ, while the creator of the world, was himself a creature of God, therefore not truly divine."[2] Arius himself stated that Jesus "has nothing proper to God in proper subsistence. For He is not equal, no, nor one in essence with Him."[3] He saw Jesus as the first of creatures, directly created by God out of nothing.

In Jehovah's Witness Christology, Jesus was the first and only direct creation of Jehovah (the Father). He is the *created logos* of John 1:1, not God but "a god." After Jehovah directly created Jesus, He created all *other* things *through* Him. Jesus is the "only begotten god,"[4] but not truly God; a divine being, but not of the *same* substance as God.[5] Like Arius, the Jehovah's Witnesses cite biblical texts such as

---

[1] The reader may have questions regarding the Trinity. See Appendix 2.

[2] Philip Schaff, *History of the Christian Church*, 8 vols. (Grand Rapids, Mich.: Wm. B. Eerdmans Publishing Co., reprinted, June 1984), 3:620.

[3] Quoted in Athanasius, *Councils of Ariminum and Seleucia*, part 2, section 15. See Philip Schaff and Henry Wace, *The Nicene and Post Nicene Fathers*, second series, 14 vols. (Grand Rapids, Mich.: Wm. B. Eerdmans, reprinted, August 1975), 4:457.

[4] Here the Jehovah's Witnesses follow the best manuscript evidence (some manuscripts have the Gr. *huios* [υἱός], "Son," rather than *theos* [θεός], "God"), as did Arius, but translate the phrase using a lower-case "g" ("only begotten god") and refer the reader back to their translation of John 1:1c, "the Word was a god."

[5] Arius denied that Christ was of the *same* substance (Gr. *homoousios*) as the Father, opting instead for a *different* substance (*heteroousios*). The middle position between the two, sometimes called semi-Arianism, views Christ as being of *like* substance (*homoiousios*). A great issue (if not *the* greatest) before,

Colossians 1:15 ("*firstborn* of all creation") and John 14:28 ("the Father is *greater* than I") to support their view that the Son was the first created being and is inferior in nature to the Father. Finally, Jehovah's Witnesses believe that Jesus in His prehuman existence was Michael the Archangel:

> In his prehuman existence Jesus was called "the Word." (Joh 1:1) He also had the personal name Michael.... "In the beginning the Word was, and the Word was with God, and the Word was a god. This one was in the beginning with God." Since Jehovah is eternal and had no beginning (Ps 90:2; Re 15:3), the Word's being with God from "the beginning" must here refer to the beginning of Jehovah's creative works. This is confirmed by other texts identifying Jesus as "the firstborn of all creation," "the beginning of the creation by God." (Col 1:15; Re 1:1; 3:14) Thus the Scriptures identify the Word (Jesus in his prehuman existence) as God's first creation, his firstborn Son.... Jesus' existence as a spirit creature began thousands of millions of years prior to the creation of the first human. The firstborn Son was used by his Father in the creation of all other things (Joh 1:3; Col 1:16, 17).... The Son's share in the creative works, however, did not make him a co-Creator with his Father[6].... the Son was the agent or instrumentality through whom Jehovah, the Creator, worked.[7]

Thus, Jehovah's Witnesses deny the pre-existent deity of Christ, teaching instead that in His pre-existence He was a created archangel.

---

during, and after the council of Nicaea was whether the Son was of the same substance as the Father, or of a different substance. Nicaea affirmed the orthodox *homoousios* over the Arian *heteroousios.*

[6]This, it seems, is unlike Arius.

[7]No authors or editors listed, *Insight on the Scriptures,* 2 vols. (New York: Watchtower Bible and Tract Society of New York, Inc., 1988), 2:394, 52. For at least the last 50 years all Watchtower publications have had no authors listed by name. In June of 1991 I visited the headquarters of the Watchtower Bible and Tract Society in Brooklyn, New York. I introduced myself and asked that I speak to one or more of the authors of their materials, and/or one of the persons responsible for the Jehovah's Witness translation of the Bible, the *New World Translation of the Holy Scriptures.* My reasons for doing so were to discuss either the Watchtower publication *Should You Believe in the Trinity?,* or several passages in their translation that rob Christ of His deity (especially John 1:1). I was approached 15 minutes later by a man from the Watchtower's writing department, who informed me that the authors and/or translators want to remain anonymous. That was virtually the end of the discussion.

Mormonism

In order to begin to unravel Mormon Christology, one must first understand the Mormon doctrine of "Eternal Progression." As it pertains to all who are now gods,[8] or those yet to become gods,[9] there is a progression involved that consists of several stages. These stages are *Intelligence, Spirit Child, Enfleshment,* and (ideally) *Godhood.*

Intelligence refers to what Mormon apostle Bruce R. McConkie calls "spirit element."[10] Spirit element is eternal, as matter is eternal, according to Mormon cosmology.[11] *Spirit children* were then formed from this eternal substance via the procreative acts of heavenly Father (Elohim) and heavenly Mother (name unknown),[12] a god and a goddess

---

[8]Mormonism is polytheistic, believing in the existence of a countless number of gods in the universe. Included in this number are the Father, the Son, and the Holy Ghost, who are three separate gods, though one in purpose. This is the Mormon definition of the Trinity.

[9]Mormonism teaches that men and women, if worthy, may progress to become gods and goddesses and produce spirit children. These spirit children then take on flesh and live on certain planets. Eventually these children, if worthy, will become gods and goddesses and populate their own planets with their own spirit children, and so on, and so on. The tenth president of the Mormon Church, Joseph Fielding Smith, stated that this process "will go on forever. We will become gods and have jurisdiction over worlds, and these worlds will be peopled by our own offspring. We will have an endless eternity for this" (Joseph Fielding Smith, *Doctrines of Salvation,* 2 vols. [Salt Lake City, Utah: Bookcraft, 1955], 2:48).

[10]Bruce R. McConkie, *Mormon Doctrine* (Salt Lake City, Utah: Bookcraft, 1979), 387.

[11]See *Doctrines of the Gospel: Student Manual* (Salt Lake City, Utah: The Church of Jesus Christ of Latter-day Saints, 1986), 13, 17, though on page 17 this source uses the phrase *"spirit and element,* which exist co-eternally with Himself [God]."* God is said to have *"organized* the earth, and all it contains" (ibid., both emphases added) from this eternal matter.

[12]In the Mormon Church's *Church News* (Salt Lake City, Utah: Deseret News Publishing Co.), then first counselor in the First Presidency (as I write this he is now the Prophet of the Mormon Church), Gordon B. Hinckley, stated that "logic and reason would certainly suggest that if we have a Father in Heaven, we have a Mother in Heaven" (October 5, 1991, p. 3).

with bodies of flesh and bones.[13] As *Doctrines of the Gospel: Student Manual* explains, "Matter always did and, therefore, always will exist, and the spirits of men as well as their bodies were created out of matter."[14] *Enfleshment* simply means that these pre-existent spirit children came to earth to take on bodies of flesh via the procreative process of earthly parents. *Godhood* is the ideal state for humanity. According to Mormon doctrine, certain people will reach their fullest potential if they become Mormons, are married in a Mormon temple, and take part in other ceremonies performed in the temple.[15] If they continue to be worthy, they will become gods and goddesses in the afterlife.

All who become gods and goddesses will receive their own planets and populate these planets with their own spirit children. To do so, they must pass through the process of eternal progression. Thus, in Mormonism, the gods did not exist from all ages past *as gods.* Rather, they *progressed* to godhood. [16]

With Christ, however, the situation is strangely different as to *when* He became a god. Mormon theology places the *attainment* of the rank of godhood by Christ in the pre-existent state of spirit child: "He is the Firstborn [of spirit children] of the Father. By obedience and devotion

---

[13]See *Doctrine and Covenants* (Salt Lake City, Utah: The Church of Jesus Christ of Latter-day Saints, 1982), 130:22, concerning the Father having a body of flesh and bones.

[14]Pg. 13.

[15]Those who do not become gods and goddesses may still be saved. There is in Mormonism a general salvation for all humanity except the "sons of perdition." These include Satan and his angels, and apostate temple Mormons. Though general salvation does not necessarily mean godhood, there are other levels of heaven reserved for those who are not Mormons, and for those who are Mormons but who have not been through the temple.

[16]"God Himself was once as we are now and is an exalted man" (the Mormon prophet Joseph Smith quoted in *Doctrines of the Gospel: Student Manual,* 7). *Achieving a Celestial Marriage* (Salt Lake City, Utah: The Church of Jesus Christ of Latter-day Saints, 1992), 132, contains this summary statement: "Our Father in Heaven was once a man as we are now, capable of physical death. By obedience to eternal gospel principles, he progressed from one stage of life to another until he attained the state that we call exaltation or godhood. In such a condition, he and our mother in heaven were empowered to give birth to spirit children whose potential was equal to that of their heavenly parents. We are those spirit children."

to the truth he attained that pinnacle of intelligence which ranked him as a God, as the Lord Omnipotent, while yet in his pre-existent state."[17]

Mormonism still does not escape the charge that the Mormon Jesus was not *always* God.[18] With Mormon Christology, Christ *attained* the rank of godhood. He was not God prior to becoming the firstborn[19] spirit child of a resurrected god and goddess. Thus, the eternal deity of Christ in the biblical sense is denied in Mormonism.

Christian Science[20]

The christological speculations of Mary Baker Eddy[21] and Christian Science antedate those of Arius! Anyone involved in exegeting the Johannine corpus has had to deal with the well known first century heretic Cerinthus.

Cerinthus very well could be the reason why John wrote his first and second epistles. He separated Jesus from the Christ, teaching that the latter was a heavenly aeon that came upon Jesus at His baptism, but left Him at His crucifixion. Consequently, this heresy was condemned by John (1 John 2:22) as a denial not only of the incarnation, but of Jesus' pre-existence as the eternal Son of God.[22] The view that Christ is some heavenly intermediary or aeon, and that Jesus is a revelator of this

---

[17]*Doctrines of the Gospel: Student Manual*, 10. See McConkie, *Mormon Doctrine*, 129.

[18]I have talked with several Mormons who try to escape this christological dilemma by stating that Christ was *potentially* or *prophetically* a god (or God). This, however, does not answer the problem. The problem remains that the Mormon Jesus was not always God.

[19]Here the Mormons quote Col. 1:15.

[20]I include here all other Mind Science cults, including Religious Science and Unity School of Christianity. They all teach a separation of Jesus from the Christ (see above) and thus are identical christologically with Christian Science.

[21]Mary Baker Eddy founded (Christian Scientists would use the term "restored") Christian Science in the latter part of the nineteenth century.

[22]This on the basis of John's statement in his first epistle: "every spirit that confesses that Jesus Christ has come in the flesh is from God" (1 John 4:2). That Jesus Christ *has come* in the flesh is evidence of John's belief in the pre-existence of the Son.

cosmic entity, is part of the gnostic Christologies of the second and third centuries as well.[23]

In like fashion Christian Science separates *Jesus* from the *Christ*.[24] A glance at the glossary of terms in Christian Science's main textbook, *Science and Health with Key to the Scriptures*,[25] reveals that Jesus is not the Christ. Jesus is "the highest human corporeal concept of the divine idea" and Christ is "the divine manifestation of God, which comes to the flesh to destroy incarnate error."[26] Thus, Jesus (who only *seemed* to be flesh[27]) had this "Christ" in Him, as all others do. Mary Baker Eddy writes, "The spiritual Christ was infallible; Jesus, as material manhood, was not Christ."[28] Thus, the "Christ" is in reality *not* Jesus, for in Christian Science the Christ is an eternal principle. *It* was

---

[23]Gnosticism, from the Gr. *gnōsis* (γνῶσις, knowledge), was very diverse in this time period. Also, its cosmogony and anthropology were quite complicated. We may, nonetheless, bring out some ingredients common in most if not all gnostic systems. First was a "spirit versus matter" dualism. Here the spirit realm revealed truth, and the material world was viewed as base and defiled. Second, the material world was birthed due to some cosmic tragedy when the True God, the *plērōma* (Gr. πλήρωμα, "fullness"), dispersed aeons or angelic intermediaries. Third, one of these intermediaries was the "Christ," and this is the main reason for the distinction between Jesus and Christ in gnostic systems. Much more information may be obtained by reading Kurt Rudolph's *Gnosis: The Nature and History of Gnosticism* (San Francisco: Harper & Row, 1987).

[24]Mary Baker Eddy's theology was also influenced by Hinduism. Early editions of *Science and Health* contain references to and from the *Bhagavad Gītā*. One may argue that Christian Science's Christ is akin to the divine soul, the *ātman Brahman*, in various Hindu philosophies, and therefore much the same as the New Age Movement's Christ. I agree that this is the logical conclusion. The case here is strong, and, given the pantheism of Christian Science (which it does not admit), is irrefutable. Christian Science, however, refrains (illogically) from *direct* statements that its Christ is God, therefore making it, on its own terms, different from the New Age Movement.

[25]By Mary Baker Eddy (Boston: The First Church of Christ, Scientist, 1971), 579-99.

[26]Pgs. 589, 583.

[27]We shall examine Christian Science's denial of the material world in chaps. 3 and 8.

[28]Mary Baker Eddy, *Miscellaneous Writings* (Boston: The First Church of Christ, Scientist, 1953), 84.

Jesus' "spiritual selfhood."[29] Finally, the "eternal Christ" is that spiritual emanation that comes to humanity to destroy error.[30]

Concerning Jesus as God the Son, we find that Christian Science's Jesus is not identified with the one who in the beginning was with God the Father and was Himself deity (John 1:1): "Jesus Christ is not God, as Jesus himself declared, but is the Son of God."[31] If He is not God, He never was God. Christian Science thus denies the eternal and pre-existent deity of Jesus.[32]

The New Age Movement

This vast movement has within it thousands of individual cults, all sharing a common christological theme (though because of its vastness there are variations within the theme). New Age Christologies share with Christian Science the gnostic view of separating Jesus from the Christ. The New Age Movement generally sees Jesus as a man from Nazareth who had no pre-existence eternally and uniquely as God the Son. Rather, the *Christ,* this cosmic quality, energy and expression of the divine,[33] incarnated itself in Jesus of Nazareth.[34] For the New Age Movement, the Christ may be eternal, as *it* has been called "the soul of the universe,"[35] but *it* should by no means be considered the eternal *logos* in the biblical sense. Further, if for the New Age Movement *Jesus* existed in the past, it was not as the eternal *logos* but rather someone else. Edgar Cayce, who is erroneously seen by some as a Christian, was asked, "Please give the important incarnations of Jesus in the world's history." He answered, "In the beginning as Amilius, as Adam, as

[29]*Science and Health,* 38.

[30]*Error* is the belief in matter as real. It has other nuances of meaning as well. See *Science and Health,* 472.

[31]*Science and Health,* 361.

[32]Because of (1) Christian Scientist's separation of *Jesus* and *Christ,* and (2) their belief that *Christ* existed long before Jesus did, we must be careful to refer specifically to *Jesus* when making statements about His deity.

[33]See David Spangler, *Reflections on the Christ* (Moray, Scotland: Findhorn Publications, 1981), 13.

[34]See ibid., 14.

[35]Ibid., 21.

Melchizedek, as Zend, as Ur, as Asaph, as Jeshua—Joseph—(Joshua)—Jesus."[36]

Baha'i

The Baha'i Faith is really a heresy of Islam that began in Persia in 1844 when Mirza Ali-Muhammad ("the Bab," lit. "the gate") announced that a soon-coming messenger of God would reveal himself to the world. In 1863 Baha'u'llah claimed to be that messenger.[37] Baha'u'llah is viewed by Baha'is to be the greatest of all the Nine Great Manifestations of deity, one of which was Jesus[38] (Krishna, Buddha, Muhammad are also numbered among the Nine Manifestations).

The Baha'i denial of the pre-existent deity of Christ follows:

> All that is mentioned of the Manifestations and Dawning-places of God signifies the divine reflection, and not a descent into the conditions of existence.... For God to descend into the conditions of existence would be the greatest of imperfections.[39]

Confusion might result when Baha'is affirm that Jesus is the pre-existent Word of God.[40] But by this phrase Baha'i Christology does not affirm Jesus in His preincarnate existence as God the Son, second person of the Trinity. Rather, to Baha'is the "Word of God" is an *impersonal* collection of the *divine perfections* of Christ:

> Before appearing in the human form, the Word of God was in the utmost sanctity and glory, existing in perfect beauty and splendor in the height of *its* magnificence.[41]

---

[36]Jeffrey Furst, ed., *Edgar Cayce's Story of Jesus* (New York: Berkley Books, 1968), 39-40.

[37]See Laura Clifford Barney, coll. and trans., *Some Answered Questions: Abdul-Baha* (Wilmette, Ill: Baha'i Publishing Trust, 1981), xi.

[38]Ibid., 149-50.

[39]Ibid., 113. What Baha'is mean by "divine reflection" is that all of the nine great Manifestations, which are analogous to perfectly polished mirrors, merely reflect the sun (God), they are not the sun themselves.

[40]See Barney, *Some Answered Questions: Abdul-Baha*, 116.

[41]Ibid., 116-117, emphasis added.

Therefore, the Word and the Holy Spirit, which signify the perfections of God, are the divine appearance.... The perfections of Christ are called the Word.[42]

Baha'u'llah is also called the Word of God in this sense.[43]

The Way International

Victor Paul Wierwille (founder) denies the eternal pre-existent deity of Christ. Consider the title of a book written by Wierwille, *Jesus Christ Is Not God*.[44] In it he asserts that the *logos* was merely a *thought* in the mind of the Father. He explains John 1:1: "How was Jesus with God in the beginning? In the same way that the written Word was with Him, namely, in God's foreknowledge."[45] Speaking of John 8:58, where Christ says, "Before Abraham was, I AM," Wierwille states that "Christ was with God in His foreknowledge before Abraham was born."[46]

The Unification Church

Sun Myung Moon's Unification Church also has no place for Christ as pre-existent deity:

Jesus, as a person who was fulfilling the Purpose of the Creation, was the ideal person God had envisioned before the Creation was created. In this sense, Jesus existed from the beginning. Some try to identify Jesus with God on the basis of the quote in John 8:58, in which Jesus said, '...before Abraham was, I am.' But Jesus didn't mean that he was God.[47]

---

[42]Ibid., 206.

[43]See George Townshend, *Christ and Baha'u'llah* (Oxford: George Ronald, 1957, reprinted, 1985), 72.

[44]Victor Paul Wierwille, *Jesus Christ Is Not God* (New Knoxville, Ohio: The American Christian Press, 1975).

[45]Ibid., 87.

[46]Ibid., 141.

[47]No authors or editors listed, *Outline of The Principle: Level 4* (New York: The Holy Spirit Association for the Unification of World Christianity, 1980), 142.

Was Jesus *eternally* God the Son? No, according to Unificationists. The key to the above quotation is "envisioned." Jesus was before His incarnation simply a *thought* in the Father's mind of what the ideal person should be.[48] There is similarity here between Wierwille (the founder of The Way International) and Moon.

The House of Yahweh

With its base in Abilene, Texas, this Yahwist cult furnishes an example of the denial of the pre-existent deity of Christ that is common in other Yahweh cults.[49] In his book, *Did Yahshua Messiah Pre-Exist?,* Yisrayl Hawkins writes, "In Yahchanan [John] 1:1, as we have proven, the word LOGOS—the Greek word translated 'Word' in the King James version, and 'preached' to be the 'savior' by those groping at the philosophical straws of paganism, trying to 'prove' the pagan doctrine of a 'pre-existent savior'—actually means PLAN!"[50] Hawkins thus translates John 1:1 as "In the beginning was the PLAN, and the PLAN was with Yahweh, and the PLAN was Yahweh's."[51] The pre-existent deity of the *logos*, and His personality, are therefore rejected by Hawkins.

United Pentecostal Church[52]

The heresy of United Pentecostal churches (known also as "Jesus Only" churches, "Oneness Pentecostals," or "Apostolic" churches[53])

---

[48]For a similar statement as that documented above, see (no author) *The Divine Principle Home Study Course,* six vols. (New York: The Holy Spirit Association for the Unification of World Christianity, 1980), 3:33.

[49]Yahweh cults are dedicated in part to the task of restoring to human understanding the true name of God, that being "Yahweh."

[50]Yisrayl Hawkins, *Did Yahshua Messiah Pre-Exist?* (Abilene, Tex.: The House of Yahweh, 1989), 223. In this quotation and the next I have not duplicated the italicized words, bold-faced words, and all the upper-case words of Hawkins.

[51]Ibid., 224.

[52]Not to be confused with pentecostals or Pentecostal churches. Here I am discussing *United* Pentecostalism.

[53]Caution is here advised, for not all churches with "Apostolic" in their designations are United Pentecostal.

pertaining to the pre-existent deity of the Son of God is of a different flavor than those of the other cults outlined in this chapter. Its heresy is that of *modalism*, which expresses the belief that there is only *one person* in the "Godhead." This person manifests Himself in different modes; at times as the Father, at other times as the Son, and at other times as the Holy Spirit.

This results in denial of the Trinity and of the pre-existent deity of the Son *as the Son.* For United Pentecostals, Jesus existed prior to His incarnation, but not as the Son of God. Rather, He existed as the Father. Consequently, the *logos* in John 1:1 was simply an *aspect* in the mind of the Father, a "Word-Image," the Son of God *in potential.* The Son was not the Son until the incarnation. At that time the Word-Image, or thought of God, manifested itself when the Father dwelled in Jesus the man. Following are several quotations from United Pentecostals:

> The Word or Logos can mean the plan or thought as it existed in the mind of God. This thought was a predestined plan [the incarnation]....
> the Son did not have pre-existence before the conception in the womb of Mary. The Son of God pre-existed in thought but not in substance.[54]

> Now I mentioned that the Word-Image [or thought of God] was only a Son in potential.... This Image or Shape or Form of God took on the form of a servant as the incarnation of God in Christ took place.[55]

> If there is only one God and that God is the Father (Malachi 2:10), and if Jesus is God, then it logically follows that Jesus is the Father.[56]

Here the eternal Sonship and deity *of Christ Himself* is rejected, along with *His* personhood before the incarnation.

Conclusion

In the preceding sections I have examined the heretical Christologies of theistic (for example, Jehovah's Witnesses),

---

[54]David K. Bernard, *The Oneness of God* (Hazelwood, Mo.: Word Aflame Press, 1983), 103.
[55]Kenneth V. Reeves, *The Supreme Godhead: Book II* (Hazelwood, Mo.: Word Aflame Press, 1984), 95, 142.
[56]Bernard, *The Oneness of God,* 66.

polytheistic (Mormonism) and pantheistic (Christian Science[57] and the New Age Movement) cults. We saw a common theme: a denial of the eternal deity of Christ, the unique deity of Christ, or both. We saw that these groups use biblical terminology. This now begs the question, "Are these terms *defined* biblically?" We turn to chapter 2 for the answer.

---

[57]Though Christian Science claims it is not pantheistic (Mary Baker Eddy even wrote a short treatise titled, *Christian Science Versus Pantheism* [Boston, Mass.: The First Church of Christ, Scientist, 1926]), it most certainly is. Mary Baker Eddy wrote that "there is in reality none besides the eternal, infinite God, good" (*Miscellaneous Writings,* 93). She also stated, "If God is Spirit, and God is All, surely there can be no matter; for the divine All must be Spirit" (*Unity of Good* [Boston: The First Church of Christ, Scientist, 1953], 31).

Chapter 2

The Biblical Witness to the Pre-existent Deity of Christ

"Tell me how it stands with your Christology, and I shall tell you who you are."—Karl Barth, Dogmatics In Outline

"This old pagan doctrine of a 'pre-existent savior,' kept alive, popular, and well by religious impostors through radio, television, and publishing, is much more dangerous than most people realize."—Yisrayl Hawkins, Did Yahshua Messiah Pre-Exist?

In this chapter I shall examine biblical passages that testify to Christ being God the Son prior to the incarnation. Some passages, such as John 8:58, were, of course, stated by Jesus in His incarnate state, but they testify to His always being God. These, therefore, will be included in this section.

John 1:1

"In the beginning was the Word, and the Word was with God, and the Word was God." John states without hesitation that the preincarnate

Christ (the Word) is God the Son before all ages. Indeed, the Word and the Father are of the same nature (ontological oneness). He affirms as well the eternal fellowship between the Father and the Son, and that the Father and the Word are distinct persons.

The three clauses of John 1:1 are,

> *en   archē   ēn   ho logos*
> in   (the) beginning   was   the Word

> *kai ho logos ēn pros ton theon*
> and the Word was with the God

> *kai   theos   ēn   ho   logos[1]*
> and   God   was   the   Word

In the beginning was the Word

John's first two words in Greek echo the LXX of Genesis 1:1: "In the beginning" (*en archē*). John's primary intent is to draw the reader back to the Genesis account, and to the point when all things in the universe were created. At this time (at the beginning of the creation), writes John, the Word (*logos[2]*) was (*ēn*). The imperfect tense form of the verb *eimi* ("I am"), thus in our text *ēn*, signifies continuous action in the past. When all things in the universe were created, the Word *continually was*, i.e., already existed. John is relating to us the eternal existence of the Word.

Note also the entirely different verb *ginomai* (γίνομαι, "I become") in John 1:3 referring to the created cosmos. This verb tells of *coming*

---

[1] Ἐν ἀρχῇ ἦν ὁ λόγος, καὶ ὁ λόγος ἦν πρὸς τὸν θεόν, καὶ θεὸς ἦν ὁ λόγος.

[2] This is not to be construed as the *logos* of Philo. David Wells, in his *The Person of Christ: A Biblical* and *Historical Analysis of the Incarnation* (Westchester, Ill.: Crossway Books, 1984), 68-69, mentions "at least three important points of difference. First, Philo's *logos* [here transliterated] was neither fully divine nor pre-existent.... Second, it is doubtful that this Word was personal as it is in John.... Third, in Philo this Word is a synonym for rational order in the cosmos or for patterns immanent in matter. It is never made identical with the self-disclosure of the 'Supreme Being.'"

into existence: "All things came into being [*egeneto*, ἐγένετο ("it became") the aorist tense form of *ginomai*] by Him..." John marks a clear distinction between the Word who *always was,* and the created order which *came into existence.*[3] Here Jehovah's Witnesses miss the point by numbering the *logos* with the rest of creation. The Word is not to be numbered among created beings, but is creator of *all* things. John 1:1a speaks of the eternal existence of the Word.

And the Word was with God

Again the imperfect tense *was* occurs. The Word *continually was* with God. "With" (*pros*) means face to face, and therefore implies two persons in eternal fellowship. Important also is the identity of "God" with whom the Word was. Not apparent in the English translations is the definite article (the) with John's first use of *theos* (God): "The Word was with *the* God." Who is "God" in this second clause of John 1:1? Our cross reference to 1 John 1:1-2 supplies the answer. Speaking of the incarnate Word in terminology reminiscent of the prologue to his Gospel, John states that He "was from the beginning," He is "the Word of Life," and that He "was *with the Father*" (*ēn*[4] *pros ton patera,* ἦν πρὸς τὸν πατέρα). So in John 1:1 the Word was with the Father.[5]

And the Word was God

This clause is either mistranslated[6] or reinterpreted[7] by cults. It teaches, however, that the Word in His *essential being* is God, even

---

[3]See Robert L. Reymond, *Jesus, Divine Messiah* (Phillipsburg, N.J.: Presbyterian and Reformed Publishing Co., 1990), 302-303.

[4]As in John 1:1, *ēn,* the imperfect of *eimi* is used, signifying timeless existence.

[5]See Reymond, *Jesus, Divine Messiah* 302-303, (see also John 1:18 cf. 6:46, and 4:23-24; 17:3).

[6]For example, the Jehovah's Witness translation, "the Word was a god."

[7]The Jehovah's Witnesses. Also, Yisrayl Hawkins (the leader of a Yahwist cult in Texas known as The House of Yahweh) denies the deity of Christ in a most (I am sad to say) amateurish fashion. This is demonstrated in his book, *Did Yahshua Messiah Pre-Exist?* (Abilene, Tex.: The House of Yahweh, 1989), 223-24. Working with *Strong's Greek Dictionary* at the back of *Strong's Exhaustive Concordance,* Hawkins enlists the *Concordance* to find John 1:1

though He is distinct from the Father in person (as we have seen from clause b). Two grammatical points will substantiate this.

First, recall that in the previous clause John uses the definite article when referring to the Father.[8] In this context it is important to note that in John 1:1c the definite article is missing before *theos: kai theos ēn ho logos* ("and God was the Word"). The text does not read *kai ho theos ēn ho logos* ("and *the* God was the Word"). Had John written "and *the* God was the Word" (and given that the identity of *the* God is the Father [clause b]), he would have taught that Jesus was the Father![9] By elimination of the article before *theos* in this clause, John carefully distinguishes the persons of the Father and the Son.[10] The distinction is

---

(translated "the Word was God"). He then notes that the Greek word for "God," *theos,* is used, and may be found in #2316 of *Strong's Greek Dictionary.* Then, and this is an enormous blunder, he goes to the *Concordance* to find the possessive "God's." Strong, of course, notes that *theos* is still the word used in the possessive (Strong gives the *lexical form,* and Hawkins does not realize it), and again points to #2316. Hawkins then says that this is how *theos* is to be understood in John 1:1, in the possessive "God's." The "Word" of God, he says, is actually the "plan" of Yahweh (he wants to restore the name *Yahweh* back into the Scripture, and omit the terrible designation "God"), and thus should be translated "and the plan was Yahweh's." Hawkins major error was his failure to know that when the possessive sense is conveyed in Greek, *theos* is employed with the possessive pronoun *autou* (αὐτοῦ, "of Him") or may simply have the genitive ending with *theos,* which would make it *theou* (θεοῦ, "of God"). Every single example Hawkins gives from *Strong's* indicating the possessive "God's" is in the genitive as just explained. John 1:1, of course, does not employ the genitive in any way as Hawkins would have his readers believe.

[8]This is not to say that John never uses the article for the Son. See John 20:28: *ho kurios mou kai ho theos mou* (ὁ κύριός μου καὶ ὁ θεός μου, lit. "the Lord of me and the God of me").

[9]If this were the case, the ancient modalists such as Praxeas, Noetus, and Sabellius (who taught of one person in the Godhead who reveals Himself in the different *modes* of Father, Son, and Holy Spirit) would be correct. Here John prophetically denies modalism. A modern form of this ancient heresy is propagated by the United Pentecostal Church, or the "Jesus Only" movement.

[10]Some may argue that John was bound by the rules of grammar to omit the article, stating that the article is naturally omitted when the predicate (in this case *theos*) precedes the verb (in this case *ēn*). But this is not always the case. See E. C. Colwell's "A Definite Rule for the Use of the Article in the Greek New Testament," *Journal of Biblical Literature* 52 (1933): 12-21. On page 17

also contextually warranted, for the Word was *with* the Father. Had John taught that the Word was the Father, it would have resulted in a contradiction of his use of *pros* ("with," "face to face") in 1:1b.

How, then, does *theos* function in 1:1c? *It functions to express what the Word is in His essence or being.*[11] In other words, the Word is Himself God by His very nature, just as the Father is. The position of *theos* in 1:1c is before the verb *was,* and therefore describes what the subject of the clause (*ho logos,* the article makes it the subject) is ontologically, or in His essential being. Translating 1:1c as "the word was a god," as Jehovah's Witnesses do, is therefore erroneous and misleading, for if John wanted to convey the idea that the Word was a god, he would have used *ho logos ēn theon, theon ēn ho logos, ho logos ēn theos* or *ho logos ēn theios.*[12]

Colwell lists the number of occurrences of predicate nouns that appear before the verb. Of the 112 examples in the New Testament, 15 have the article (97 do not have the article, one of which is John 1:1). This, of course, is a small percentage. Yet, it still shows that John would be well within the rules of grammar if he chose to use the article with *theos* in 1:1c.

[11]*Theos* is an anarthrous (without the article "the") predicate nominative, *qualitative* in force, as we shall see above. See also Philip B. Harner, "Qualitative Anarthrous Predicate Nouns: Mark 15:39 and John 1:1," *Journal of Biblical Literature* 92 (1973): 75-87. On page 75, Harner states "that anarthrous predicate nouns preceding the verb may function primarily to express the nature or character of the subject."

[12]See ibid., 84-85, for the latter two. The last example using *theios* is adjectival, which was certainly at John's disposal had he wanted to communicate that the Word was some sort of divine being. His use of *theos* rather than *theios* suggests his want to convey that the Word, being *theos,* is of the same substance as the Father (the antecedent use of *theos* to describe the Father in 1:1b); thus the ontological deity of the Son.

More should be said concerning the Jehovah's Witness translation of John 1:1c ("the Word was a god"). *First,* they admit that *theos* in 1:1c is a predicate without the article, and that this "points to a quality about someone" (New World Bible Translation Committee, *The Kingdom Interlinear Translation of the Greek Scriptures* [New York: Watchtower Bible and Tract Society of New York, Inc., 1985], 1139). This is what I have concluded as well. *Second,* they attempt to downplay the above statement by stating that Jesus is "a god or divine or godlike." They then draw the conclusion that this terminology "does not mean that he was the God with whom he was" (ibid.). In other words, they must view 1:1c as the *logos* being *a god* because "if He were God, He would be with Himself (1:1b), and that is an unreasonable thing to say!" This apologetic

To conclude and summarize, John 1:1 teaches that the Son is eternal (clause a), is eternally with the Father (clause b), and is Himself God by nature, sharing the same essence as the Father (clause c).

John 8:58[13]

"Jesus said to them, 'Truly, truly, I say to you, before Abraham was born, I AM.'" Christ here claims for Himself pre-existent deity.

The first thing that stands out is Jesus' use of the phrase "I AM" (*egō eimi,* ἐγὼ εἰμι). It stands alone, without any predicate. We may

---

on the Witnesses' part is drawn from a fallacious premise, namely that the two uses of *theos* in John 1:1 function grammatically in the same way. As was shown above, 1:1b teaches that the *logos* was *with the Father,* not with Himself, and that John's second use of *theos* in clause c functions differently from its use in clause b. *Third,* some Jehovah's Witnesses are convinced that because *theos* in 1:1c lacks the definite article in Greek, it must therefore be translated with the indefinite article *a* or *an,* thus "a god." But this as well is erroneous, as we have seen from a grammatical point of view. Moreover, if this were true, then we would also have to translate 1 John 4:8, 16 as "God is a love," for *ho theos agapē estin* (ὁ θεὸς ἀγάπη ἐστίν) also has the anarthrous *agapē* (love) preceding the verb. Such a translation, however, would not be accurate, and even the Jehovah's Witnesses translate the phrase correctly to read "God is love." Also, there are several other places in the Jehovah's Witness *New World Translation* where *theos* lacks the article, yet they translate it simply as "God" (see, for example, John 1:6, 12, 18).

More informed Jehovah's Witnesses call upon the Watchtower Society's list of predicate nouns without the article where the translation is best understood with the indefinite article. "A prophet" (Mark 11:32; John 4:19), "a slanderer" (John 6:70), "a thief" (John 10:1), are cited as examples (ibid., 1140). But in these examples *the essential meaning of describing the nature of someone is still prevalent.* The prophet is *by nature* a prophet, and every bit a prophet as another prophet! (see Robert M. Bowman, *Jehovah's Witnesses, Jesus Christ, and the Gospel of John* [Grand Rapids, Mich.: Baker Book House, 1989], 47-48). The same may be said of the slanderer and the thief. Thus, the "a god" rendering would not fail to communicate that the Word is every bit God as the Father. In fact, the Jehovah's Witnesses would not dare to reduce *Jehovah* to "godlike" status (as they do Jesus) on the basis of their translation of the anarthrous predicate *theos* in Luke 20:38, which refers to Jehovah: "He is a God, not of the dead" (*theos de ouk estin nekrōn,* θεὸς δὲ οὐκ ἔστιν νεκρῶν) (ibid., 48-49).

[13]See also the introduction of this book for a treatment of John 8:24, 58.

use the phrase "I am," but we would do so with the predicate either implied or directly stated. For example, in answer to the question, "Are you going to the store?", we may say, "I am." Here the predicate, "going to the store," is implied in our answer. We might say, "I am going to Ephesus." Here "going to Ephesus" is the predicate phrase directly stated. But in John 8:58 "I AM" is absolute. There is no implied or direct predicate. The reason for this is that there is no predicate phrase that could possibly be implied from the context.

Second is the way Jesus distinguishes Himself from the created order, a fact we have already witnessed with reference to the *logos* in the prologue to John's Gospel.[14] Before Abraham ever *came into existence*, Jesus always existed ("I AM"). This is reminiscent of the "come into existence/always existed" contrast between the created order and God in Psalm 89:2 in the LXX (English 90:2): "Before the mountains came into existence..., You [i.e., God] are." The present tenses translated "I AM" and "You are" in John 8:58 and Psalm 89:2 carry the meaning of continuous action, thus, "I always existed," and "You always existed."

Third, and the crux of our concern, is what the phrase "I AM" means. Simply put, it is "in the style of deity."[15] It is representative of the "I AM" statements in the LXX[16] that are attributed to Yahweh. In Deuteronomy 32:39, *Yahweh* states, "Behold, Behold, that I AM." Isaiah 41:4c, 43:10a, and 46:4a read, respectively, "I, God, the first, and to all the things coming, I AM;" "You are my witnesses.... that you may know... that I AM;" "I AM, and until you grow old, I AM" (see also Isa. 45:18). John opens his Gospel with a declaration of the pre-existent deity of the Son, and continues that witness in John 8:58.

Note on John 8:24

Taken in light of the LXX citations above, and the above observations regarding John 8:58, the I AM statement in John 8:24 is a most urgent warning to those who knowingly deny who Jesus claimed

---

[14]See John 1:1, 3, and this chapter under John 1:1. John 1:1 states that the *logos always was* (the imperfect tense of the verb *eimi* ["I am"]). But the created order in 1:3 *came to be* (the aorist tense of *ginomai,* γίνομαι).

[15]Leon Morris, *The Gospel According to John* (Grand Rapids, Mich.: Wm. B. Eerdmans Publishing Co., 1971), 473.

[16]Ibid.

to be. Just as Yahweh confronted the rebellious people Israel in the Old Testament to believe "that I AM" (*hoti egō eimi,* ὅτι ἐγώ εἰμι, see the LXX of Deut. 32:39; Isa. 43:10), Jesus confronts the rebellious leaders of Israel in John 8:24b: *"For unless you believe that I am (hoti egō eimi), you shall die in your sins."*[17] Jesus is Yahweh the Son, and He affirms His pre-existence in the previous verse: "You are from below, I am from above." He then warns of the consequences of denying who He claimed to be (v. 24).[18]

It is imperative, therefore, for one to have the *correct view* of Christ in order to have the faith that is able to place one in the Christian camp. A defective view of Christ, a denial of the biblical view of Christ, makes it impossible for one to be a follower of the biblical Christ.[19]

---

[17]My translation. Quite interesting is the claim of John that "we beheld His glory" (1:14), and in spite of this the people "who were His own did not receive Him" (1:11). This same phenomenon occurs in the Old Testament, where Yahweh states that in spite of all seeing His glory, they would not listen to Him (Num. 14:22)! In John 8:24 Jesus is "being" Yahweh in the same sense.

[18]In John 13:19 Jesus instructs his disciples that He would fulfill Psalm 41:9 (see John 13:18). He states, "From now on I say to you before it happens, in order that you may believe, whenever it happens, that I am" (my translation). Here the *hoti egō eimi* ("that I am") continues in the style of deity from Isaiah 43:10.

[19]Though the Jehovah's Witnesses translate *ego eimi* in John 8:58 as "I have been" rather than "I AM," they still translate the same phrase in 8:24 as "I am [he]" (brackets original)! To buttress their "I have been" rendering, the Jehovah's Witnesses cite two grammarians (G. B. Winer, *A Grammar of the Idiom of the New Testament* [Andover, 1897], 267, and Nigel Turner, *A Grammar of New Testament Greek* [Edinburgh, 1963], 62) who place the *egō eimi* of 8:58 in a category of verbs that may be translated as expressing a past action beginning (Turner?) in the past and continuing in the present (see *The Kingdom Interlinear Translation of the Greek Scriptures,* 1145). They correctly cite these grammarians, but that does not guarantee that we *must* place John 8:58 in this category. *Context* must rule in the dynamic equivalent English (or any other language) translation, for we must endeavor to accurately convey the *intent* of the biblical author. It is precisely at this point that two observations are raised. *First,* we must ask ourselves if the Jews would stone Jesus for claiming to be a created angel who came into existence at a certain time before Abraham was born (see John 8:59; cf. 10:33 [Here the Jehovah's Witnesses' translation "make yourself a god" is inconsistent with their translation of John 1:18. If they were consistent, it would read "no one has seen *a* god at any

Sadly, this is the case with the cults, as they make Jesus anything but God the Son, second person of the Trinity.[20]

John 17:5

"And now, glorify Thou Me together with Thyself, Father, with the glory which I had with Thee before the world was." In His high priestly prayer Jesus acknowledges His eternal pre-existent glory which He shared with the Father. If stated publicly, as He did His "I AM" statements, this surely would have provoked stoning, for He was not only calling God His Father, he was also claiming to share God's glory.

That Christ in His pre-existence displayed His glory is evident in John 1:1, 14. He eternally was, eternally was with the Father, was Himself God, and manifested His already experienced glory to the eye of humanity by becoming flesh. John cannot *add* anything to that, except to bring out phrases that elaborate on this central opening theme. In other words, John in 1:1 sets the tone with a strong ontological

---

time..." They also fail to see that because of 1:18, which refers to "God," the translation of 10:33 should be "make yourself God," thus warranting stoning.]). Such a claim has in Scripture no reason for stoning, though blaspheming "The Name" does (Lev. 24:16; see also John 19:7). *Second,* the theme "coming into existence/always existing" has been demonstrated with reference to Yahweh in the Old Testament (Ps. 90:2 [LXX 89:2]; see also Ps. 102:25-27). In the context of John this is also clear as regards the Son and all creation (1:1, 3; see also Heb. 1:10-12). It is inescapable in our immediate context that John is contrasting the *coming into existence* of Abraham, and the *continuous* existence of the Son. John continues this theme to the end, with the creation (Thomas) actually confessing Jesus as God (John 20:28). In concluding, I wonder whether the Jehovah's Witnesses deny this text's witness to Christ being eternally God because of their misunderstanding (and subsequent misrepresentation) of the doctrine of the Trinity. When all is said and done, they make the final argument that "Jehovah and Jesus are never identified as being the same person" (*Kingdom Interlinear,* 1146). See the next note for another example of this, this time exhibited by the Unification Church.

[20]The Unification Church states that by the expression I AM, "Jesus didn't mean that he was God.... If Jesus were God, how could he intercede with himself?" (*Outline of The Principle: Level 4* [New York: The Holy Spirit Association for the Unification of World Christianity, 1980], 142). Like the Jehovah's Witnesses, the Unification Church misrepresents the doctrine of the Trinity, then tears down this misrepresentation.

affirmation of Christ's deity, then subsequently affirms it in different ways as his Gospel continues to unfold.

He does just that in 17:5. The glory Christ had was His before the world was.[21] What kind of glory could this be, except the glory that He had with the Father because He is the Father's unique Son? After all, as John writes, "we beheld His glory, glory as of the unique one from the Father" (John 1:14).[22] As we shall see in chapter 4 (see under John 1:14), when John speaks of the Son's "glory," he has in mind the highest conception of glory due only to God, for the Son has "tabernacled" with us (John 1:14), a covenantal theme referring back to the "glory of Yahweh" filling the *tabernacle* in Exodus 40:34-35. With this strong language in John 17:5, and in light of these observations from John's first chapter, Jesus can only mean the glory that was His eternally as Yahweh the Son!

Zechariah 12:10

"They will look on Me whom they have pierced; and they will mourn for Him, as one mourns for an only son." The speaker here is Yahweh, the maker of heaven and earth (see v. 1),[23] and the statement, John says, was fulfilled in Christ (John 19:37; John's citation of the Zechariah passage strongly implies the pre-existent deity of Christ).

The text, however, is not without its seeming difficulties, and has led some to amend the text and its pronoun shift.[24] The curious change from the *first* person to the *third* ("they will look on *Me*... and they will mourn for *Him*") in the Hebrew text suggests two persons, that is, the speaker who is pierced and the one who is mourned. But Kenneth L.

---

[21]The Jehovah's Witnesses often point to John 17:3 ("that they may know Thee, [Father,] the only true God, and Jesus Christ whom thou hast sent"), stating, "here Jesus says that Jehovah is the only true God. How, then, can Jesus be God?" They miss the point that in the Gospel of John, God (*theos,* θεός) is often a synonym for the Father (see 6:46 cf. 1:18; 4:23-24).

[22]My translation.

[23]Cf. Keil and Delitzsch, *Commentary on the Old Testament,* 10 vols. (Grand Rapids, Mich.: Wm. B. Eerdmans Publishing Co., 1986), 10:387, and E. W. Hengstenberg, *Christology of the Old Testament* (Grand Rapids, Mich.: Kregel Publications, 1970), 361.

[24]See R. T. France, *Jesus and the Old Testament* (London: Tyndale, 1971), 153.

Barker notes that such a change in person is not at all uncommon in Hebrew,[25] thus it is possible to see one person speaking ("They will look on Me... and they will mourn for Me").

Most important is John's application of Zechariah 12:10. In Zechariah, Yahweh is clearly the one speaking. John continues his witness of the pre-existent deity of the Son with a reference to Zechariah 12:10a (which in Zechariah is in the *first* person: "They will look on *Me* whom they have pierced"), and places it in the *third* person: "And again another Scripture says, 'they shall look on *Him* whom they pierced'" (John 19:37).[26] John means to communicate that Jesus is this

---

[25]For example, in the note for Zechariah 7:13 Barker states that "the use of קָרָא (*qara,* third person, "he called") instead of the expected קָרָאתִי (*qarathi,* first person, "I called"), to agree with the following וְלֹא אֶשְׁמָע (*velo eshma,* first person, "I would not listen"), is explained in the NIV Preface: 'And though the Hebrew writers often shifted back and forth between first, second and third personal pronouns without change of antecedent, this translation often makes them uniform, in accordance with English style and without the use of footnotes'" (Frank E. Gaebelein, ed., *The Expositor's Bible Commentary,* 12 vols. [Grand Rapids, Mich.: Zondervan Publishing House, 1985], 7:648-49; see also Barker's comments on Zechariah 9:10 in the notes on p. 664). In other words, the Hebrew text in Zech. 7:13 actually reads, "just as *He* called and *they* would not listen, so *they* called and *I* would not listen." Reading this in context, the logical sequence of pronouns should match in the English translation, thus the NIV rendering, "When I called, they did not listen; so when they called, I would not listen." The point is that the Hebrew has the "He, they/they, I" sequence, but *intends* the meaning of "I, they/they, I." So the translation and/or interpretation must reflect the *meaning* and *intent* for our benefit. Barker interprets the "me" in Zech. 12:10 as referring to the coming Messiah, and points his readers to his notes on 7:13 and 9:10 for the pronoun shift (pp. 683-84; 688 in the notes).

[26]The LXX is not cited here because of its "mocked" instead of "pierced" (probably due to the LXX mistaking the Heb. *rqd,* רקד for *dqr,* דקר). Therefore, John does not follow the LXX (see Morris, *The Gospel According to John,* 823, n. 105). Still interesting, however, is its "they will look to *me... and* they will mourn for *him.*" Some have suggested that since Aquila and Theodotion agree with John, there may have been an LXX manuscript in John's time that reads as John, though there is no *existing* manuscript of such sort. The LXX versions of Aquila and Theodotion, however, are dated in the second century. Therefore, to state that John *may* have had access to such a manuscript is speculation (see ibid.). Leon Morris is correct when he states that John most likely used the Hebrew (ibid.). In addition to Morris' observations, Merrill C. Tenney adds that

Yahweh of Zechariah. Merrill C. Tenney observes that John is "footnoting" an Old Testament passage.[27] John does so not only in 19:37, but one verse before as well. In verse 36 John alludes to the prohibition against breaking the bones of the passover lamb in Exodus 12:46 (see also Num. 9:12). Psalm 34:20 states that the Lord keeps all the bones of the righteous, and that "not one of *them* is broken." John applies these passages to Christ, referencing Him in the third person singular: "Not a bone of *Him* shall be broken." It is no wonder, then, that John does the same in verse 37, taking Yahweh's statement in Zechariah, "they shall look on Me whom they have pierced," and applying it to Christ in the third person: "they shall look on Him whom they pierced."[28] E. W. Hengstenberg notes, "In Zechariah the Messiah Himself speaks, John speaks *of* Him."[29] With John's context clearly in the crucifixion of Jesus, there can be no doubt that Zechariah's Yahweh is indeed the pre-existent Son of God.

Micah 5:2[30]

"But as for you, Bethlehem Ephrathah, too little to be among the clans of Judah, from you One will go forth for Me to be ruler in Israel.

John was "footnoting" from the Hebrew text (see the next note), taking *vehibbitu elay eth asher daqaru* (וְהִבִּיטוּ אֵלַי אֵת אֲשֶׁר־דָּקָרוּ, "they will look to me whom they have pierced") to read in the Greek, *opsontai eis hon exekentēsan* (ὄψονται εἰς ὅν ἐξεκέντησαν, "they will look to the one whom they have pierced").

[27]See Tenney, "The Footnotes of John's Gospel," *Bibliotheca Sacra* 117 (1960): 350-64, and his commentary on the Gospel of John in *The Expositor's Bible Commentary,* 9:185. D. A. Carson, in his commentary on Matthew, cites the same phenomenon for Matthew 27:9-10 (*The Expositor's Bible Commentary*, 8:565). Hengstenberg makes the same point in his *Christology of the Old Testament,* 362.

[28]The Jehovah's Witness *New World Translation* of Zechariah 12:10 is characteristically misleading: "they will certainly look to the One whom they pierced." Such a translation is not from the Hebrew or any LXX existing in John's time. To give credentials to their rendering, they cite Theodotion's version of the LXX (second century) and John 19:37! But translating the Hebrew on the basis of John 19:37 is not sound practice, and is evidence of the Watchtower Society's intentional misleading of people.

[29]Hengstenberg, *Christology of the Old Testament*, 362, emphasis added.

[30]5:1 in the Hebrew text.

His goings forth are from long ago, from the days of eternity." This prophecy was fulfilled in Christ, who was born in Bethlehem (Matt. 2:4-6, 8-11; John 7:42). The last part of this verse tells of Christ's eternal nature. He has always existed, and only God has existed from all eternity.

Though it is true that the Hebrew words for "His goings forth" (*motsaothayv,* מוֹצָאֹתָיו), "from long ago" (*miqedem,* מִקֶּדֶם), and "from the days of eternity" (*mime olam,* מִימֵי עוֹלָם), do not *in and of themselves* always connote timeless eternal existence, they do at times. Context, then, must determine meaning.

His "goings forth," i.e. His activities, if appearing in the text *without* the following words, would express only activities or "doings," and thus carry no implication of eternality. But the activities must be viewed with the qualifiers put to them, namely "from long ago, from days of eternity."

"From long ago" may refer simply to "from of old" or "ancient times," with a point in time as the beginning point. But it may also refer to that which has no beginning, as in the phrase "the eternal God" (*elohe qedem,* אֱלֹהֵי קֶדֶם) in Deuteronomy 33:27, or "the one who sits enthroned from of old" (*yosheb qedem,* יֹשֵׁב קֶדֶם) in Psalm 55:19 (Heb. 55:20).

"From the days of eternity" likewise has two options, either a specific beginning point in time, or eternity, as in texts which express the nature of God (*el olam,* אֵל עוֹלָם, "the eternal God" [Genesis 21:33 and Isa. 40:28] and *che ha olam,* חֵי הָעוֹלָם, "Him who lives forever" [Daniel 12:7]).[31]

With the above in mind, context must govern. The ruler who is to come obviously is a figure of supernatural origin. The words above drive us to that conclusion even if they are not taken in the strict sense of *eternal.* Further, this supernatural King is to be born in Bethlehem. This therefore warrants a brief examination of Matthew 2:6[32] and *its* context to see how it is treated in this synoptic Gospel.[33] "And you, Bethlehem, land of Judah, are by no means least among the leaders of

---

[31]For all the preceding, see H. W. F. Gesenius, *Gesenius' Hebrew-Chaldee Lexicon to the Old Testament* (Grand Rapids, Mich.: Baker Book House, 1979), 723-24; 612-13.

[32]Micah 5:2 is also alluded to in John 7:42.

[33]Matthew follows neither the Hebrew text or the LXX.

Judah; for out of you shall come forth a ruler who will shepherd My people Israel."[34] Matthew's citation of Micah 5:2 establishes the identity of this supernatural figure of Micah. He is the Messiah. Matthew has already stated that the Messiah is "God with us" (*Immanuel*, 1:23). Further claims to deity for the Messiah are found in Matthew 1:21, where he applies Psalm 130:8 to Christ's redeeming work ("And she will bear a Son; and you shall call His name Jesus [Heb. *yehoshua*, the LORD saves], for it is He who will save His people from their sins"). In the Psalm it is Yahweh who will His people from their sins. In Matthew it is Jesus Himself, for He is Yahweh, the LORD who saves.[35] Matthew, in these texts clearly calling the Messiah Yahweh, then states in 2:6 that this Messiah was born in Bethlehem.

In light of all this, the Messiah to come in Micah exists eternally in the strictest sense. He always *was,* and always was Yahweh.[36]

The Son who was "Sent"

The texts already examined in this chapter have witnessed the eternal deity of the pre-existent Son of God. We may safely be within biblical grounds, therefore, to conclude that the pre-existent Son of God is God the Son who was sent into the world. (Jesus did not *become* the Son of God. He was always, is now, and forever will be the Son of God.) Passages in the New Testament teach that God *sent* His Son into the world. The Father *sending* His Son into the world to redeem His people presupposes that the Son existed before the event of sending.

The phraseology of the Son being sent appears in Matthew 10:40, Mark 9:37, and Luke 9:48. There are multiple references in the Gospel of John (see, for example, 3:17; 5:30, 36, 37; 6:29, 38, 39, 40, 44, 57; 7:16, 28, 29; 8:16, 18, 26, 42; 9:4; 12:44, etc.). It appears outside the

---

[34]Matthew, though leaving out the portion in Micah beginning with "His goings forth...", pulls into his quotation of Micah 5:2a an allusion to Micah 5:4a. It appears here that Matthew, having already established Messiah's deity (Matt. 1:23; cf. 1:21 and see above), does not need to further establish Messiah's deity in 2:6.

[35]And just as it is *Yahweh's* people in the Psalm, signifying ownership and thus another attribute of deity, in Matthew it is Jesus' people, signifying the same! More on this in chap. 4.

[36]We may add here that Matt. 1:21, 23 are references to Isa. 7:14. This Messiah to come is to Isaiah the Mighty God (Isa. 9:6).

Gospels (Rom. 8:3; Gal. 4:4; 2 Cor. 8:9; 1 John 4:9, 10, 14). We may add to this Jesus' own witness that He has "come into the world" (see John 9:39; 12:46), and Martha's confession: "I believe that You are the Christ, the Son of God, *even* He who comes into the world" (John 11:27).[37] Having established that the Son of God preexisted,[38] and that He was Himself God, I shall now examine the *irony* of the phrase "Son of God."

"Son of God"

Some suppose that because Jesus is the Son of God, He therefore cannot be God. In light of John 8:24, this must not be taken lightly.

Ironically the phrase "Son of God" *means* "God the Son." I shall discuss this title *only as it applies to Christ* in His preincarnate glory with the Father, for that is the subject of this chapter. In chapter four and in following chapters the title will surface repeatedly in the context of the incarnate state of Christ. But first a preceding point: the phrase "son(s) of God" may carry several meanings, depending on the context. As David Wells writes,

> It is true, of course, that there is a general usage of the title "son(s) of God" in the Old Testament. It is used of heavenly beings (Gen. 6:2; Job 1:6; 38:7; Ps. 29:1; 89:7), and it is used of God's people (Exod. 4:22, 23; Jer. 31:9; Hos. 11:1; Deut. 14:1; 32:5; Isa. 43:6). Finally, it is used of the Davidic King, the king's relation to God being described in terms of a son-to-father relationship (2 Sam. 7:12-14; 1 Chron. 17:13). In the New Testament, however, this title is used in a specialized sense when applied to Christ.[39]

---

[37]The Greek of this phrase is precise, the Son of God is the one who comes into the world (*ho huios... ho erchomenos,* ὁ υἱὸς... ὁ ἐρχόμενος).

[38]The title "Son of Man" is also used by Christ in the context of pre-existence. Of Himself Jesus states, "What then if you should behold the Son of Man ascending where He was before?" (John 6:62).

[39]David F. Wells, *The Person of Christ: A Biblical and Historical Analysis of the Incarnation* (Westchester, Ill.: Crossway Books, 1984), 70. I am sure Wells would also agree that in the New Testament the title is not used only of Christ. It is used, for example, of believers (by adoption; Rom. 8:14). Thus, Wells has carefully stated that the title, "when applied to Christ," carries a special meaning. Parenthetically, it is interesting to note that John never uses the title to refer to anyone else. He uses it only of Christ. Believers, on the other

Son of God Means God the Son

In our texts in this chapter, we have seen that Christ is truly God. And He is Yahweh the Son *who was sent*. The theological significance of "Son of God" when referring to Christ is ontological *and* functional: He is described in the clearest sense as sharing the same essence as the Father (ontological), as creator of the universe along with the Father (functional), as "with" the Father "in the beginning" (functional), Himself being by nature God (ontological), being with the Father and sharing the Father's glory (functional), and bringing all things into existence (functional).

As the Son of God, Christ comes eternally from the Father in a Son-to-Father relationship. Now it is true that the son of anyone shares in the same nature of his father, and it is no different with Christ who *eternally* comes from the Father[40] (the Jews most assuredly had this understanding, for when Jesus states "my Father," they took it to mean that Jesus was making Himself *equal* to God [John 5:17-18[41]]). He is the Son of the Father, and therefore shares in the same nature as the Father.[42] "Son of God" therefore means "God the Son."

---

hand, are said to be the "children of God" in John 1:12. It seems that John is ever so careful, given all that the title implies in his Gospel, to distinguish between Christ (who is Son by virtue of His nature) and believers (who are children of God by adoption).

[40]See my exposition of John 1:18 in chap. 4.

[41]In the Synoptic Gospels Jesus uses the phrase "my Father," and "Son of God" as well. Robert Reymond points these out (Matt. 11:27 [Luke 10:22], 21:37-38 [Mark 12:6, Luke 20:13], 24:36 [Mark 13:32], 28:19, as well as others in John [6:40, 10:36, 11:4, 14:13, 17:1]), and states that by these sayings Jesus was claiming "essential divine oneness with God" (*Jesus, Divine Messiah,* 68).

[42]In my experience the title "Son of Man" has never been challenged by heretics, perhaps because they assume that it deals exclusively with His humanity. But just like "Son(s) of God," this title is used in various ways in the Old and New Testaments. One of these is to testify to Christ's pre-existent and incarnate deity, as Mark 2:5-7, 10 (Matt. 9:6; Luke 5:24; only God can forgive sin), Matt. 19:28 (His sitting on His *glorious* throne), Matt. 24:30 (Mark 13:26; Luke 21:27; Daniel 7:13; Yahweh is the only "cloud-rider;" see Pss. 18:9-11; 104:3; Isa. 19:1; Nah. 1:3), and John 3:13 (He has come *from* heaven) show. I shall have more on the Son of Man in chap. 4.

Jude 4, 5, 9, 14

The way in which Jude uses the title "Lord"[43] is representative of his high view of Christ. In verse 4 of the epistle it is crystal clear that he applies this title to the already incarnate and glorified Christ (*"For certain persons have crept in unnoticed... and deny our only Master*[44] *and Lord, Jesus Christ"*).[45] Our remaining three verses of focus, however, tell of Christ's pre-existent deity.[46]

In verse 5 Jude, after calling Jesus "our only Master and Lord" (v. 4), reminds his readers "that the Lord, after saving a people out of the land of Egypt, subsequently destroyed those who did not believe." Of course it was *Yahweh* who performed this act, and here Jude applies this to Christ, saying it was He who did so. Obviously this occurred *before* the incarnation. There are at least two strong reasons why we should see "Lord" here referring to Jesus. *First* is that immediately before verse 5, Jude in verse 4 confesses Jesus as "our only Lord." *Second,* it is not as though Jude is ambiguous in his references to the Father and the Son. In verses 1, 4, 21, and 25 Jude specifically refers to the Father by the titles "Father" and "God," showing that he can make the distinction.[47]

---

[43]See the discussion of the title "Lord" in chap. 5 under Romans 10:9, 13, and nn. 21, 22.

[44]"Master" and "Lord" are two nouns that are governed by one definite article. Thus the two nouns refer to *one* person, Jesus Christ (cf. 2 Pet. 2:1; and see the discussion in chap. 5 under Titus 2:13). The fact that Jude calls Christ "Master" denotes Christ's ownership of His covenant people (in v. 1 Jude claims to be "a bond-servant of Jesus Christ"), and thus His deity, for in the Old Testament it is *Yahweh* alone who owns His people (cf. Isa. 43:10 and the discussion in chap. 5 under Romans 1:1).

[45]Thus this reference should be included among the many texts in chap. 7 attesting to the incarnate deity of Christ.

[46]See Reymond, *Jesus, Divine Messiah,* 284-85.

[47]Regarding the identity of the "Lord" in verses 5, 9, and 14, the objection may be raised that "Lord" alone is used in these verses, while in other verses where "Lord" is used to refer to Christ, Jude is careful to use the phrase "Lord Jesus Christ" (vv. 17, 21, 25). Thus the conclusion drawn is that "Lord" in vv. 5, 9, 14 may refer to the Father, since Jude does not specify who the Lord is in these verses, as he has in vv. 17, 21, and 25. I draw attention again, however, to the connection between vv. 4 and 5. In v. 4 Jude calls Jesus "our only Lord," and then proceeds to write of the "Lord" who brought a people out of Egypt.

Jude also refers to Jesus as Yahweh in verses 9 and 14. Though in these verses Jude *quotes* (but see n. 48) from non-biblical sources (The Assumption of Moses[48] and 1 Enoch 1:9, respectively), he nonetheless *alludes* to either Old Testament verses or themes where Yahweh is the referent. For example, Jude 9 states, *"But Michael the archangel, when he disputed with the devil and argued about the body of Moses, did not dare pronounce against him a railing judgment, but said, 'The Lord rebuke you.'"* Though here Jude *may* have quoted from an extra-biblical source, we still find in Zechariah 3:2 the words spoken to Satan, "the LORD (*Yahweh*) rebuke you." Jude 14 states [alluding to 1 Enoch 1:9]: *"And about these also Enoch, in the seventh generation from Adam, prophesied, saying 'Behold, the Lord came with many thousands of His holy ones.'"* There is here a parallel with Deuteronomy 33:2, where "the LORD (*Yahweh*)...came from the midst of ten thousand holy ones." I conclude therefore that Jude views Christ not only as pre-existent, but pre-existent as Yahweh the Son.

Conclusion

The Bible proclaims the pre-existent deity of Christ. The Christian Church has therefore historically proclaimed Jesus as God the Son before all ages, who was sent by God the Father to redeem sinners. Though denials and attacks of this doctrine are many, they have failed to steer the Church off course from this historic confession, simply because the unchanging Scriptures thrust us to no other conclusion. We now proceed to chapter three to examine heresies pertaining to the incarnate deity of Christ.

---

[48]That Jude 9 comes from *The Assumption of Moses* is not certain, though some have stated that it does. See James H. Charlesworth, ed., *The Old Testament Pseudepigrapha*, 2 vols. (New York: Doubleday, 1983), 1:924: "Jude 9 refers to the story of the dispute between Michael and Satan for the body of Moses, an account that does not appear in our text [*Testament of Moses*]. That the episode was contained in the lost ending of the Testament of Moses or in a cognate work, properly called the Assumption of Moses, is possible; but our present information does not warrant any positive conclusion." This being the case, my remarks above regarding Zech. 3:2 as the cross reference of Jude 9 take on more weight.

Chapter 3

Heresy and the Incarnate Deity of Christ

"Were such a God to become incarnate in the concrete, limited form of a man He would thereby immediately cease to be God."—Richard Backwell, The Christianity of Jesus

"The Word had become flesh: a real human baby. He had not ceased to be God; He was no less God then than before."—J. I. Packer, Knowing God

This chapter documents various heresies concerning the deity of Christ in His incarnate state. First, though, I shall offer an orthodox affirmation.

Christian Doctrine Explained

Christians believe that the eternal Son of God *came* into the world to save sinners. As the pre-existent Son of God He was also God the Son. At His incarnation He remained fully God, God the Son, but added to His person a full human nature. After His bodily resurrection[1] He remained God the Son, and since His bodily ascension to the right hand of God the Father He remains God the Son. Yet, modern heresies, like their ancient predecessors, deny this essential teaching of Scripture.

Jehovah's Witnesses

The saga of the creature Michael the Archangel continues into the birth of Jesus Christ. Jehovah's Witnesses state, "Scriptural evidence indicates that the name Michael applied to God's Son before he left heaven to become Jesus Christ."[2] Further, in order for the birth of Jesus to take place, "Jehovah God caused an ovum, or egg cell, in Mary's womb to become fertile, accomplishing this by the transferal of the *life* of his firstborn Son from the spirit realm to earth."[3] And in order for this to occur, Michael the Archangel, this first and only direct creation of Jehovah, *ceased to be in the form of an archangel*: "His becoming flesh meant nothing less than that he ceased to be a spirit person."[4] Jehovah then transferred his "life essence" into the virgin's womb, producing the perfect man Jesus: "This is far different from saying that he clothed himself with flesh as in a materialization[5] or as an incarnation.... [W]e do not find once that John says that the Word became a God-Man, that is, a combination of God and man."[6] Finally, the Witnesses state that at His resurrection and ascension (which are *not* bodily) Jesus keeps His name, but also resumes His heavenly name, "Michael." As such He is a spirit creature once again.

---

[1]The same body that died on the cross was raised (John 2:19-21).

[2]No authors or editors listed, *Insight On The Scriptures,* 2 vols. (New York: Watchtower Bible and Tract Society of New York, Inc., 1988), 2:393.

[3]Ibid., 2:56, emphasis mine.

[4]No authors or editors listed, *The Word According to John* (New York: Watchtower Bible and Tract Society, 1962), 11. The Watchtower cites Phil. 2:5-8 as evidence of this, stating that "he 'emptied himself' of his heavenly glory and spirit nature and 'took a slave's form'" (*Insight On The Scriptures,* 2:67).

[5]Though Jesus is an angel, Jehovah's Witnesses say his coming to earth was not like the rest of the angels, who in Scripture *clothed* themselves with flesh in their materializations.

[6]*The Word According to John,* 11.

Mormonism

Mormon belief holds that the firstborn spirit child of heavenly Father (Elohim, an exalted man) and heavenly Mother (name unknown, an exalted woman) now must take a body on earth. And though we (also spirit children of heavenly Father and Mother) were sent to earth to inhabit bodies that were formed through the sexual union of our earthly fathers and mothers, for Jesus it was different. Sexual union remained the vehicle by which this firstborn spirit child took a body on earth, but the partners in this sexual union were quite unusual, one in particular. I shall state the doctrine, and then I shall support it with several quotations from Mormon sources.[7]

Mormonism teaches that *Elohim Himself* (the Father, an exalted man) came down and had sexual union with the virgin Mary in order to clothe the spirit child Jesus with a body.

> That child to be born of Mary was begotten of Elohim, the Eternal Father, *not in violation of natural law* but in accordance with a higher manifestation thereof; and, the offspring from that association of supreme sanctity, *celestial Sireship*, and pure mortal maternity, was of right to be called the "Son of the Highest."[8]

> The Church of Jesus Christ of Latter-day Saints proclaims that Jesus Christ is the Son of God in the most literal sense. The body in which He performed His mission in the flesh was sired by that same Holy Being we worship as God, our Eternal Father. Jesus was not the son of Joseph, nor was He begotten by the Holy Ghost. He is the Son of the Eternal Father.[9]

---

[7]Mormons tend to be insulted when details of *how* the conception took place are stated. They simply do not believe it, or they affirm that the details are a mystery to them. For this reason I have included several quotations.

[8]No authors or editors listed, *Doctrines of the Gospel: Student Manual* (Salt Lake City, Utah: The Church of Jesus Christ of Latter-day Saints, 1986), 9, quoting James E. Talmage, *Jesus the Christ,* third edition (Salt Lake City, Utah: The Church of Jesus Christ of Latter-day Saints, 1924), 81. Emphases mine.

[9]Ezra Taft Benson, *The Teachings of Ezra Taft Benson* (Salt Lake City, Utah: Bookcraft, 1988), 7. Some may recognize this 13th Prophet of the Mormon Church as former United States Secretary of Agriculture in the Eisenhower administration. His statement that Jesus was not begotten by the Holy Ghost is in direct disagreement with the Bible (see Matt. 1:18, 20).

The birth of the Saviour was as natural as are the births of our children; it was the result of natural action. He partook of flesh and blood—was begotten of His Father, as we were of our fathers.[10]

In relation to the way in which I look upon the works of God and his creatures, I will say that I was naturally begotten; so was my father, and also my Saviour Jesus Christ. According to the Scriptures, he is the first begotten of his father in the flesh, and there was nothing unnatural about it.[11]

When the time came that His first-born, the Saviour, should come into the world and take a tabernacle, the Father came Himself and favored that spirit with a tabernacle instead of letting any other man do it.[12]

Christ was begotten of God. He was not born without the aid of Man, and *that Man was God!*[13]

This heretical twist in the "virgin" birth of Mormonism carries with it the denial of the biblical deity of Christ at the incarnation. He was not *always* God,[14] but became a god in the spirit child stage of progression.

---

[10]From a discourse of Brigham Young in 1860, contained in George Q. Cannon, ed., *Journal of Discourses*, 27 vols. (London: George Q. Cannon, 1861), 8:115.

[11]Ibid., 211. Discourse by Heber C. Kimball in 1860.

[12]Ibid., 4:218. Discourse by Brigham Young in 1857.

[13]Joseph Fielding Smith, *Doctrines of Salvation,* 2 vols. (Salt Lake City, Utah: Bookcraft, 1955], 1:18, emphases original. Regarding the citation of sources from Mormon authorities that are not directly published by "The Church of Jesus Christ of Latter-day Saints," it should be noted by the reader that Mormons may at times use this tactic as an apologetic to dismiss what has been stated by these authorities. Yet, we at times find these very citations in "official" Mormon publications! For example, this very quotation from Joseph Fielding Smith is found in the *Book of Mormon Student Manual* (Salt Lake City, Utah: The Church of Jesus Christ of Latter-day Saints, 1989), 74.

[14]For the logical fallacies of such a doctrine, see Francis J. Beckwith and Stephen E. Parish, "The Mormon God, Omniscience, and Eternal Progression: A Philosophical Analysis," *Trinity Journal* 12NS (1991): 127-38. One problem mentioned in this article is the Mormon doctrine of "progressing" to godhood and infinite knowledge. Such a doctrine is incoherent, for infinity can never be reached in a finite progression. One would never arrive.

This spirit child god was then clothed in a mortal body and is presently a god, one of billions[15] of gods in the universe.

Christian Science, Unity School of Christianity, Religious Science

We have seen that Christian Science denies Jesus was eternally God. Thus there is no continuation of His deity at and throughout the incarnation: "Jesus Christ is not God, as Jesus himself declared, but is the Son of God." Christian Science also imparts to its adherents the teaching that "Jesus, as material manhood, was not Christ."[16] There is therefore an ontological (nature, essence) difference between Jesus and the Christ. Jesus is not the Christ, though the Christ dwells in Jesus.

Concerning the virgin birth of Jesus, the question is asked in a Christian Science publication, "Do you believe in the virgin birth?" The answer is, "Yes, we believe that Jesus was born of a virgin."[17] But what Christian Science *means* by "virgin birth" immediately follows: "As we understand it, *Mary's pure concept of God* as the Father of man[18] *was the avenue or means* by which the Christ [not Jesus], Truth, found expression in the human Jesus."[19] Thus, the virgin birth is conceived of in non-materialistic terms. The virgin birth was brought about by Mary's *thoughts:*

> Christ was not born of the flesh. Christ is the Truth and Life born of God—born of Spirit and not of matter. Jesus, the Galilean Prophet, was born of the Virgin Mary's spiritual thoughts of Life and its manifestation.[20]

---

[15]If not millions. On one occasion in 1975, Mormon Prophet Spencer W. Kimball stated: "Brethren, 225,000 of you are here tonight. I suppose 225,000 of you may become gods. There seems to be plenty of space out there in the universe" (quoted from *The Ensign,* November 1975, p. 80, in Jerald and Sandra Tanner, *Mormonism: Shadow or Reality?* [Salt Lake City, Utah: Utah Lighthouse Ministry, 1982], 172-A).

[16]See chap. 1 for the bibliographical data on both quotations.

[17]No authors or editors listed, *Questions and Answers On Christian Science* (Boston, Mass.: The Christian Science Publishing Society, 1974), 6.

[18]Christian Science redefines "man" as well. Man is a divine idea of God and is not material.

[19]*Questions and Answers On Christian Science,* 6, emphases mine.

[20]Mary Baker Eddy, *The First Church of Christ, Scientist and Miscellany*

To begin to understand the above, the Christian must first understand the worldview[21] of Christian Science, for it is the "lens" through which the Christian Scientist interprets the biblical text. The material world, says Christian Science, is illusion. Matter is unreal; sin, evil and death are unreal. This belief grows out of the Christian Science view of God, which is pantheistic.[22] Flowing from this erroneous premise that all is God, one may follow Christian Science reasoning that "if God is Spirit, and God is All, surely there can be no matter; for the divine All must be Spirit."[23] Moreover, "there is in reality none besides the eternal, infinite God,[24] good. Evil is temporal: it is the illusion of time and mortality."[25] Consequently, "sin is a lie from the beginning—an illusion,"[26] and death is "an illusion."[27]

With their brand of absolute pantheism (*absolutely* all is God[28]) it is no wonder that Christian Science denies both the pre-existent eternal

---

(Boston, Mass.: The First Church of Christ, Scientist, 1941), 261.

[21]Everyone, from the atheist to the satanist, has a worldview. *Worldview* is defined as a person's belief regarding the universe, and that person's function and/or purpose in it.

[22]From the Gr. *pan,* παν ("all"), and *theos,* θεός ("God"). Christ Scientists rebel at being called pantheists. A booklet by Mary Baker Eddy titled *Christian Science Versus Pantheism* (Boston, Mass.: The First Church of Christ, Scientist, 1926), tries to make the case that Christian Science is not pantheistic.

[23]Mary Baker Eddy, *Unity of Good* (Boston, Mass.: The First Church of Christ, Scientist, 1936), 31.

[24]Thus *monism.* Monism is the philosophy that there is only one reality, and that reality is God.

[25]Mary Baker Eddy, *Miscellaneous Writings* (Boston, Mass.: The First Church of Christ, Scientist, 1924), 93.

[26]Mary Baker Eddy, *Message to The Mother Church, 1901* (Boston, Mass.: The First Church of Christ, Scientist, 1929), 13.

[27]Mary Baker Eddy, *Science and Health with Key to the Scriptures* (Boston, Mass.: The First Church of Christ, Scientist, 1971), 584.

[28]In addition to Christian Science's gnostic christological separation of Jesus and the Christ, and its similarity to the ancient docetic view that Jesus' body was not real (the Docetists [from the Gr. *dokeō,* δοκέω, "I seem"] believed that Jesus' body only *seemed* to be real; thus, He was not true humanity), there is the strong flavor of the philosophy of Hinduism's *Advaita Vedānta* in the writings of the cult. *Advaita Vedānta* (non-dualism) was popularized by the Hindu sage Shankara (788-820). In this philosophy Shankara proposed that all is God, and that the material world is illusory. For more on the *Advaita Vedānta* connection with Christian Science, see Steven

deity of Jesus and His deity at the incarnation. Regarding the former, there is for Christian Science no *personal logos* (Word) who was with the Father in the beginning, and who was Himself God the Son from all eternity. Regarding the latter, there can be no incarnation of the eternal Son of God in the biblical sense, because Christian Science denies Jesus' real humanity (the result of its absolute pantheism).

As for the Unity School of Christianity and Religious Science,[29] their Christologies are identical to that of Christian Science.[30] They both deny that Jesus was the eternal personal *logos* who was with the Father in the beginning, and who was eternally God the Son. Further, a separation of Jesus and the Christ is fundamental. The Unity School of Christianity explains that it believes in "Jesus—The Man of Nazareth." Yet, "Christ existed long before Jesus."[31] Speaking of Christ, Religious Science says that "*It* [is] the One and Only Power in the Universe," and that "we must understand that Christ is not a person."[32] As a result, the gnostic separation of Jesus and Christ occurs: "Jesus—The name of a man. Distinguished from the Christ."[33]

It should be noted that Christian Science, Unity and Religious Science teach that the Christ dwells within each person, just as *It* dwelled in Jesus (though no one has reached the heights of a display of the Christ Principle to the extent that Jesus has; thus Jesus is the "way-shower," not "the way"). Unity and Religious Science, however, have gone on record stating that *we* may become the Christ, just as Jesus did. "Reveal yourself to yourself by affirming, *"I am the Christ, son of the living God.""*[34] "Each partakes of the Christ nature, to the degree that

---

Tsoukalas, "A Consideration for Christian Scientists: Worldview Imposition," *The Sounding Board* 1:2 (Dec. 1994): 1. To obtain, write to Sound Doctrine Ministries, P. O. Box 1962, Exeter, NH, 03833.

[29]Unity publishes the magazines *Daily Word* and *Unity*. Religious Science publishes *Science of Mind* magazine.

[30]With the exception that they may not hold to a docetic view of the humanity of Jesus.

[31]Both quotations from Charles Fillmore, *The Revealing Word* (Unity Village, Mo.: Unity School of Christianity, 1985), 110, 34.

[32]Ernest Holmes, *The Science of Mind* (New York: Dodd, Mead and Co., 1938), 357, 359, emphasis mine.

[33]Ibid., 603.

[34]Containing the teaching of Charles Fillmore, *Metaphysical Bible Dictionary* (Unity Village, Mo.: Unity School of Christianity, 1931), 150, emphases original.

Christ is revealed through him, and to that degree he becomes the Christ."[35] Thus the denial that Jesus is *uniquely* the Christ; thus the denial that Jesus is the *unique* Son of God.

The New Age Movement

In many ways the Christology of the New Age Movement is similar to that of Christian Science, Unity, and Religious Science, namely that there is a fundamental distinction between the Christ and Jesus. He is not the unique Son of God in the biblical sense. Rather, as David Spangler states, "Jesus was one of a line of spiritual teachers, a line that continues today, but he was the first to directly incarnate and reveal the Christ in such a planetary and cosmic fashion."[36] Spangler's further comments are most revealing:

> Jesus demonstrated God immanent, and by so doing he revealed the Christ, the consciousness of God, the I am that I am, here, there, everywhere.[37] Unfortunately, the past conditioning of man was still externally oriented, with the result that Jesus was removed from the kinship of human revelation and made a God himself, exclusively.... The true Christian has only rarely been seen because a Christian has largely been defined as someone who worships and follows Christ as God, but not someone who actually follows him to the source and realization of one's own divinity and godhood and Christhood, and then is himself a revelation of this fact. Jesus is a way-shower, not the end or the goal.[38]

---

[35]*The Science of Mind,* 357.

[36]David Spangler, *Reflections On the Christ* (Moray, Scotland: Findhorn Publications, 1981), 28.

[37]This is standard New Age thinking. Consider, for example, the popular *A Course In Miracles,* a revelation from "The Voice" given to Helen Schucman in the middle 1960s into the early 1970s (Tibouron, Calif.: Foundation For Inner Peace, 1985): "The name of *Jesus* is the name of one who was a man but saw the face of Christ in all his brothers and remembered God.... The man [Jesus] was an illusion" (Manual for Teachers, 83). Here *A Course In Miracles* also displays elements of *Advaita Vedānta* (see above under Hinduism) and Docetism (an element of both incipient Gnosticism and the later fully developed Gnosticism of the second and third centuries).

[38]Spangler, *Reflections On the Christ,* 29. Here the Christ may be identified with the *Self,* the "God-Soul" in everyone (see above under Hinduism). *A*

Even in spite of new agers' wide acceptance of Spangler's words on the Christ and Jesus, which get right to the point of disagreement with Christianity, we still must exercise caution in dialogue with new agers. It is not outside the parameters of New Age belief to call Jesus "God." For the new ager, Jesus is God, but only in the pantheistic sense that all is God. He is God only in the sense that you and I are, and He is the Christ in the sense that He revealed the "Christ" to humanity in such a way that would have us recognize that we, too, are Christs. As Spangler notes, "In human terms, this means it is a time when we learn to *be* at one with God ourselves, to be Christs ourselves."[39] Christians, then, must be careful to define the terms "Jesus" and "Christ."[40]

The Unification Church

One of the best examples of the similarity of language between the cults and Christianity is seen in the Unification Church's *Divine Principle*. It states, "The Principle does not deny the attitude of faith held by many Christians that Jesus is God, since it is true that a perfected man is one body with God."[41]

What if in conversation a Unificationist were to state only the first part of the preceding? If it were not for the second phrase in this statement, which defines what Unificationists mean by "Jesus is God," we would never know the difference, and that difference is that any man who is by their definition "perfected" is one with God. The difference continues. After citing John 14:9-10, 1:10, and 8:58, the *Divine Principle* states that Jesus "can by no means be God Himself,"

Course In Miracles states that the Christ is "the Self we share.... the holy Self, the Christ Whom God created as His Son" (Workbook, 421). Regarding recognizing our own divinity, godhood and Christhood, *A Course In Miracles* teaches, "Is He [Jesus] the Christ? O yes, along with you" (Manual for Teachers, 83).

[39]Ibid., emphasis original.

[40]Biblically Jesus *is* the Christ (Matt. 16:16; see 1 John 2:22 regarding those who deny this). His name is Jesus of Nazareth, and He is the Christ, i.e. the anointed one, the historic *person* (not a cosmic force, principle, or the *Self*) expected by God's people in the Old Testament. Jesus the Christ is the only one who is both God and man. He is the unique Son of God.

[41]No authors or editors listed, *Divine Principle* (New York: The Holy Spirit Association for the Unification of World Christianity, 1973), 209.

Knowing Christ in the Challenge of Heresy

and that John 1:10 "does not signify that he was the Creator Himself."[42] Thus the Unification Church denies the biblical definition of the incarnate deity of Christ.

The Way International

Victor Paul Wierwille, with no ambiguity, denies the incarnate deity of Christ: "Jesus Christ is not God. Biblically he is the Son of God. This in no way detracts from the uniqueness of Christ. His position is second only to God, being God's 'only begotten Son.'"[43]

Baha'i

The Baha'i Faith's Christology is well represented by Richard Backwell, who "was for some years a part-time manager of the Baha'i Publishing Trust."[44] He states,

> Many people have come to suppose that Jesus should be regarded as God Himself come down from heaven occupying human form until release after death on the cross. *This strange view* seems to have arisen from interpreting certain statements made by Jesus Himself, taken in isolation, or from the supposition that certain of the recorded miracles, considered literally, could only have been performed by the Godhead.[45]

Backwell then goes on to list certain attributes of God, and to draw the conclusion that "[w]ere such a God to become incarnate in the concrete, limited form of a man He would thereby immediately cease to be God."[46]

Further, the Baha'i Faith does not acknowledge Jesus as unique in the biblical sense. For them Jesus is one of Nine Great Manifestations of God who came to bring peace and the teaching of God. Speaking of the belief that Christ is the unique incarnation of God, George

---

[42]Ibid., 210-11.

[43]Victor Paul Wierwille, *Jesus Christ Is Not God* (New Knoxville, Ohio: The American Christian Press, 1975), 60.

[44]Richard Backwell, *The Christianity of Jesus* (Wellington Place, Peterhead, Scotland: Volturna Press, 1972), back of dust jacket.

[45]Ibid., 23, emphases added.

[46]Ibid., 29.

Townshend, a former Anglican priest converted to Baha'i, states, "there is nothing in Christ's own statements, as recorded in the Gospel, to support this view."[47] Thus Jesus as *a* Manifestation of God is joined by Krishna, Buddha, Muhammad, etc. And Jesus is not even the greatest among these. Baha'u'llah (otherwise known as Mirza Husayn Ali), "the Greatest Name,"[48] in 1863 declared that he was one to bring in an age of peace for all mankind.

Unitarian Universalism

Though quite diverse theologically, the Unitarian Universalist movement displays a common theme: Jesus Christ never was God, is now not God, and never will be God. "Unitarian," as it applies to the nature of God, is by definition not "Trinitarian" (that is, for Unitarianism there only one person who is God, not three persons who are the one God). Thus Unitarianism ends up rejecting Jesus as God the Son.

Illustrating this diversity and this common theme, we read,

> *On Jesus:* There is a belief in the Galilean as the highest model of the religious life, on the one hand; and, on the other, a belief in Jesus which equates his ministry to that of Moses, Buddha, Socrates, and Mohammed.[49]

This diversity of the Unitarian Universalist movement is further manifested with a belief in the separation of Jesus and the Christ, as was seen above with Christian Science, its related movements, and the New Age Movement:

> The Unitarian Universalist begins with the humanity of Jesus, which is the same humanity in all people, and accepts the divinity in Jesus

---

[47]George Townshend, *Christ and Baha'u'llah* (Oxford: George Ronald, 1957, reprinted, 1985), 25.

[48]See Laura Clifford Barney, coll. and trans., *Some Answered Questions: Abdul-Baha* (Wilmette, Ill.: Baha'i Publishing Trust, 1981), 149.

[49]Harry Scholefield, ed., *The Unitarian Universalist Pocket Guide* (Boston, Mass.: Unitarian Universalist Association, 1981, revised 1983), 8, emphases original.

(sometimes called 'the Christ') only insofar as it says something about universal human nature *in potentia.*[50]

Quoting the nineteenth century British Unitarian James Martineau, the pamphlet containing the preceding states, "The incarnation is true, not of Christ [Jesus] exclusively, but of Man universally."[51]

Yet another view in the Unitarian Universalist pool of beliefs about Jesus follows:

> Matthew, Mark, Luke, and John put into their pictures of Jesus what they needed to have there in order to make him what they believed him to be, the supreme human who was also God. Many writers have since done that sort of thing. Our Christian culture puts into its concept of Jesus what it needs to have there in order to make him what they believed him to be.... I find it exhilarating to believe that the perfection we have poured into the figure of Jesus has come from the minds of human beings, from human imagination, and ethical aspiration. Today it is a greater perfection than it was for the gospel writers. My faith is that it will grow better as human experience is added to it. I'm for a better and better Jesus, born from the aspiring heart of humanity.[52]

In all this the common thread is a denial of the deity of Christ, though Christians must be careful to discern at times the Unitarian use of the term "divinity." For example, William Ellery Channing is quoted as saying, "We do not deny it [Jesus' divinity].... We firmly believe in the divinity of Christ's mission and office, that he spoke with divine authority, and was a bright image of the divine perfections."[53] A few sentences later Channing denies the deity of Christ in the context of his misunderstanding of the doctrine of the Trinity:

---

[50]Statement by Richard M. Fewkes in Daniel G. Higgins, Jr., ed., *Unitarian Universalist Views of Jesus* (Boston, Mass.: Unitarian Universalist Association, n.d.), 5, emphases original.

[51]Ibid.

[52]Ibid., 8-9. Statement by John G. MacKinnon.

[53]Prescott B. Wintersteen, *Christology in American Unitarianism* (Boston: The Unitarian Universalist Christian Fellowship, 1977), 17.

Trinitarianism teaches that Jesus Christ is the supreme and infinite God, and that he and his Father... are strictly and literally one and the same being. Now to us this doctrine is most unspiritual and irrational.... Now we affirm, and this is our chief heresy, that Jesus was not and could not be the God from whom he came.[54]

Finally, we read, "Jesus' authority is derived from the Father, but that does not make him Almighty God himself."[55]

This is a Jesus far removed from the biblical Christ. Rather than the Jesus attested to by the New Testament record, the Jesus who will come to judge the living and the dead, this Jesus has been craftily decked out in an attractive dress, a dress manufactured after the biblical record had been stripped of its authority, historical validity, and reliability. It is a Jesus that rests on the absolute of the whims of human wishful thinking.[56]

Liberal Protestantism

I may just as well have included in the above section the extreme doctrinal liberalism of churches and individuals who mark themselves not only as Protestants of different denominations, but mark themselves as Christians as well. In reality they are Unitarian in their doctrine of God. The mark of distinction carried by designations of groups clearly outside the boundaries of Christianity (such as Jehovah's Witnesses, Mormons, etc.) is blurred when we talk of heretical churches carrying the designations of Methodist, Episcopal, Baptist, Congregational, and the like. (I do not mean to say that all churches with these titles are heretical. By no means. There are many *Christian* Baptist, Congregational, Episcopal, and Methodist churches.) It would be naive to assume that there are no christological heresies within the four walls

---

[54]Ibid.

[55]Ibid., 41.

[56]According to *The Unitarian Universalist Pocket Guide*, 8, people who are atheists and agnostics (!) may be members of Unitarian Universalist churches. Illustrating the diversity among Unitarians is a series of pamphlets prepared by the Unitarian Universalist Association in Boston. The list includes, *The Faith of a Religious Atheist, The Faith of a Humanist, The Faith of a Theist, The Faith of a Liberal Christian,* and *The Faith of a Feminist.*

of any church simply because of a Protestant designation. This affords all the more reason to discuss Liberal Protestantism, if only briefly.

In this movement we find most of the heresies discussed up to this point. It all depends on the church, the minister, and the members of these churches. They may teach that Jesus was only a man, or one of many spiritually enlightened teachers, or that the Christ was in Jesus just as *IT* is in you. Or perhaps for these ministers the issue of just who Christ is carries no importance, and therefore they never mention it in their sermons.

Perhaps they have been reading about Robert Funk and the "Jesus Seminar," or have a copy *The Five Gospels: The Search for the Authentic Words of Jesus,*[57] produced by the Seminar. This work is the product of the examination of the sayings of Jesus. The sayings attributed to Jesus in these Gospels are color-coded to tell us whether or not Jesus *really* said them (red), *most likely* said them (pink), *could* have said them (gray), or *definitely did not* state them (black). Funk is quoted as saying that Christians "don't want the real Jesus. They want one they can worship."[58]

With Liberal Protestantism comes the basic denial of Christ as exclusively God the Son and exclusively Savior.[59]

---

[57]A new translation and commentary of the four Gospels *plus* the Gospel of Thomas by Robert W. Funk, Roy W. Hoover, and the Jesus Seminar (New York: Macmillan, 1993).

[58]Robert Funk, quoted from the Feb. 24, 1994 *Los Angeles Times*, in Luke Timothy Johnson, *The Real Jesus: The Misguided Quest for the Historical Jesus and the Truth of the Traditional Gospels* (San Francisco: HarperCollins Publishers Inc., 1996), 12. This is an excellent summary and critique of the Jesus Seminar's methodology and conclusions.

[59]I have talked with ministers of churches who affirm the deity and humanity of Christ, and even the Trinity, but who deny that Christ is the only way of salvation. Such a belief, however, by necessity cancels out what is affirmed. The biblical record shows Christ as exclusively God the Son, and exclusively the Savior. If Christ is not the only way, then there are other saviors and other means to heaven. Thus the *unique* incarnate deity of Christ is denied, and therefore He is not the "only (unique) begotten" Son of God that we encounter in the Gospel of John, and His work on the cross is rendered non-essential if there are other ways of salvation. Such a view flies in the face of the purpose of the incarnation. Such a view, therefore, ultimately denies that Christ has come in the flesh. Consequently, we end up with a Jesus that is foreign to the New Testament; we end up with a counterfeit Christ who by implication

The Word-Faith Movement

This heretical[60] movement within Christianity has other labels: Positive Confession, Name It and Claim It, Word of Faith, and Health and Wealth. It is represented by such notables as Fred Price, John Avanzini, Casey Treat, Charles Capps, Paul Crouch, Morris Cerullo, Benny Hinn, and Jerry Savelle. Other leading voices in this movement are Kenneth Copeland and Kenneth E. Hagin.

Though Word-Faith teachers at times assert the deity of Christ, other statements made by them are heretical concerning His *uniqueness* as the Son of God. For example, Kenneth Copeland stated, "Now listen! From the Book of Acts, all the way through all of the epistles, all the way through the Revelation of John, Jesus is no longer called the only begotten-Son of God."[61] Copeland has even equated Adam with Jesus: "Adam is as much like God as you can get, just the same as Jesus."[62] Further, due to the Word-Faith doctrine that we are "little gods," Kenneth Copeland once stated, "And I say this with all respect, so that it don't upset you too bad. But I say it anyway. When I read in the Bible where He [Jesus] says, 'I AM,' I just smile and say, 'Yes, I AM too.'"[63] Kenneth E. Hagin as well enters into heresy regarding the uniqueness of Christ when he makes the statement, "The believer is as much an incarnation as was Jesus of Nazareth."[64]

---

cannot be God the Son. On another occasion I visited a church where I heard the minister speak of "sharing Christ" with the world. Only after speaking with him, and asking him pointed questions, did he admit that Jesus was only a man and the "Christ" was the Holy Spirit in Him.

[60]In addition to the heretical doctrine soon to be discussed, the Word-Faith Movement also espouses that believers are little gods, that faith is a cosmic force, that the force of faith is carried by the actual words one speaks, and that by this practice God is bound to act on our behalf for health and prosperity.

[61]Kenneth Copeland, (audiotape) *What Happened from the Cross to the Throne* (Fort Worth, Tex.: Kenneth Copeland Ministries, 1990). See also his *Now Are We In Christ Jesus* (Fort Worth, Tex.: Kenneth Copeland Ministries, 1980), 24, where Copeland states, "Jesus is no longer *the only-begotten* Son of God" (emphases original).

[62]Kenneth Copeland, (audiotape) *Following the Faith of Abraham* (Fort Worth, Tex.: Kenneth Copeland Ministries, 1989).

[63]Kenneth Copeland, "Believer's Voice of Victory" broadcast, TBN, July 19, 1987.

[64]Kenneth E. Hagin, "The Incarnation," *Word of Faith* magazine,

Unfortunately, there is more. Kenneth Copeland gave a prophecy wherein Jesus was speaking through Copeland. What follows is most alarming: "They crucified Me for claiming that I was God. *But I didn't claim I was God*; I just claimed I walked with Him and that He was in Me. Hallelujah. That's what you're doing."[65] Finally, Paul Crouch, while listening to Kenneth Copeland expound upon the "born again Jesus" doctrine (Jesus died and went to hell "as a mortal man sin" and then was born again out of the pit of hell[66]), stated about Jesus after He went to hell, "and soon His divinity returned."[67] This, of course, carries with it at least two major heretical implications. First is that Jesus at one point was not God, and second that the Triune God was at one point not a Trinity.

Islam, Hinduism and Buddhism

The reader may wonder why I have included Hinduism, Buddhism,[68] and Islam in what should only be deviations of Christian doctrine. The answer is two-fold. First, if Christ is indeed God, He is the God of the universe, and *any* deviation from that teaching I consider heretical. Second, these three groups are no longer limited to their specific domains in the East. Beginning in the last part of the nineteenth century the West has witnessed a tremendous proliferation of Hindus, Buddhists and Muslims. Consequently, due to the Judeo-Christian roots

---

(December 1980): 14.

[65]Kenneth Copeland, "Take Time to Pray," *Believer's Voice of Victory* magazine 15, 2 (February 1987): 9, emphases added. In response to questioning, Copeland later stated: "I didn't say Jesus *wasn't* God. I said He didn't *claim* to be God when He lived on the earth" (Kenneth Copeland, "Question & Answer," *Believer's Voice of Victory* 16, 8 [August 1988]: 8, emphases original). But there is still a problem with this. Regarding the prophecy, did Jesus speak through Copeland, or not? Obviously the original claim was that Jesus was speaking (note the pronouns). Jesus would never have said what was spoken through Copeland, and even if Jesus was not speaking through Copeland, his Christology is still heretical, for Jesus claimed to be God when He lived on the earth.

[66]More on this in chap. 8.

[67]TBN "Praise-a-Thon" program, November 6, 1990. Tape on file from the Christian Research Institute.

[68]It may be better to speak of Hinduisms and Buddhisms, the plural signifying the different types within the two systems.

of the early settlers to this country from Europe, and subsequent Christianized generations stemming from them, adherents of these structures coming to the United States needed to have *something* stated about who Christ was (if they had not already, which is the case with Islam). They could not remain silent about this central figure of history. Thus, as soon as statements about who Christ was were penned by adherents of these religions, heresy *specifically* targeting the biblical text was born.

Islam

For Islam the case of heresy is simple. The Qur'ān, the Muslims' holy book, denies that Jesus is the Son of God, and thus God the Son. Concerning the Christian doctrine of the Trinity (which they viewed as the Father, Mary, and Jesus the Son), the Muslim Scriptures state: "Christ Jesus the son of Mary was (no more than) an apostle of God.... So believe in God [Allah] and His apostles. Say not 'Trinity.' Desist. It will be better for you. For God is One God. Glory be to Him. (Far Exalted is He) above having a son."[69]

Hinduism

There are thousands of cults comprising Hinduism today. Since there is no mention of Christ in the various holy books of classical Hinduism, Hindu spiritual teachers have viewed Christ within the framework of their own worldviews taken from these Hindu holy books. In other words, Hindu teachers view Christ from within the context of their views of God and humanity. I shall discuss the two types of Hinduism most prevalent in the West, and then document some of the statements about Christ given by teachers within these two types.

The first type is *Advaita Vedānta*. *Vedānta* means "the end of the Vedas." *Veda* means "knowledge, sacred teaching, sacred knowledge" in Sanskrit. It is also a title for the oldest holy texts of Hinduism. *Vedānta* thus refers to the philosophy gathered from an examination of a collection of philosophical treatises at the end of the Vedas called the *Upanishads.*

---

[69]A. Yusaf Ali, *The Holy Qurān: Text, Translation and Commentary,* 2 vols. (Brentwood, Md.: Amana Corp., 1983), 1:234 (Sūrah 4:171).

Advaita Vedānta is the philosophy of *non-dualism* (the meaning of the word *advaita*). The most important teacher of this philosophy was Shankara (788-820). Here God is *Brahman,* and Brahman alone is real (*monism:* there is only one reality, and that is God). Thus, the material world ultimately is an illusion.[70] In its concept of humanity, the only *real* part of a person is *ātman.* The *ātman* is the soul (or Self) which *is* Brahman (God). And Brahman, conversely, is *ātman.* Thus, the inner part of each and every person, that part which alone is ultimately real, is *ātman Brahman* (the God-Self). It is the spark of divinity in everyone.[71]

Second is that of *Vishishtādvaita Vedānta,* or *qualified non-dualism.* This philosophy, explicated by the Hindu sage Ramanuja (1055-1137), states that Brahman is God and is real, but that the world of appearance is equally real, yet not independent of Brahman (and this is the "qualification"). The world has its reality in Brahman. The soul, or *ātman,* of a person also has its basis and reality in Brahman.

Swami Vivekananda

The greatest modern-day proponent of *Advaita Vedānta* in the West was Swami Vivekananda. His visit to the World's Parliament of Religions in Chicago in 1893 was the catalyst for the spread of his brand of Hinduism in the United States. He founded the "Vedanta Society" in New York in 1894.

The Swami had interesting, though heretical, things to say about Jesus Christ. Due to his holding the philosophy of *Advaita Vedānta,* Vivekananda denied the biblical incarnation of Jesus: "He [Jesus] had no other idea of Himself, no other except that He was Spirit. He was disembodied, unfettered, unbound Spirit."[72] He also denied the

---

[70] An analogy given for this world view is that of a person walking in the dark and mistaking a piece of rope for a snake. Only as the person's consciousness changes the illusory perception (as he walks closer to the source of this illusion) is he able to see what the object truly is. So it is with a person and Brahman. One's perception must change in order to see Brahman (the rope) and not the illusion (the snake).

[71] I believe *Advaita Vedānta* to be *the* major philosophical force behind today's New Age Movement.

[72] S. Vivekananda, *Inspired Talks* (New York: Ramakrishna-Vivekananda Center of New York, 1958), 192.

uniqueness of Jesus: "Let us, therefore, find God not only in Jesus of Nazareth, but in all the Great Ones who preceded Him, in all who have come after Him, and all who are yet to come."[73] He further states, "The Trinitarian Christ is elevated above us; the Unitarian Christ is merely a mortal man. Neither can help us."[74]

With Vivekananda we also find the separation of Jesus and Christ: "Christ and Buddha were the names of a state to be attained; Jesus and Gautama were the persons to attain it."[75] Second, after proclaiming that "Jesus was imperfect,"[76] he states that "we must not pin our faith on any man, however great; we too must become Buddhas and Christs."[77] To sum up, this Hindu philosophy (taught by thousands of teachers today) contains no affirmation of Jesus Christ as uniquely God in human flesh. Even if a proponent of this philosophy were to state, "Jesus was God," the phrase would not be defined biblically; it would be defined in the way that the Self (*ātman*) of Jesus, the only reality, was identical to Brahman (God).[78]

Vivekananda's philosophy has been called "non-duality at its starkest,"[79] and at this point the reader may wonder how it is that Vivekananda can even speak of "Jesus of Nazareth," of us not pinning our faith in any *man,* and of other "Great Ones" who were *incarnations.* All these imply at the least a recognition of the material. To state it another way, if the only reality is God, why even make mention of these, for do they not imply fleshly existence? Perhaps Vivekananda would say, "Indeed, all material existence is not real, but I must communicate on your level." Or perhaps he would say, "Ah, now you are beginning to comprehend; you are now much closer to Brahman realization!"

---

[73]Ibid., 200.
[74]Ibid., 20.
[75]Ibid., 52.
[76]Ibid.
[77]Ibid., 113.
[78]Vivekananda says that "the Soul [Self, *ātman*] is the unity of all personalities.... It is at rest, eternal, unchangeable, It is God" (ibid., 38).
[79]R. C. Zaehner, *Hinduism* (New York: Oxford University Press, 1966), 168.

A. C. Bhaktivedanta Swami Prabhupada

Prabhupada introduced the Hare Krishna movement to the United States in the 1960s. This form of *Vishishtādvaita Vedānta* has attracted celebrities such as former Beatle George Harrison. According to the Hare Krishna Movement, *Krishna*[80] is the eighth incarnation of the god Vishnu. As such he is the Supreme Lord. He is the personal Lord of each adherent. Every follower of Krishna is devoted to him. Prabhupada, like Vivekananda, had interesting yet heretical things to say about Jesus. "Jesus Christ Was a Guru" is the title of a section in Prabhupada's *The Science of Self Realization.*[81] Though Prabhupada states that he recognizes Jesus as "the son of God, the representative of God,"[82] he denies the uniqueness of Jesus by stating, "anyone who is preaching God's glories must be accepted as a *guru.* Jesus Christ is one such great personality."[83]

Jesus preached God consciousness.[84] Further, "whether you call God 'Christ'...or 'Krishna,' ultimately you are addressing the same Supreme Personality of Godhead."[85] In practice, however, the one in whom Hare Krishna adherents are to place their devotion (Sanskrit *bhakti*) is Krishna. Prabhupada, and consequently all devotees to Krishna, do not recognize Jesus as uniquely God the Son.

Buddhism

There are many expressions of Buddhism. Some involve the acknowledgment of deities and the incarnations of these deities, called *Bodhisattvas.*[86] Bodhisattvas are enlightened beings who, for a time, postpone their achievement of *Nirvāna* (eternal bliss) in order to bring

---

[80]An adjective in Sanskrit meaning "black." In Hindu mythology, Krishna was born as a result of the god Vishnu plucking out one strand of his black hair, which in turn entered the womb of Krishna's mother, Devaki.

[81](Los Angeles: The Bhaktivedanta Book Trust, 1980), 134.

[82]Ibid., 135.

[83]Ibid., 136.

[84]See ibid., 136.

[85]Ibid., 126.

[86]This is found in *Mahāyāna* Buddhism.

truth to human beings.[87] Others acknowledge no divine being or beings at all and are largely systems of ethics.[88]

The most popular figure in Buddhism today is the Dalai Lama.[89] The Dalai Lama's Tibetan Buddhism (a form of *Mahāyāna* Buddhism) believes in the existence of Jesus Christ, but, like other eastern religions, redefines who He is. The Dalai Lama sees Jesus as just another Bodhisattva: "For me, as a Buddhist, my attitude toward Jesus Christ is that he was either a fully enlightened being or a bodhisattva of a very high spiritual realization."[90]

Along with his denial of Jesus Christ as the unique Son of God, we find in the following the Dalai Lama's inference that Jesus is not the Christ. Rather, Jesus is only the "historical personification" of the "Christ." Drawing upon his Buddhism, were there is an ontological separation between the Buddha (a person) and the "Truth" (suchness) embodied by the Buddha, the Dalai Lama states concerning Jesus and the Christ.

> In order to actually see the Buddha, you must realize that the *dharmakāya*—the Truth of the Buddha[91]—is suchness. This is what it means to actually see the Buddha. Similarly, these passages [John 12:44-50] point out that it is through the historical personification of

---

[87] See Lewis M. Hopfe, *Religions of the World* (New York: Macmillan, 1991), 163.

[88]Such as *Theravāda* Buddhism. The ideal of this form of Buddhism is to achieve enlightenment by oneself, though among the laity there may be those who express some sort of devotion to divine beings (see Hopfe, *Religions of the World*, 160).

[89]*Lama* means "superior one." *Dalai* means "sea." Thus it "indicates the vastness and depth of the person" (ibid., 172-73).

[90]Dalai Lama, *The Good Heart: A Buddhist Perspective on the Teachings of Jesus* (Boston, Mass.: Wisdom Publications, 1996), 83.

[91]Originally the *dharmakāya* meant the body of teachings of Gautama Buddha. Later it merged into meaning the *true nature* of all the enlightened ones (buddhas). All buddhas have this essential nature (see Stephen Schuhmacher and Gert Woerner, eds., *The Encyclopedia of Eastern Philosophy and Religion* [Boston, Mass.: Shambala Publications, Inc., 1989], 377). It is evident as the quotation proceeds that the Dalai Lama is equating the *dharmakāya* with the "Christ" essence or Truth.

the Christ [i.e., Jesus] that you are actually experiencing the Father that he represents. Christ is the gateway to this encounter with the Father.[92]

The reader should note that the Dalai Lama's teaching regarding the uniqueness of Jesus Christ and the separation of Jesus and the Christ (the Christ being synonymous with the Buddha nature, or *dharmakāya*) may be found in many types of Buddhist philosophies.

---

[92]Dalai Lama, *The Good Heart,* 112.

Chapter 4

The Four Gospels: The Incarnate Deity of Christ

"Brethren, we must think of Jesus Christ as God."—*Clement,* Second Letter to the Corinthians

"Jesus Christ is not God."—*Victor Paul Wierwille,* Jesus Christ Is Not God

The Gospels' witness to the deity of Christ at and through His incarnation is our subject for this chapter. I shall work through them (not exhaustively) to build evidence supporting the doctrine that Christ at His incarnation and beyond was God the Son.

The Synoptic Gospels

Matthew, Mark and Luke comprise what are known as the Synoptic[1] Gospels. As we work through the Gospels, one all-important

---

[1]"The word 'Synoptic,' from Gr. *syn* ('together') and *opsis* ('view'), means 'giving a common view' of the Gospel story, and is used to refer to these three Gospels. The word emphasizes their agreements, but must not be allowed to

theme will continually emerge: Jesus is consistently pictured by the four Gospel writers as doing and saying that which only Yahweh can do and say. This attribution of the deeds and words of Yahweh to the Son of God are evidence that they see in Jesus the coming of Yahweh the Son, God with His people, and thus the inauguration of the kingdom of God among men.

Matthew 1:21-23 (28:20)

"And she will bear a Son; and you shall call His name Jesus, for it is He who will save His people from their sins. Now all this took place that what was spoken by the Lord through the prophet might be fulfilled, saying, 'Behold, the virgin shall be with child, and shall bear a Son, and they shall call His name Immanuel,' which translated means 'God with us.'" This passage dealing with the forthcoming incarnation of the Son of God strongly implies His deity. Here the divine attributes of *saving, ownership,* and *presence* are manifest in the Son at His coming.

Yahweh Saves

In Psalm 130:8 the cry of the heart is that Yahweh will redeem His people from their sins. Yahweh saves, and in Matthew 1:21 it is *Jesus Himself*[2] (as His name in Hebrew, *yehoshua* [Yahweh saves], states) who will save His people. This is *why*[3] the Son of God is to be called "Jesus."

Yahweh Owns

The phrase "His people" is ripe with divine significance. Psalm 130:8 states that Yahweh will redeem Israel [*His* people]. The covenant people Israel were Yahweh's (Exod. 4:22; Isa. 43:10), and it was

---

obscure their differences" (F. V. Filson, s.v. "Gospels, Synoptic," in Geoffrey W. Bromily, gen. ed., *The International Standard Bible Encyclopedia,* 4 vols. [Grand Rapids, Mich.: Wm. B. Eerdmans Publishing Co., 1982], 2:532).

[2]The Jehovah's Witnesses, who relegate the divine functions of Christ to Jehovah acting *through* Christ, totally miss the intent of Matthew, which is that *He* (Jesus) will save.

[3]*"For* (Gr. *gar,* γὰρ) it is He..." (v. 21) signals a ground (or reason) clause.

Yahweh who came to the aid of His own people (see Exod. 4:31). In Matthew all this is said about the person of the Son. Jesus has come to the aid of *His* people. Here the immediate reference is to the godly remnant of Jews who were Jesus' people (though later, of course, the believing Gentiles would be included). The people who are to be "saved from their sins" belong to Yahweh the Son in a covenant relationship, and Christ as Yahweh, by divine implication, owns—they are "*His* people."

Yahweh's Presence

In the Old Testament *the* characteristic that set the nation of Israel apart from all other nations was the "divine presence." Yahweh was *with* His people. He was with His people in many ways. As Walther Eichrodt points out, Yahweh's presence among His people may be manifested by the *malak Yahweh* (מַלְאַךְ יְהוָה, "the angel of the LORD") who is Yahweh Himself (see Gen. 16:11, 13), the *kebod Yahweh* (כְּבוֹד־יְהוָה, "the glory of the LORD") in the form of a cloud (Exod. 24:16, 17; see Luke 1:35!), and the *pene Yahweh* (פְּנֵי יְהוָה, "the face of the LORD"), indicative of the presence of the LORD (Exod. 33:14).[4] The Ark of Yahweh also signified His divine presence (see 2 Sam. 6:14, 15, 21).[5] It cannot be denied that the presence of Yahweh was the important ingredient in the relationship between Him and His people. Indeed, there was an indissoluble link between the "presence" and the covenant (Ezek. 37:26-27).

For Matthew, Yahweh has visited His people, and it is in the person of the Son. Thus he is able to state that God is with us (*Immanuel,* 1:23).[6] And with the quoting of Isaiah 7:14 it is to be the event of the virgin birth, the birth of one who is the "Mighty God" (Isa. 9:6; 10:21) that will bring forth "God with us." This should not be viewed as God being with His people *through* the Son, as if the Son is some sort of intermediary (as the Jehovah's Witnesses state). Rather, Yahweh Himself in the person of the Son of God is with His people.

---

[4]Walther Eichrodt, *Theology of the Old Testament,* trans. J. A. Baker, 2 vols. (Philadelphia, Pa.: The Westminster Press, 1967), 2:24, 30, 37-38.

[5]Ibid., 270.

[6]Matthew follows almost perfectly the LXX of Isa. 7:14.

Jesus is the incarnate Son of God, the incarnate God the Son. He has visited His people and marked the divine presence of Yahweh with us in the most unique way, by taking upon Himself a perfect and full human nature in the womb of the virgin by the agency of God the Holy Spirit (Matt. 1:18, 20). As the unique Son of God, He as Yahweh promises to be with His covenant people "always, even to the end of the age." This declaration of Christ in Matthew 28:20 is in the style of deity, for only Yahweh can declare His presence with His people.

Matthew 3:3; Mark 1:3; Luke 3:4 (John 1:23)

The Synoptics' witness to the deity of Christ continues as Isaiah 40:3 is quoted: *"The voice of one crying in the wilderness, 'make ready the way of the Lord, make His paths straight.'"*[7]
John the Baptist is "the voice," and Jesus is "the Lord." Matthew, Mark and Luke apply Isaiah 40:3 to John the Baptist, and the Baptist applies it to himself in John 1:23. Isaiah 40:3 reads, "A voice is calling, 'Clear the way for the LORD [*Yahweh*] in the wilderness; Make smooth in the desert a highway for our God.'" According to this text, someone is going to come to prepare the way for *Yahweh*. In the Gospels it is John the Baptist who comes[8] to prepare the way for Jesus (Luke 1:17, esp. 1:76).
Jesus is the Yahweh spoken of in Isaiah 40:3. All the events in the Gospels evidence this: the Isaiah text is quoted (Matt. 3:3; Mark 1:3; Luke 3:4; John 1:23), John the Baptist is introduced (Matt. 3:4; Mark 1:4; Luke 3:2; John 1:6), and Jesus is introduced (Matt. 3:13; Mark 1:9; Luke 3:21; John 1:29).
John the Baptist is the "messenger" of Malachi (Mal. 3:1; 4:5), who is the instrument used to prepare the way of Yahweh, to "make His paths straight." This phrase refers to the bringing of repentance,[9] which

---

[7]Matthew, Mark and Luke quote the passage from the LXX.
[8]In the spirit (same prophetic ministry) and power of Elijah (Luke 1:17; see Matt. 11:14; 17:12-13; Mark 9:11-13, where John the Baptist *is* Elijah, in the sense of the same type of prophetic ministry). In these Gospel verses there is also an allusion to Malachi 3:1a: "Behold, I [Yahweh] am going to send my messenger, and he will clear the way before Me." Malachi 4:5 states that Elijah the prophet will be sent "before the coming of the great and terrible day of the LORD [*Yahweh*]."
[9]See D. A. Carson, *Matthew,* in Frank E. Gaebelein, ed., *The Expositor's*

was the focus of John's ministry as he prepared the way for Yahweh the Messiah, Son of God.[10]

Matthew 9:2-3; Mark 2:5-7; Luke 5:20-21

In Mark 2:5 Jesus says to the paralytic, *"My son, your sins are forgiven"* (see Matt. 9:2; Luke 5:20). Here the functional implies the ontological. By Christ forgiving sins He is taking upon Himself only what God can do, thereby implicitly claiming to be God in the ontological sense.[11] The Jews follow Jesus' pronouncement with a pronouncement of their own, "He is blaspheming; who can forgive sins but God alone?" And they were quite correct! God alone can forgive sins: "I, even I, am the one who wipes out your transgressions for my own sake; and I will not remember your sins" (Isa. 43:25). In Isaiah, to forgive sin is the prerogative of Yahweh the Redeemer, the Holy One of Israel (Isa. 43:14). In Matthew, Mark and Luke, to forgive sin is the prerogative of the Son of Man, who is Yahweh, Redeemer, the Holy One of Israel.[12] How can it be otherwise, for Jesus is "God with us" (*Immanuel*) who has come to "save *His* people from their sins" (see Matt. 1:21, 23).

Bible Commentary, 12 vols. (Grand Rapids, Mich.: Zondervan Publishing House, 1984), 8:102.

[10]Matthew 3:3 is further evidence of "God with us" (1:23), and further evidence that this phrase does not mean that Jesus was merely a "royal envoy" (see Carson, *Matthew,* 102), one who only *represents* Yahweh.

[11]I have often read with excitement these kinds of functional christological passages in the New Testament, only to be saddened that heretical groups do not see in these passages Christ "being" God. His actions are one giant attestation to His being God, as the Old Testament background shows. For other occurrences of this theme, D. A. Carson, in his *Matthew,* 325, directs the reader to Philip B. Payne, "Jesus' Implicit Claim to Deity in His Parables," *Trinity Journal* [1981]: 3-23.

[12]A common conception among Christians (and, as Robert Reymond points out, even among early Church theologians such as Ignatius [*Ephesians,* 20:2], the writer of *The Epistle of Barnabus* [12:10], Irenaeus [*Against Heresies,* 3:16; 7; 17:1], and Justin Martyr [*Dialogues,* 76:1; 100]; see Robert L. Reymond's *Jesus, Divine Messiah* [Phillipsburg, N.J.: Presbyterian and Reformed Publishing Co., 1990], 67, n. 55) is that the term "Son of Man" denotes Jesus' humanity *alone,* while Son of God signifies His deity *alone.* This, however, is not the case. "Son of Man" most certainly signifies Jesus' deity.

Matthew 13:41

"The Son of Man will send forth His angels, and they will gather out of His kingdom all stumbling blocks and those who commit lawlessness." Here the actions of Jesus imply that He is God, and again the functional implies the ontological. Yahweh is the eschatological judge who will gather out of His kingdom all lawlessness (see Zeph. 1:3, 18). In our text it is the Son who does this (see also 2 Tim. 4:1, 8).

Moreover, the Son of Man will be seen "coming on the clouds of the sky with power and great glory" when He sends forth His angels (Matt. 24:30-31). Yet, in the Old Testament Yahweh is the only "cloud-rider" (see Pss. 18:9-11; 104:3; Isa. 19:1; Nah. 1:3). The Jews knew this, for when Jesus asserts once again that He will be coming on the clouds of Heaven, they charge him with blasphemy (Matt. 26:64-65;[13] Mark 14:61-64; cf. Lev. 24:16).

Our text also states that the "kingdom" belongs to the Son of Man. The kingdom of the Son of Man (denoting ownership, a claim of deity; see 2 Tim. 4:18; 2 Pet. 1:11) is the same as the Father's kingdom (Matt. 13:43). Still yet, what the Son of Man *does* in His kingdom shows that He is God the Son. As Yahweh is the Lord of the harvest (Hos. 6:11; Joel 3:11-14), so is the Son of Man (Matt. 13:24-30, 36-42; in this pericope [meaning a unit or section] the Son of Man "gathers," signifying the harvest motif). As Yahweh is the sower (Isa. 5:7; Jer. 2:21; 11:16-17; 12:2; 24:6); So is the Son of Man (Matt. 13:24-30).[14]

---

[13]Jesus' answer in light of the question is interesting. The question in Matt. 26:63 was for Jesus to tell the chief priest and the council whether he was the Christ, the Son of God. Jesus answers this question of ontological oneness with the Father by stating that He *as the Son of Man* will be seen sitting at the "right hand of power" (denoting supreme rule and authority, a claim of cosmic proportions) and "coming on the clouds of heaven" (v. 64). Thus, if the phrase "Son of God" has high ontological significance, and Jesus' answer seems to equate "Son of Man" with "Son of God," can we not assume that the former carries with it ontological connotations?

[14]For the references to the Lord of the harvest and the sower, I am indebted to Philip B. Payne, "The Authenticity of the Parables of Jesus" in R. T. France and David Wenham, eds., *Gospel Perspectives: Studies of History and Tradition in the Four Gospels*, 6 vols. (Sheffield, England: JSOT Press, 1981), 2:339. I add to this list the claim by Christ, "The Son of Man is Lord of the Sabbath" (Matt. 12:8; Mark 2:28; Luke 6:5). Lord of the Sabbath gives to Christ the divine prerogative of ownership over all that has to do with the

A word must be said about Jesus and *His* angels. They belong to Christ, which is implicitly an attribute of deity. The Old Testament mentions Yahweh's angels in Psalm 103:20 (see also Ps. 148:2). The context in this Psalm is one of Yahweh's sovereign power (v. 19), and one of the effects of His sovereignty is that the angels belong to Him and "perform His work" (v. 20). Further, Zechariah 14:5b states, "Then the LORD [*Yahweh*], my God, will come, and all the holy ones with Him[15]" (cf. Matt. 25:31!).[16] So it is with the Son of Man. The angels are His and perform His work of divine judgment (another implicit attestation to Christ's deity, for angels of the LORD executing divine judgment is seen in the Old Testament [see Gen. 19:13; 2 Sam. 24:16; 2 Kings 19:35; Ezek. 9:1,[17] 5, 7]).

Matthew 14:27; Mark 6:50 (John 6:20)

The scene in these three Gospel passages depicts Jesus walking on the water during a storm to meet the disciples in their boat. The disciples were frightened because they saw someone on the water, but Jesus said, *"Take courage, I Am [egō eimi, ἐγώ εἰμι]."*

I believe Christ is claiming to be God, and therefore *egō eimi* should be translated "I AM" instead of "it is I," as most translations read. Christ's identification of Himself to the disciples goes beyond the simple mode of recognition ("It is I") for the following reason. We know from the text that the sea must have been rough, for Matthew records that the wind was strong and the disciples' boat was being battered by the waves (14:24). Yet Jesus, who had on another occasion stilled a storm (see Matt. 8:26; Mark 4:39; Luke 8:24[18]), walked on the

---

Sabbath, including what is to be observed and what is not. This right belongs to Him as Yahweh.

[15]The Hebrew has "with You" (*immak,* עִמָּךְ); the LXX reads "with Him" (*met' autou,* μετ' αὐτοῦ).

[16]See 2 Thess. 1:7-10 (esp. 7-8).

[17]In the Ezekiel text the Hebrew *pequdoth* (פְּקֻדוֹת) may be understood as human executioners, but see C. F. Keil and F. Delitzsch, *Commentary on the Old Testament,* 10 vols. (Grand Rapids, Mich.: Wm. B. Eerdmans Publishing Co., reprinted, July 1985), 9:126.

[18]I am indebted to G. K. Beale for bringing to my attention the cross reference to Ps. 107:29 and its surrounding verses. In the Psalm it is Yahweh who is the storm-stiller and the LORD of the seas. Thus, all the evangelists

water toward them. In the Old Testament Yahweh is the "storm stiller" (see Pss. 89:9; 107:29). He rules the swelling of the sea (Ps. 89:9). Here Jesus is the Yahweh who rules the sea, and the disciples' recognition of this is evident, for they "*worshipped* Him, saying, 'You are certainly God's Son'" (Matt. 14:33). And when the contexts of Psalm 107 and Matthew 14 (and Matt. 8) are further compared, we notice the theme of distress and crying out to the Lord (Ps. 107:27-28 crying out to Yahweh; Matt. 8:25; 14:30 crying out to Jesus). Matthew, then, sees Jesus as the Yahweh of Psalm 107. Jesus, by His actions in fulfillment of that which only Yahweh can do, is rightly worshipped and does not rebuke the disciples for their act of devotion.[19] Thus, the *egō eimi* ("I Am") here should be regarded as Jesus' self-identification as God, who is the *egō eimi* of Deuteronomy 32:39, Isaiah 41:4; 43:10, etc. (LXX).[20]

Matthew 16:27

After Jesus states to His disciples that they must take up their cross and follow Him (Matt. 16:24), He as the Son of Man makes another implicit claim to deity: *"For the Son of Man is going to come in the glory of His Father*[21] *with His angels; and will then recompense every man according to his deeds"* (v. 27).

In Psalm 62:12 it is God who "dost recompense a man according to his work." This is yet another self-conscious statement of deity made by the Son of Man, for it is He who will recompense (see also Isa. 66:6). Further, ownership of the angels belongs to the Son of Man, another implicit attribute of His deity (see my comments under Matt. 13:41). Finally, the glory he has is that which He shares with His

---

follow their pericopes of *Jesus* stilling the storm (Matt. 8:18-27; Mark 4:35-41; Luke 8:22-25) with pericopes of the demoniac's (or demoniacs') multiple demons entering into the swine and Jesus' sending of them into the sea! Yet another example of Jesus "being" God.

[19]Certainly Christ would have rebuked them if He were only a man. See Peter's words to Cornelius in Acts 10:26 (see also Rev. 19:10; 22:8).

[20]D. A. Carson notes concerning the translation "It is I": "Although the Gr. *egō eimi* can have no more force than that ["It is I"], any Christian after the resurrection and Ascension would also detect echoes of 'I am,' the decisive self-disclosure of God" (*Matthew*, 344).

[21]Luke states that Christ will come in His glory, and the glory of the Father (9:26).

Father, a fantastically blasphemous claim if Christ were anything less than God (Yahweh Himself states that He will not give His glory to another [Isa. 42:8]). Christ is not only prophesying that He will do the work of God in the eschatological judgment (see also Matt. 7:21-23; and esp. 19:28; 25:31, where He "will sit on the throne of *His* glory"[22]); He is also intimating that by sharing glory with the Father, His intimate relationship with the Father is one that no creature can ever experience.

Matthew 21:12; Mark 11:15; Luke 19:45

The Synoptics are rich with the functional Christology that points to Jesus as God. We continue with this theme as *"Jesus entered the temple and cast out all those who were buying and selling in the temple, and overturned the tables of the moneychangers and the seats of those who were selling doves."*

What significance this carries! Here Jesus is the Lord[23] of Malachi 3:1 who "will suddenly come to His temple." He is the "God of justice" (Malachi 2:17) who will come, and come He does, in the person of Christ. The possessive "His" in Malachi 3:1 is also significant. It is Jesus' temple, and He as God is Lord over it and can exercise immediate divine judgment on the moneychangers and those selling doves. He does so in fulfillment of Scripture, particularly Isaiah 56:7 and Jeremiah 7:11. In these two Old Testament passages it is the LORD, Yahweh, who speaks of *His* house [temple]: "For My house will be called a house of prayer for all the peoples" (Isa. 56:7b); "Has this house, which is called by My name, become a den of robbers...?" (Jer. 7:11a). Thus Jesus can state, "It is written, 'My house shall be called a house of prayer; but you are making it a robbers' den'" (Matt.

---

[22]Gr. *Thronou doxēs autou,* θρόνου δόξης αὐτοῦ; lit. "the throne of His glory." Here Jesus equates Himself with "The Ancient of Days" of Daniel 7:9. Phenomena that occur in Matthew and in Daniel are the same, making Christ equating Himself with the Ancient of Days incontestable. Both contain judgment motifs (Dan. 7:10-12, 18, 22; Matt. 19:29-30; 25:32-46), and both contain the setting up of thrones (Dan. 7:9; Matt. 19:28).

[23]Heb. *adon,* אָדוֹן. For *adonay* being synonymous (though not always) with *Yahweh,* see later in this chapter under Luke 20:41-44. True, here Malachi distinguishes between *adon* and *Yahweh,* but the distinction is not ontological, for 2:17 refers to the "God of justice," and its first referent is *adon* in 3:1. The distinction, therefore, points to the separate persons of the Trinity.

21:13; see Mark 11:17; Luke 19:46). Jesus' use of "My house" differs from His statement "My Father's house," which He uttered at the time of the first cleansing of the temple in John 2:16.[24] Here it is Jesus' house, signifying His ownership of the temple.[25]

As the pericope continues, further claims to deity emerge, buttressing His earlier claim to divine authority (the temple is "My house"). In Matthew 21:14 Jesus heals the blind and the lame. The children then cry out praise to Christ, and the scribes become indignant (21:15). They ask Jesus, "Do you hear what these are saying?" (v. 16a). Jesus' answer in verse 16b defends the children's praise of Him by citing Psalm 8:2,[26] where God ordains *for Himself* the praise of children (see Ps. 8:2 in the NIV[27])!: "Yes; have you never read, 'Out of the mouth of infants and nursing babes thou hast prepared praise for Thyself'?" (v. 16b). In his commentary on this verse, D. A. Carson notes that Jesus was "justifying the praise of the children by applying to himself a passage of Scripture applicable only to God."[28]

Matthew 24:35; Mark 13:31; Luke 21:33

"Heaven and earth will pass away, but My words shall not pass away." Here Jesus makes a startling claim: His words will never pass away. His word endures forever.

The claim is startling because this theme is indicative of the eternality of "Yahweh's word" in the Old Testament. Yahweh's word endures forever. Isaiah 40:8 states, "The grass withers, the flower fades, but the word of our God stands forever." Though "heaven" and "earth" are substituted in the Gospels for "grass" and "flower," the meaning is the same, that being the eternal nature of the word of God "established by contrast with the natural order."[29] The same may be said of

---

[24]See Robert Reymond, *Jesus, Divine Messiah*, 101. Leon Morris argues the possibility of two temple cleansings. See his, *The Gospel According to John* (Grand Rapids, Mich.: Wm. B. Eerdmans Publishing Co., 1971), 190-91.

[25]Reymond, *Jesus, Divine Messiah*, 101.

[26]8:3 in the Hebrew text.

[27]The Hebrew *oz* (עז) may be translated "praise," as in the NIV. See *Gesenius' Hebrew-Chaldee Lexicon to the Old Testament* (Grand Rapids, Mich.: Baker Book House, 1979), 616.

[28]*Matthew*, 443.

[29]R. T. France, *Jesus and the Old Testament* (London: Tyndale Press,

statements found in Psalm 119:89, 160, which read, "Forever, O LORD [*Yahweh*], Thy word is settled in heaven," and "The sum of Thy word is truth, and every one of Thy righteous ordinances is everlasting." R. T. France notes that "Jesus' own words in Matthew 5:18 and Luke 16:17... show that the permanence of the word of God was a common idea."[30] How, then, could Jesus, knowing the sacred Scriptures as He did, claim for His own words that which is characteristic of *Yahweh's* words if He Himself were not Yahweh the Son? The words of Christ in Matthew 24:35, Mark 13:31, and Luke 21:33 are indicative of Yahweh who has come as the person of the Son, whose words, since He is God, shall never pass away.

Matthew 28:19-20

"Go therefore and make disciples of all nations, baptizing them in the name of the Father and the Son and the Holy Spirit, teaching them to observe all that I commanded you; and lo, I am with you always, even to the end of the age." Concentrating on the very important command of Christ to make disciples of all nations, Christians sometimes miss the divine implications of Jesus' words in this passage.

First is the mention of "the Father and the Son and the Holy Spirit." As believers are baptized, this signifies coming into a covenant relationship with the Father. But then Christ links Himself and the Spirit to the Father in this relationship. This is to say that the Son and the Spirit are mentioned on equal ground with the Father. The three persons comprise the one "name" (note *name* is singular). This covenant relationship also denotes that the Trinity *owns* believers, for believers are the Father's people, the Son's people, and the Holy Spirit's people. Since we are talking specifically about Christ we may tie all this together to say that Christ is placed on an equality with the Father, and that the new covenant people belong to Christ (a theme reminiscent of *Yahweh's* covenant people in the Old Testament). Both these aspects strongly imply deity.

Second is that the covenant people of God (the Father and the Son and the Holy Spirit) are to be taught everything that *Christ commanded* the disciples. Yahweh's covenant people are always charged to obey the

---

1971), 151.
  [30]Ibid., 151.

commands of the LORD in covenant relationship (see, for example, Deut. 6:24), and this is no different! Christ as God must be followed and obeyed.

Third is Christ's promise of His eternal presence with His covenant people ("lo, I am with you always"). The context of this passage is covenantal, so it should not be interpreted as a mere presence in the mind of Christians (or anything else that would lessen its impact). No, the language of Christ is that of Yahweh, whose presence with His covenant people Israel was the one crucial factor that set that nation over all the other nations in the land. Yahweh was with His people (Isa. 43:5: "Do not fear, for I am with you"). Here Christ is always with His people. This can only be true if Christ is God (for more on this theme, see this chapter under Matthew 1:21-23, *Yahweh's presence*).

Luke 5:8

The disciples had been out all night with no catch of fish. Jesus commanded Simon Peter to let the boat out one more time. He then instructed Peter to let down the nets for a catch. Peter said, "Master,[31] we worked hard all night and caught nothing, but at your bidding I will let down the nets" (Luke 5:5). They caught so much fish that their nets began to break and the boat (and, by this time, the rescue boat) began to sink (vv. 6-7). Peter then *"fell down at Jesus' feet, saying, 'Depart from me, for I am a sinful man, O Lord!*[32]*'"* (v. 8).

Peter's action and subsequent words speak volumes about *who* Christ is. Robert Reymond begins the argument:

> Peter's act of prostrating himself at Jesus' knees, accompanied with his acknowledgment of his sinfulness, is an act of religious worship. Whereas godly men and angels always condemned such prostration before them as an act of misplaced devotion, indeed, as an act of idolatry (cf. Acts 10:25-26; 14:11-15; Rev. 19:9-10; 22:8-9), Jesus issued no such prohibition to Peter.[33]

B. B. Warfield then finishes the argument. Remarking on Peter's reaction, he states:

---

[31]Gr. *epistata*, ἐπιστάτα.
[32]Gr. *kurie*, κύριε (vocative of *kurios*).
[33]*Jesus, Divine Messiah*, 169.

[It] seems to be an ascription to Jesus of a majesty which is distinctly recognized as supernatural: not only is the contrast of "Lord" with "Master" here expressed (cf. v. 5), but the phrase "Depart from me; for I am a sinful man" (v. 8) is the natural utterance of a sense of unworthiness which overwhelms men in the presence of the divine [cf. Job 42:5-6; Isa. 6:5; Dan. 10:16; Luke 18:13; Rev. 1:12-17], and which is signalized in Scripture as the mark of recognition of the divine presence.[34]

In short, this whole scene depicts Jesus being God.

Luke 19:10

In this verse Jesus assumes the role of Yahweh:[35] *"For the Son of Man has come to seek and to save that which was lost."*

Our cross reference is Ezekiel 34:16a, where *Yahweh* states, "I will seek the lost, bring back the scattered, bind up the broken, and strengthen the sick." Interesting as well are Yahweh's words in verse 11: "I Myself will search for My sheep and seek them out." In Ezekiel 34 Yahweh says that He will no longer put up with the shepherds of Israel who take from the flock and feed themselves. The day will soon come when *He Himself* will seek the flock, feed the flock, bind up the broken, strengthen the sick, deliver them (v. 22),[36] and judge the people (v. 17). In the pericope containing Luke 19:10, and in pericopes on both sides of it (18:35-43; 19:11-27, 28-48; 20:1-8, 9-18),[37] it is Jesus who performs all these acts, not to mention His confrontation with the false shepherds of Israel (20:1-8)!

---

[34]Quoted in Reymond's *Jesus, Divine Messiah,* 169-70. The bracketed information may be Reymond's. Warfield's remarks are from his *The Lord of Glory* (Grand Rapids, Mich.: Baker Book House, reprinted, 1974), 142.

[35]See R. T. France, *Jesus and the Old Testament,* 150, 156. France states that "Jesus was not averse to taking upon himself what in the Old Testament was said of Yahweh" (151).

[36]Here the LXX has the Gr. *sōzō* (σῴζω) for "deliver." In Luke 19:10 the verb translated "save" is *sōzō.*

[37]Indeed not only in these pericopes, but throughout all of Luke.

Luke 20:41-44

Prior to this passage, Luke records the questioning of Jesus by the Sadducees regarding marriage at the resurrection (Luke 20:27-33). Jesus responds that at the resurrection believers "neither marry, nor are given in marriage" (v. 35). Neither will they die, for they are sons of the resurrection (v. 36). Verse 37 then reads, "But that the dead are raised, even Moses showed, in the passage about the burning bush, where he calls the Lord[38] the God of Abraham, and the God of Isaac, and the God of Jacob."

Luke 20:41-44 is connected with Luke 20:27-40 (and thus 20:37) for a reason. After Jesus relays to His listeners that Moses called *the Lord* the God of Abraham, the God of Isaac, and the God of Jacob, He goes on to ask, *"How is it that they say the Christ is David's Son? For David himself says in the book of Psalms [110:1[39]], 'The Lord[40] said to my Lord,[41] Sit at My right hand, until I make Thine enemies a footstool for Thy feet.' David therefore calls Him 'Lord,' and how is He his son?"* (Luke 20:41-44) The parallel between verse 37 and verse 44 links Jesus with deity: "Moses calls the Lord the God of Abraham..." and "David calls Him [the Christ] 'Lord.'"

Could Luke (and, of course, Jesus) subtly be implying that "the Lord" who is the God of Abraham, Isaac, and Jacob in Luke 20:37 is "the Lord" of David in Luke 20:42, 44? It is plausible, given (1) that Jesus in His question to the Jewish leaders (v. 41) is looking for more than merely the human lineage of the son of David (His main focus seems to be on the Lordship of Messiah *over* David [v. 44]), and (2) that Psalm 110 *as a whole* "entitles Him [Messiah] to sit on God's throne and to exercise universal and everlasting dominion."[42] Moreover, when the whole of Psalm 110 is read in the light of Hebrews 1:5-13[43] (where the Psalm is quoted [see Heb. 1:13]), one cannot help but draw the conclusion that the Son by His very nature is God, and that He will judge among the nations from His place of universal

---

[38]Gr. *kurion,* κύριον (accusative of *kurios*).

[39]LXX 109:1.

[40]Gr. *kurios.* Hebrew in the Psalm is *Yahweh.*

[41]Gr. *kurio,* κυρίῳ (dative case of *kurios*). Hebrew in the Psalm is *adoni,* אֲדֹנִי.

[42]Both points are taken from Robert Reymond, *Jesus, Divine Messiah,* 14.

[43]Again I am indebted to Reymond (ibid.) for this.

authority. Therefore, in Luke 20:42-44 Jesus identifies Himself as "the Lord, the God of Abraham, Isaac, and Jacob" (20:37[44]).

Still yet, Luke 20:41-44 *alone* is evidence for the deity of Christ when read in light of Psalm 110, which it partially quotes. Though some might argue that the psalmist makes a distinction between *Yahweh* and *adoni,* and conclude that Jesus (who is prophetically *adoni* in the Psalm) is not Yahweh, there are strong contextual reasons to conclude that this passages implies Christ's deity.

As mentioned, Jesus quotes Psalm 110:1 and applies it to Himself. In the Hebrew text we read, "The LORD [*Yahweh*] said to my Lord [*adoni*]..." The rest of Psalm 110 shows that the psalmist's use of *adon* does not exclude the coming Messiah as God. Verse five reads, "The Lord [*adonay*[45]] is at Thy [*Yahweh,* implied] right hand; He will shatter kings in the day of His wrath." I mentioned earlier Robert Reymond's observation of Jesus being viewed here as the one who will exercise universal and everlasting dominion (only God does this). Moreover, the wrath to come in Psalm 110:5 is *adonay's* wrath, and therefore He is the eschatological judge (see also Ps. 2:5, 12). The point here is that in the Old Testament there are clear references to the wrath of Yahweh (Exod. 15:7; 22:24; 32:10, 11, 12; Num. 11:33; 25:11; see esp. Pss. 21:9; 38:1; 78:31, 38, 49; 79:6), and that therefore this divine attribute belonging to Yahweh also belongs to the Son. *Second,* the objection that *adonay* cannot be God (*elohim*) is made without reference to other Psalms where God and *adonay* are synonymous. Psalm 59:10-11 (vv. 11-12 in

---

[44]In Matthew and Mark the account of the identity of the Lord at the burning bush does not immediately precede Jesus' question about the Son of David (see Matt. 22:23-45; Mark 12:18-37). Both these Gospels precede the Son of David question with Jesus' answer to the question, "which is the greatest commandment?" (see Matt. 22:36; Mark 12:28). Jesus' answer, "Love the Lord your God..." follows. Mark then has the scribe stating, "Right, teacher..., He is one, and there is no one else beside Him" (12:32). Jesus' question about David's son then follows (12:35). Matthew has no such statement by the scribe, but records Jesus proceeding directly to the question (22:42). This, however, does not change my observation, for in the Matthean and Markan accounts the antecedent to the Son of David question is "love the Lord (*kurios*) your God..." It is still quite interesting that after this, Jesus shares that He is David's Lord! (Note: in both Matthew and Mark it is *God* rather than the *Lord* who states, "I am the God of Abraham, and the God of Isaac, and the God of Jacob" [Matt. 22:31-32; Mark 12:26].)

[45]The basic root noun is *adon;* "*i*" and "*ay*" are merely the suffixal endings.

Heb.) states: "My *God* [*elohim*] in His lovingkindness will meet me; *God* [*elohim*] will let me look triumphantly upon my foes. Do not slay them, lest my people forget; scatter them by Thy power, and bring them down, O Lord [*adonay*], our shield."

Third, there is evidence that *adonay* is also *Yahweh,* signifying that the terms are interchangeable. Exodus 23:17 states: "Three times a year all your males shall appear before the Lord [*adonay*] Yahweh [*Yahweh*]." In Isaiah 6 "the Lord [*adonay*] sitting on the throne" (v. 1) is identified as "the King, the LORD [*Yahweh*] of hosts" (v. 5). One more example shall suffice: "For the LORD [*Yahweh*] your God [*elohim*] is the God of gods and the Lord [*adonay*] of Lords" (Deut. 10:17). When all this evidence is considered, the *adonay* in Psalm 110, the coming Messiah, should be viewed as God.

Summation of the Synoptics

The Synoptic Gospels contain a high view of Christ. All three evangelists portray Him in the highest sense, as God in human flesh. The phrases "Son of God" and "Son of Man" set forth Christ as Yahweh. As the Son of God[46] and the Son of Man He makes statements that only God can make, and acts as only true deity can.

Sadly, it is abundantly clear that the cults have totally missed the biblical witness to the deity of Christ. They have failed to see the Old Testament background in the words and actions of Christ in the Synoptics, a background that portrays Him as Yahweh the Son.

We now move to the witness of the incarnate deity of Christ in the Gospel of John.

---

[46]Son of God, when it pertains to Christ, also carries the sense of "uniqueness." We shall see this spelled out in clearer fashion in John's Gospel, but in the Synoptics it is most strongly implied in Matt. 11:27 (Luke 10:22): "No one knows the Son, except the Father; nor does anyone know the Father, except the Son, and anyone to whom the Son wills to reveal Him." This intimate filial relationship between the Son and the Father is unique, for no one knows the one except the other. In the case of knowing the Father, we may know Him, says Christ, but only under the condition of Christ willing it to be. Thus, we may know the Father, but not directly, as the Son does in a unique way. Rather, we may know the Father *through* the Son.

The Gospel of John

The purpose of the Gospel of John is "that you may believe that Jesus is the Christ, the Son of God; and that believing you may have life in His name" (John 20:31). As we set out to examine certain passages in this Gospel pertaining to the incarnate deity of Christ, we do so keeping with John's purpose (in part). The purpose of John is to lay out for His readers *who* Christ is, and to exhort them to place their trust in *this* Christ alone.

John 1:14[47]

"And the Word became flesh, and dwelt among us, and we beheld His glory, glory as of the only begotten from the Father, full of grace and truth." The Word who always was; the Word who always was with the Father; the Word who always was God (John 1:1), has now taken to Himself humanity in the historic person of Jesus Christ.

As the *eternal* Word He can never stop being God. Thus we must not take the phrase "the Word *became* flesh" to mean that the Word *changed* to humanity. The fact that God must by definition always be God prohibits this.[48] His *flesh* became.[49] God the eternal Word united with Himself full humanity when His flesh "became" in the womb of the Virgin by the agency of God the Holy Spirit (Matt. 1:18, 20). John perhaps used the term "flesh," denoting *real* humanity, because it was so repugnant to the Docetists (those who denied the real humanity of Christ, saying His body was a mere illusion) who viewed the material world as base and defiled. God, they said, could never have united Himself with humanity or join Himself in any way with humanity. Today this docetic opinion is expressed in the statements of Christian Science.

The next two phrases, "and dwelt among us, and we beheld His glory" are covenantal, implying the deity of the Son. First, God in the

---

[47]John 1:1 (and 8:58) are discussed in chap. 2.

[48]Moreover, as we shall see, John 1:18 states that the only begotten is *eternally* in the bosom of the Father.

[49]The Gr. verb *ginomai* (γίνομαι) indicates coming into existence. See chap. 2 under John 1:1. Also, "flesh" (*sarx*, σάρξ) in John 1:14 emphasizes the human *essence* that the eternal Word as God took upon Himself (it is an anarthrous predicate nominative, qualitative in force).

person of Christ is "dwelling" (the divine presence!) with His people. In the person of Christ we have the Old Testament tabernacle of God among men (the Greek verb *eskēnōsen* [ἐσκήνωσεν], translated "dwelt" in John 1:14, comes from the noun *skēnē* [σκηνή], "tabernacle"). Second, in the Old Testament, God's presence was "His glory" revealed in the cloud in the *tabernacle*: "Then the cloud covered the tent of meeting, and the glory of the LORD filled the tabernacle" (Exod. 40:34).[50] Ezekiel 37:26-27 looks to the time when Yahweh will make an everlasting covenant with His people (v. 26), and will *dwell* with His people and be their God (v. 27).[51] This is fulfilled in Christ. In Him ("as of the only begotten") we behold the glory of Yahweh Himself: He has tented among us; He is the "Shekina," the glory of God (see also Acts 1:9, 11,[52] 2 Cor. 4:4, 6); He is God in the flesh, and God manifest to flesh (humanity).

"Only begotten" in no way conveys the heretical idea that Jesus was begotten by the Father in the sense that the Father (an exalted man) came down and sired Jesus, as the Mormons believe. Nor does it communicate that Jesus, as the Word, was the first and *only* creature (and thus *only* "begotten" from the Father) directly created by Jehovah

---

[50]See Leon Morris, *The Gospel According to John*, 103.

[51]These, of course, are only a sampling of the plethora of glory passages in the Old Testament.

[52]The passage in Acts is certainly covenantal, but implies as well Jesus being the eschatological judge at the consummation of the ages. From Acts 1:12 we understand that Christ's ascension took place on the Mount of Olives. (I must make an additional point pertaining to the deity of Christ. Here Jesus speaks to His disciples on a mountain. This is significant from an Old Testament perspective, where the Deity dwelled on the mountain and conversed with His covenant mediators. This, coupled with "the cloud" indicating the glory of Yahweh, speaks loudly that Christ is Yahweh the Son.) Jesus' commands (also characteristic of Yahweh) to His disciples take place on the Mount of Olives (see Acts 1:12). The cloud events of Acts 1:9, 11 speak of the glory of the LORD (see Exod. 24:16, 17). The words of the two men clothed in white tell us that Jesus "will come in just the same way as you have watched Him go into heaven" (Acts 1:11). Thus the Son of Man will come on the clouds of heaven, indicating that He is Yahweh the cloud-rider (see Isa. 19:1). Also strongly implied in Acts (since He ascends from the Mount and will come back "in just the same way") is that He will return to the Mount of Olives in "the day of Yahweh" as the Yahweh (the eschatological judge) spoken of by the prophets Zechariah (see 14:4, 7, 8 cf. Rev. 22:1, 2) and Ezekiel (11:23).

God, as the Jehovah's Witnesses teach. Rather, it means "unique." Jesus is God the Father's *unique* Son. First, the Greek word *monogenes* (μονογενής, "only begotten") derives from *monos* (μόνος, "alone," "only") and *genos* (γένος, "kind"). Christ is "one of a kind," or unique. Second, the context supports this, for in verse 12 John intentionally calls believers "the children [note, Gr. *tekna* (τέκνα, "children"), not *huioi* (υἱοί, "sons")] of God." John sets apart those who *become* children of God, from the one who is the *only begotten* and thus the *unique* Son of God.

The phrase "full of grace and truth" is also covenantal and implies in the strongest sense the deity of the only begotten. These words of John to describe the Lord of glory are directly attributed to Yahweh in Exodus 34:6, just after (interestingly!) Yahweh descends in the cloud (see 34:5). As Yahweh *dwells* with Moses on mount Sinai, He describes Himself as "full of grace and truth"[53] (see also 2 Sam. 2:6; Neh. 9:17; Ps. 25:10; Joel 2:13; Jon. 4:2).

In conclusion, the whole of verse 14 bursts with Old Testament imagery that can only be true of Yahweh. As God tenting among humanity, we may behold the glory of the unique Son of God, who is full of grace and truth.

John 1:18

"No man has seen God at any time; the only begotten God, who is in the bosom of the Father, He has explained Him." Though cited by ancient and modern heretics to teach that the Son had a beginning at a point in time,[54] this verse ironically teaches that Jesus is God incarnate.

Sometimes Trinitarians are accused of believing a contradiction, namely that if Jesus is God and people have seen Him, then it contradicts John's statement that "no man has seen God at any time." This seeming contradiction is solved by realizing that John's use of the Greek word *theos* (θεός, "God") in the phrase "no man has seen God at

---

[53]My translation of the Hebrew *rab chesed ve emeth* (רַב־חֶסֶד וֶאֱמֶת).

[54]Arius and the Valentinians, Jehovah's Witnesses and the Mormons. Here the phrase "only begotten" is viewed either as the Father directly creating Jesus (Jehovah's Witnesses), or as Elohim the Father (with body parts) coming to earth to have a sexual union with Mary in order to give the spirit-child Jesus a body (Mormons). As we have seen in the previous section on John 1:14, *monogenes* ("only begotten") carries neither of these meanings.

any time" refers to the *Father.* Throughout his Gospel, John uses *theos* as a synonym for *the Father* (see John 4:23-24;[55] 5:37; esp. 6:46;[56] though not always, see John 1:18b; 20:28). The second clause of John 1:18 ("the only begotten God, who is in the bosom of *the Father,* has revealed *Him*") makes it clear that John's first use of *theos* in 1:18 refers to the Father (i.e., "Him" refers to "the Father," which refers to the first use of "God" in 1:18a). In short, John wishes to communicate that no one has ever seen God (the Father), but the only begotten God who is in His (the Father's) bosom has revealed Him (referring back to the Father). Thus, going back to John 1:18, when the *whole* verse is considered, the second clause helps to interpret the first, and no contradiction occurs with Trinitarian theology.

John 1:18 proclaims Jesus as God the Son. First, the weight of manuscript evidence favors "the only begotten *God*" rather than "the only begotten *Son.*"[57] Second, it is quite plausible to translate the phrase[58] not only as the NASB has it ("the only begotten God, who is in the bosom of the Father..."), but also as "the only begotten, God, who is in the bosom of the Father..." I opt for this translation, for it continues

---

[55]John 4:23-24 makes it most clear that *theos* is synonymous with *patēr* (πατήρ, "Father"). Verse 23 tells us that "the true worshippers shall *worship the Father in spirit and truth.*" Verse 24 serves as a reiteration of this thought: "*God* is spirit; and those who *worship Him* (God) must worship *in spirit and truth.*" Here "God" (v. 24) is "the Father" (v. 23).

[56]This is true throughout the rest of the New Testament as well. See, for example, 2 Cor. 13:14 (here *theos* most certainly refers to the Father), and Gal. 1:1 (theos *patēr,* "God the Father"). For more on this, see Murray J. Harris, *Jesus as God: The New Testament Use of Theos in Reference to Jesus* (Grand Rapids, Mich.: Baker Book House, 1992), 271.

[57]Manuscripts known as P66, the original of *Aleph,* B, and the original of C evidence "[the] only begotten God," while p75 and the first copyist of *Aleph* still have *theos,* but place the definite article before *monogenēs* (*"the* only begotten"). The reading of *huios* (υἱός, "Son") is evidenced by A and the *third* (!) copyist of C. Leon Morris makes the excellent point that since the phrase "only begotten Son" is the usual Johannine expression, this would make it all the more reasonable that later copyists would insert "Son" for "God" in the process, thus implying that "God" was the original rendering (see Morris, *The Gospel of John,* 113).

[58]Gr. *monogenēs theos ho ōn eis ton kolpon tou patros,* μονογενὴς θεὸς ὁ ὢν εἰς τὸν κόλπον τοῦ πατρὸς.

the thrust of John 1:1, where the Word is called God.[59] Thus, I understand John to describe Christ as "the only begotten [or "unique one," see comments on John 1:14], God [cf. John 1:1], the one who is *continually* [eternally[60]] in the bosom of the Father..."[61] The only begotten's existence with the Father is timeless. Not only is He God, but because He is God the Son He is unique, being eternally in the bosom of the Father (signifying the eternal unique relationship between the Father and the Son).

John 5:18—Son of God means God the Son

"For this cause therefore the Jews were seeking all the more to kill Him, because He not only was breaking the Sabbath, but also was calling God His own Father, making Himself equal with God." The irony of the cults' denial of Christ as God because "He's the Son of God!" is that "Son of God" strongly implies an ontological equality that, in this passage, is backed up by His functional equality with the Father.

Claiming to be the Son of God[62] means claiming equality with God the Father.[63] The reason the Jews sought to kill Jesus was most likely blasphemy (see Lev. 24:16). In verse 17 Jesus states, "My Father is working until now, and I Myself am working." Beside the obvious functional christological parallel between "God working" and "I am working," where Jesus *does what God does*, the claim of Jesus that God is His Father ("My Father") communicates to the Jews that Jesus is

---

[59]Just as in John 1:1, where the ontological oneness between Father and Son is expressed along with the distinctness of the two persons, so it is here. In this verse the only begotten is Himself God, yet He exists in the bosom of the Father.

[60]This is the force of the present participle *ōn* (See Morris, *The Gospel of John,* 114, and Reymond, *Jesus, Divine Messiah,* 306). The present tense many times signals continuous action.

[61]Morris mentions that this translation is possible, making it a three-titled description: "Christ: 'Only-begotten, God, He who is in the bosom of the Father'" (*The Gospel of John,* 313-14).

[62]And Son of Man (see 5:27).

[63]One may argue that the phrase "Son of God" is not used in this pericope. The *phrase* is not, but certainly *Son* is used. Moreover, this pericope (John 5:17-23) is put forth by John to fulfill the purpose of his Gospel, that we may believe Jesus is the *Son of God* (20:31).

claiming *equality*, ontological oneness, with God (v. 18[64]). Only God can do what God does, and John proceeds to put flesh to his argument of equality in verses 19-32. In verse 19 it is the Son who does what He sees the Father doing (and He does it in like manner[65]).[66] As the Father raises the dead, so does the Son, and it is whom *He* wills[67] (v. 21; cf. Deut. 32:39; 1 Sam. 2:6; 2 Kings 5:7, where *Yahweh* does this). As the Father has life in Himself, so does the Son (v. 26). The Father even defers[68] to the Son by giving all judgment to the Son (v. 22), and as the Son of Man Jesus will come to execute divine judgment (v. 27; cf. Dan. 7:9-10[69]). It is *His* voice that the dead will hear at the judgment (vv. 28-29; cf. Ezek. 37:12-13, where *Yahweh* does this). The purpose[70] for this giving of judgment to the Son is "that all may honor the Son *just as* they honor the Father" (v. 23). Here the Son is honored equally with the Father. Simply put, this statement by John would be blasphemous if Jesus were not God the Son. Further, the Son loves the Father within this equality, and defers to Him by doing only what the Father wills (John 5:30).[71]

---

[64]See also John 10:18, 25, 29, 37. These verses surround John 10:30, where Jesus specifically claims ontological oneness with the Father.

[65]The Son does it as God the Father does it. No mere *imitation*, but an actual performance of deeds as only God can do them.

[66]The marvelous reason for this is, "For [or "because"] the Father loves the Son" (v. 20). This love of the Father for the Son expresses itself in the Father showing the Son all the works He does (v. 20).

[67]This shows the sovereignty of the Son of God, an attribute of deity. He is sovereign as God is sovereign.

[68]See Royce G. Gruenler's *The Trinity in the Gospel of John* (Grand Rapids, Mich.: Baker Book House, 1986), where Gruenler argues *deference* over *subordination*. In this study Gruenler shows that the three persons of the Trinity are in continual deference to one another. With *deference* meaning "yielding," he cites example after example where the Son defers to the Father (John 5:30; see above), and where the Father defers to the Son (John 5:22; see above).

[69]In Daniel 7:9 the divine judge described is the "Ancient of Days." Jesus is described in the same way in Rev. 1:14.

[70]Signaled by the Gr. *hina* (ἵνα), "in order that..."

[71]We must not forget the Spirit in this mutual deference, divine unity, and love within the Triune God. For example, in John 14:26 the Spirit defers to the Father in the Father's sending of Him (in the authority of the Son!). Yet on the other hand the Father and the Son defer to the Spirit, in that it is the Spirit who will teach the disciples all things. But it does not stop there; this inexhaustible

John 10:30

"I and the Father are one." Here Jesus asserts His ontological oneness with His Father. Following are my reasons.

First, throughout the passage (10:22-42) Jesus calls God His Father (vv. 25, 29, 37; see also 10:18). We have seen the theological and ontological implications of this claim of Christ (see the previous section on John 5:18). With such a statement Jesus is claiming equality with the Father. Second, the Jews understood this, for immediately after His assertion of oneness with the Father, they "took up stones again to stone Him" (v. 31). Upon Jesus' question as to why they wanted to stone Him, His opponents answered, "because You, being a man, make yourself out to be God" (v. 33). Again, Levitical law made blaspheming "the Name" a cause for stoning (Lev. 24:16), and it was precisely this that warranted such action by the Jews. In their eyes, stoning Jesus was necessary, for He was a man, and a man could not be God.

Adding weight to the claim that "Son of God" means "God the Son" is the parallel between the Jews' reason for stoning Jesus in John 10:33 ("because you... make *yourself out to be God*") and their reason in John 19:7 that Jesus should die ("We have a law [Lev. 24:16], and by that law He ought to die because He *made Himself out to be the Son of God*"). In John 10:33 and 19:7 the reason the Jews claimed Jesus should die is that He was blaspheming "the Name." Doing so involved claiming to be God (10:33) and the Son of God (19:7). They are synonymous.

"I and the Father are one" testifies that Jesus is essentially one with the Father. His *essence,* His very *nature,* is the same as that of His Father. "One" (Gr. *hen,* ἕν) is in the neuter, and therefore may refer to a thing, thus *essential unity*[72] (being of the same nature). Both the Father and the Son are one substance, God.[73] It is *not* in the masculine (*heis,*

---

divine love and unity manifests itself with the Spirit deferring to the Son by teaching what the Son has said to the disciples. I am greatly indebted to Royce Gruenler for his concept of deference within the Godhead (see his *The Trinity in the Gospel of John*).

[72]See Leon Morris, *The Gospel According to John,* 522.

[73]Some may object to this interpretation, citing 1 Cor. 3:8 ("Now he who plants and he who waters are one [the neuter *hen*]") as an example of simple "unity" (i.e. purpose). But, as seen in my opening remarks for this verse, there is much more to the context than mere unity. The Jews' desire to stone Jesus

εἰς), hence "one person," which would make a strong case in support of the modalism of the United Pentecostal Church, or "Jesus Only" movement.[74] With the context of Christ calling God "My Father," we should view "I and the Father are one" as a metaphysical statement, a statement that Christ and the Father are of the same nature. Hence, Jesus in His incarnate state is God the Son.

---

was not because of a claim to unity of will with the Father. Morris, in his *The Gospel According to John,* 523, quotes Hoskyns, who states, "the Jews would not presumably have treated as blasphemy the idea that a man could regulate his words and actions according to the will of God." Morris himself then writes, "But they did regard this as blasphemy as the next verse [10:31] shows. They had asked Jesus for a plain assertion of His messiahship, and they got more than they had bargained for." Merrill C. Tenney cites 1 Cor. 3:8 as proof that *hen* "asserts unity of nature or equality" in John 10:30 (see *The Gospel of John,* contained in *The Expositor's Bible Commentary,* 9:112). In an earlier commentary, Tenney stated that the *hen* in John 10:30 "without a doubt... has metaphysical implications that transcend those of 1 Corinthians 3:8, for the remark was understood clearly as an assertion of deity" (*John: The Gospel of Belief* [Grand Rapids, Mich.: Wm. B. Eerdmans Publishing Co., 1976], 168).

[74]Not to be confused with Pentecostals. As stated in chap. 1, United Pentecostal churches deny the doctrine of the Trinity. They are modalists (after the ancient modalistic heresies of Noetus, Praxeus, and Sabellius), teaching that there is *only* one person in the Godhead. "Father," "Son," and "Holy Spirit" are but "attributes" contained within Jesus of Nazareth, who, as the God of the New Testament, "sent *Himself* into the world as the Son of God" (see Robert A. Herrmann, *Oneness, the Trinity and Logic* [Arnold, Md.: Antioch Publishes The Word, 1984], 86-87). As for the ancient heresy of modalism (popular in the second through fourth centuries), Augustine (354-430) once stated, "'I and the Father are one.' He said not, I am the Father; or, I and the Father *is* one person; but when He says, 'I and the Father are one,' hear both, both the *one, unum,* and the *are, sumus,* and thou shalt be delivered both from Charybdis and from Scylla. In these two words, in that He said *one,* He delivers thee from Arius; in that He said *are,* He delivers thee from Sabellius" (*On the Gospel of John,* XXXVI.9; contained in Philip Schaff, ed., *The Nicene and Post Nicene Fathers,* first series, 14 vols. [Grand Rapids, Mich.: Wm. B. Eerdmans Publishing Co., reprinted, 1974], 7:212, emphases original). Here Augustine is stating that by "one," Jesus asserts He is one substance with the Father and equal with the Father, and thus Arius (and, for our purpose, Jehovah's Witnesses) is in error. By "are," Augustine rightly sees in the text the two persons ("I and the Father, *we* are one"), thus refuting the claims of Sabellius and other modalists (and, for our purpose, United [Oneness] Pentecostals).

John 17:11, 22

In objection to the phrase "I and the Father are one" as evidencing the deity of Christ, Jehovah's Witnesses call upon John 17:11 and 22, where Christ states regarding believers, *"that they may be one [Gr. hen, ἕν] just as We are one."* They explain that in these verses, "He used the same Greek word (*hen*) for 'one' in all these instances. Obviously, Jesus' disciples do not all become part of the Trinity. But they do come to share a oneness of purpose with the Father and the Son, the same sort of oneness that unites God and Christ."[75]

The conclusion reached by the Jehovah's Witnesses seems devastating to the Christian interpretation of oneness of nature between the Father and the Son in John 10:30. Yet, their conclusion is based on a subtle misreading of the text. John 17:11 and 17:22 *never* state that the disciples are "one" with the Father and the Son! The two verses *do* state, however, that believers may be one "just as" the Father and the Son are one. The situation is one of analogy. Believers are to be one *in the same way* that the Father and the Son are. Thus, believers are to be one in nature with each other,[76] and they are, given that they are of the new birth and have been changed within by the regeneration of the Holy Spirit.[77]

John 17:21, 23, however, employ the preposition "in" (Gr. *en, ἐν*) when speaking of believers' relationship with the Father and the Son, and the adjective "one" (*hen*) *only* when speaking of believers' relationship with *each other*:

> (21) that they may all be one [*hen*]; even as Thou, Father, art in [*en*] Me, and I in [*en*] Thee, that they also may be in [*en*] Us.... (23) I in [*en*] them, and Thou in [*en*] Me, that they may be perfected in unity [*hen*].

Here the issue is not "one" (*hen*), denoting sameness of essence, when the relationship between believers and the Father and/or the Son

---

[75]No authors or editors listed, *Reasoning from the Scriptures* (New York: Watchtower Bible and Tract Society of New York, Inc., 1985), 422.

[76]See Tenney, *The Gospel of John* in *The Expositor's Bible Commentary*, 9:164: "The unity mentioned [in John 17:11] is not simply a unity achieved by legislation. It is a unity of nature because it is comparable to that of the Son and the Father."

[77]Ibid.

is the topic. Rather, the issue is "in" (*en*), denoting the belonging of believers to the Father and the Son,[78] a unity of purpose, and that the works of believers have their foundation and power "in" the Father and the Son.[79]

To summarize, the following chart is helpful:

One (hen): of the same nature	*In (en): belonging*
Father with Son-10:30; 17:11, 22	Father in Son-17:21, 23
Believer with Believer-17:11, 22	Son in Father-17:21
Believers with Father and Son-None	Believers in Father and Son-17:21
	Son in Believers-17:23

Therefore there is no problem with the interpretation of John 10:30 (that Jesus is one in essence with the Father) and the above verses in John 17.

John 12:41

"These things Isaiah said, because he saw His glory, and he spoke of Him." The "things Isaiah said" are found in Isaiah 53:1 and 6:10 and are quoted in John: "Lord, who has believed our report? And to whom has the arm of the Lord been revealed" (John 12:38 cf. Isa. 53:1); "He has blinded their eyes, and He hardened their heart; lest they see with their eyes, and perceive with their heart, and be converted, and I heal them" (John 12:40 cf. Isa. 6:10).

Of whom does John speak in 12:41 when he states that Isaiah saw *His* glory, and Isaiah spoke of *Him*? It is Jesus. The use of "Him" in verses 37 and 41 is significant. In verse 37, though Jesus was performing many great signs, they were not believing in *Him*. In verse 41 Isaiah saw *His* glory, and Isaiah spoke of *Him*. Since "Him" in verse

---

[78]See John 17:11 where Jesus prays, "Holy Father, keep them in (*en*) Thy name, which Thou hast given Me."

[79]This interpretation is sustained by John 15:4, where the Son states: "Abide in [Gr. *en*] Me, and I in [*en*] you [Jesus' followers]. As the branch cannot bear fruit of itself, unless it abides in [*en*] the vine, so neither can you, unless you abide in [*en*] Me." Here the fruit one bears is the result or natural outgrowth of abiding *in* the Son (and vice versa). The same may be said of the Father and the Son. In John 10:38 the works that the Son does bear witness that the Father is in (*en*) the Son and vice versa.

37 clearly refers to Jesus, and since there is in this whole passage no reference to the Father, "Him" in verse 41 must refer to Jesus. Additionally, in 6:1 Isaiah sees "the Lord,"[80] and later identifies this Lord as "the King, the LORD of Hosts" (6:5).[81] John therefore states that Isaiah beheld Yahweh the Son in His preincarnate glory.

By applying the Isaiah text to the Son, John is adding proof to his claims about the Son in the first 18 verses of his Gospel, especially John 1:14, where the new covenant people see Jesus' glory.

John 18:6 (5, 8)

"When therefore He said to them, 'I am He' [Gr. egō eimi, ἐγώ εἰμι], they drew back and fell to the ground." Though this is one instance where the predicate *may* be supplied (i.e., "I am *Jesus the Nazarene*"),[82] due to the soldiers stating that they seek Jesus the Nazarene (see vv. 5, 7), I believe that Jesus' use of "I am" here is absolute (no predicate implied) and refers to Him being God. Also, as verse 5[83] is "in the style of deity,"[84] so is verse 6.[85]

Throughout his Gospel John intends that his readers know that Jesus is God the Son. Because of this *and* the reaction of the soldiers ("they drew back, and fell to the ground"), I see John's intent continuing here. John even seems *intensely determined* to communicate that the Son of God is also God the Son. As pointed out in Leon Morris' *The Gospel According to John,* assertions are repeated in John to draw the reader's attention to a given truth (such as "your son lives,"

---

[80]Heb. *adonay,* אֲדֹנָי.

[81]Heb. *ha melek Yahweh tsebaoth,* הַמֶּלֶךְ יְהוָה צְבָאוֹת.

[82]The predicate acts as an object of a sentence, completing its thought. Here *Jesus the Nazarene,* though not in the text, may be supplied in the thought of the sentence. Some I AM statements of Jesus in John's Gospel are inarguably absolute (stand absolutely without the predicate), such as John 8:58. I will argue that Jesus' *egō eimi* in this passage should be understood as absolute, and thus is a claim to deity on the part of Christ.

[83]Jesus asks the soldiers in v. 4, "Whom do you seek." "They answered Him, 'Jesus the Nazarene.' He said to them, 'I am *He*'" (v. 5).

[84]See Morris, *The Gospel According to John,* 743.

[85]Morris states that "what concerns John [in verse 6] is the majesty of Jesus" (ibid., 744).

in 4:50, 51, 53).[86] We find this sort of repetition with "I am" in 18:5, 6, 8:

> They answered Him, "Jesus the Nazarene." He said to them, "I am *He*".... When therefore He said to them, "I am *He*", they drew back and fell to the ground.... Jesus answered, "I told you that I am *He*; if therefore you seek me, let these go their way."

In light of this repetition theme that Morris points out, it seems hardly the case that John would embark on emphasizing Jesus being a Nazarene (the *supposed* implied predicate), since that was not the focus of the first 18 verses of the Gospel. Rather, he emphasizes the deity of the Son.

How, then, should we view the reaction of the soldiers? Again, since John is quite intent on relating the deity of the Son, we should view John's intent of their reaction as one of *coming into the presence of deity.* This is not outside the theology of John, for in Revelation 1:17 he employs this phenomenon of falling down before the deity. As was the case with the soldiers in John 18:5, Jesus Christ, who is God (see Rev. 1:14 cf. the "ancient of days" in Daniel 7:9; see also Rev. 1:17, the "first and the last" cf. Isa. 44:6), comes before John. John falls at His feet as though dead, just as those before him had done when in the presence of Yahweh (cf. Gen. 17:3; Ezek. 1:28; 3:23). The parallel is strong, and the implication strong as well: John intends to let us know that Jesus is God.

John 20:28

"Thomas answered and said to Him, 'My Lord and my God!'"[87] The Gospel of John opens with a declaration that the preincarnate Son

---

[86]Pg. 743, n. 11. Morris here gleans from C. H. Dodd's *Historical Tradition in the Fourth Gospel* (Cambridge, 1963), 75, n. 2.

[87]Gr. *ho kurios mou kai ho theos mou,* ὁ κύριός μου καὶ ὁ θεός μου; lit. "the Lord of me and the God of me." I have often asked Jehovah's Witnesses, "Who is *THE* God of you?" I may phrase it another way: "Who is *THE* God?" Since they have been taught that Jesus is *a* god (via their own translation of John 1:1), there is in their minds a huge difference between *a* god and *THE* God, between Jesus and Jehovah. Thus their answer: "Jehovah is." I then ask them to read from their own New Testament translation, *The Kingdom Interlinear Translation of the Greek Scriptures* (New York: Watchtower Bible

is God, continues throughout to tell us that the incarnate Son is God, and now begins to close with the declaration of Thomas that the risen Son is God. We see exemplified in Thomas' confession John's reason for writing his Gospel; by confessing Christ as *Lord* and *God*, Thomas has *believed* "that Jesus is the Christ, the Son of God" (see 20:31).[88]

Far from being an exclamation of surprise,[89] or a separation of persons addressed,[90] John includes this historic confession of Thomas in his Gospel because it suits his purpose: Jesus is Himself God the Son (the Son of God). Thomas echoes an Old Testament passage, a confession that *Yahweh* is "my God and my Lord" (Ps. 35:23). The Hebrew text reads *elohay va [a]donay* (אֱלֹהַי וַאדֹנָי), and *Yahweh* is the one addressed (see 35:1, 10, esp. 22 and 24)! What is even more startling is that the LXX of this Psalm (34:23) reads the same as the Greek in John's Gospel: *"ho theos mou kai ho kurios mou"* ("My God and my Lord"). Though the order of phrases is reversed (John, "My Lord and my God"; LXX and Hebrew, "My God and my Lord"), the impact is not lessened; such a confession would *never* cross the lips of Thomas without rebuke by Jesus if He were not God. Instead, Jesus affirms Thomas' confession (see v. 29). Incidentally, this verse is, in my opinion, the most powerful of biblical texts to share with someone who denies the deity of Christ.[91]

---

and Tract Society of New York, Inc., 1985), page 513. Here the Greek text appears on the left of the page with word-for-word English under the Greek words. On the right of the page is their translation of the Greek. I ask them to read Thomas' confession in the English under the Gr. *"ho kurios mou kai ho theos mou."* It reads, "The Lord of me and the God of me." Jesus is called *THE* God. Thus, Jesus is Jehovah the Son!

[88]Yet another reason that "Son of God" is synonymous with "God the Son." By confessing that Jesus is God (20:28), Thomas has believed "that Jesus is the Christ, the Son of God" (20:31).

[89]As in "Oh, my God!" Those appealing to this apologetic take a modern-day idiomatic expression and place it on the lips of Thomas! This is an example of reading into the text something never intended by John or Thomas.

[90]As in another popular Jehovah's Witness argument that Thomas said to Jesus, "my Lord," and then to Jehovah, "my God." Robert Reymond states that this notion of Jehovah's Witnesses is incorrect. He quotes Bruce Metzger, who makes the point that such an interpretation overlooks the introductory phrase, "Thomas said *to Him* [Jesus], 'My Lord and my God'" (see Reymond, *Jesus, Divine Messiah*, 213).

[91]The Christian should be aware of at least four defenses on the part of

Summation of the Gospel of John

John speaks of Jesus as the pre-existent Yahweh the Son (1:1; 8:58), as the incarnate Yahweh the Son (1:14, 18; 10:30), and as the still incarnate but risen and glorified Yahweh the Son (20:28). He does so in no uncertain terms for the purpose that all who read his Gospel might believe in Jesus as the Son of God, and that believing they would have life in His name.

Conclusion

Matthew, Mark, Luke and John provide us with the highest view of Christ, proclaiming Him as God the Son, Yahweh among us, Yahweh

---

those who are confronted with John 20:28. *First* is the defense that never really answers the text in question, but merely resorts to traveling to *other* texts to refute the biblical doctrine of Christ's deity. *Second* is the defense that stays in John 20, but draws attention to v. 31, from which comes the argument, "Jesus is the Son of God, not God!" This argument has already been answered, for I have shown that the phrase "Son of God" means "God the Son." *Third* is to again stay in John 20, but to draw attention to v. 17, where Christ says to Mary, "I ascend to My Father and your Father, and My God and your God." A few observations are in order: (A) Jesus is careful not to say "to *our* Father and to *our* God." Instead, He makes a separation ("to My Father and your Father, to My God and your God"), indicating His special filial relationship which He alone shares with the Father. Though believers are allowed to call God their Father, it is by adoption. God is *not* our Father in the same sense that He is Jesus' Father, for Jesus is God's *unique* Son. Moreover, as Reymond observes, nowhere in the teachings of Jesus does He speak of God to His disciples as "our Father." The Lord's prayer, Reymond then notes, is not an exception, since Jesus is here instructing His disciples to pray *among themselves* (see *Jesus, Divine Messiah,* 210). (B) By virtue of His humanity, and in keeping with biblical Trinitarianism, Jesus may state that the Father is His God, and at the same time not deny that He is God *the Son. Fourth* is to interpret the phrase *ho kurios mou kai ho theos mou* as "my godly lord," as followers of The Way International have been taught. Here founder Victor Paul Wierwille (*Jesus Christ is not God* [New Knoxville, Ohio: American Christian Press, 1981], 36-37) states that the phrase is a *hendiadys,* meaning that two nouns are used to express one thought, and that therefore one of these nouns may function adjectivally (hence, "my godly [adj.] lord [noun]"). But this is erroneous and misleading, for (A) both nouns (*kurios* and *theos*) have definite articles before them, and (B) *both* nouns are followed by the possessive pronoun *mou.*

who saves, God in the flesh, God who forgives, Yahweh the cloud-rider, God the eschatological judge, and Yahweh the storm-stiller. The same may be said of the rest of the New Testament witness to the incarnate deity of Jesus Christ. It is to this that we now turn, beginning with the writings of the apostle Paul.

Chapter 5

Paul: The Incarnate Deity of Christ

"He being begotten by the Father before the ages, was God the Word, the only-begotten Son, and remains the same forever."—*Ignatius,* Epistle to the Magnesians

"Now listen! From the Book of Acts, all the way through all of the epistles, all the way through the Revelation of John, Jesus is no longer called the only-begotten Son of God."—*Kenneth Copeland,* What Happened from the Cross to the Throne

Paul's Jesus is no less than that of Matthew, Mark, Luke and John: Jesus is truly God. There is as high a Christology in the writings of this great apostle and theologian as there is in the Gospels. It shall be an interesting and edifying journey as we travel through the corpus of the apostle who was visited by God the Son Himself on the road to Damascus (Acts 9:1-8).

Romans 1:1

In the very first verse of Paul's Epistle to the saints in Rome we have the affirmation that Christ is God the Son: *"Paul, a bond-servant of Christ Jesus, called as an apostle, set apart for the gospel of God."*

Of whom is Paul a servant? Jesus. Paul is owned by Christ. Paul belongs to Christ. And the Old Testament background to this statement by Paul affords to Jesus that which belongs to Yahweh. The startling claim that he was a "servant of *Christ Jesus*" (see also Gal. 1:10; Phil. 1:1[1]) draws one immediately to those who were servants of *Yahweh*. Abraham (Gen. 26:24; Ps. 105:6, 42), Moses (Num. 12:7, 8; Deut. 34:5; Josh. 1:1, 2, 7; Ps. 105:26), Joshua (Josh. 24:29; Judg. 2:8), David (2 Sam. 7:5, 8; Pss. 78:70; 89:3, 20; Isa. 37:35), Isaiah (Isa. 20:3), the prophets (Ezra 9:11; Jer. 7:25; Dan. 9:6; Amos 3:7; Zech. 1:6), and other believers (Pss. 34:22; 113:1; Israel as a people, 136:22 and Isa. 43:10 cf. 1 Cor. 4:1; Col. 4:12; Eph. 6:6) are called servants of Yahweh. Paul, no doubt, is identifying Jesus as his Lord, the one of whom he is a servant. In so doing he places Jesus in the Old Testament position of LORD. In effect he calls Christ Yahweh.

One other interesting feature of our focus verse is Paul's phrase, "the gospel of God." For him this phrase is synonymous with "the gospel of Christ."[2] Here the gospel belongs to God; it is *His* gospel (see also 1 Thess. 2:2). But Paul elsewhere states that it is *Christ's* gospel (Gal. 1:7; 1 Thess. 3:2). For Paul the two go hand in hand, and he has no second thought about placing Christ on equal ground with God the Father regarding ownership of the gospel.

---

[1]Paul is not alone among other New Testament writers in calling himself a servant of Christ. See James 1:1; 2 Pet. 1:1; Jude 1. Quite interesting is that the Scripture also labels believers as bond-servants of God the Father (Rev. 19:5). The ease with which the New Testament writers call themselves "bond-servants of Christ," while the biblical option of "bond-servants of God [the Father]" was available, lends weight to the argument that Christ was considered ontologically equal to the Father.

[2]We may take the genitive here as subjective (i.e., it is God's gospel) rather than objective (i.e., the gospel *about* God), especially in light of v. 3, where God's gospel is "concerning His Son."

Romans 8:9

Though quite subtle (as our previous verse), Romans 8:9 provides a most implicit claim to Christ's deity: *"However you are not in the flesh but in the Spirit, if indeed the Spirit of God dwells in you. But if anyone does not have the Spirit of Christ, he does not belong to Him."*

The parallelism is simple: "Spirit of God" (Gr. *pneuma theou*, πνεῦμα θεοῦ) and "Spirit of Christ" (*pneuma Christou*, πνεῦμα Χριστοῦ). The Holy Spirit, the third person of the Godhead, belongs to the Father[3] and to Christ. The Spirit's relation to the Father is the same as His relation to the Son, as is evident in the other writings of Paul (cf. 2 Cor. 3:17; Gal. 4:6; Phil. 1:19; 1 Pet. 1:11).[4]

Romans 9:5

The Greek of Romans 9:5 is as follows: *hōn hoi pateres kai ex hōn ho Christos to kata sarka, ho ōn epi pantōn theos eulogētos eis tous aiōnas, amēn* (ὦν οἱ πατέρες καὶ ἐξ ὦν ὁ Χριστὸς τὸ κατὰ σάρκα, ὁ ὢν ἐπὶ πάντων θεὸς εὐλογητὸς εἰς τοὺς αἰῶνας, ἀμήν), *"Whose are the fathers, and from whom is the Christ according to the flesh, who is overall, God blessed forever. Amen."* There is a difference of opinion as to the translation of the Greek in this verse. For example, the NASB, Jerusalem Bible, Phillips, NKJV, and the NIV prefer the above rendering. The RSV, NEB, NAB, Goodspeed, and Moffatt prefer a second rendering, which is a doxology to God the Father. Here a period is placed after "from whom is the Christ according to the flesh." The doxology then follows: "May God [the Father], who rules overall, be praised forever." I believe the first to be proper, thus evidencing the deity of Christ.

Those who prefer the second rendering do so "principally on the basis that Paul elsewhere never calls Christ God."[5] Even if this were

---

[3]Paul as well uses *theos* as a synonym for the Father. See also Rom. 1:7.
[4]See also Acts 16:7.
[5]Barclay M. Newman and Eugene A. Nida, *A Translator's Handbook on Paul's Letter to the Romans* (London: United Bible Societies, 1973), 180. See also John Murray, *The Epistle to the Romans*, 2 vols. (Grand Rapids, Mich.: Wm. B. Eerdmans, 1965, reprinted, 1980), 2:247. Murray states that the "chief argument" for the second rendering is that Paul never calls Jesus God, and contests it.

true, are we on this basis *ruling out* that Paul could not have said it once? Nonetheless, if it can be shown that Paul elsewhere calls Jesus God, the principal argument is defeated, and little (if any) reason is left for the second rendering.[6]

First is Paul calling Christ "Lord" (*kurios*) in Romans 10:9, only to refer in parallel to an Old Testament passage, where he substitutes "Lord" (*kurios*) for the Hebrew *Yahweh,* thus equating Christ with Yahweh (Rom. 10:13). In 10:9 we have, "if you confess with your mouth Jesus as Lord..." In 10:13 Joel 2:32[7] is quoted, "Whoever will call upon the name of the Lord will be saved." *Second* are several passages in Paul's writings[8] where Christ is called God. More detail will be given these later in this chapter, but consider for now Philippians 2:5-6 ("Christ Jesus, who, although He existed in the form of God..."), Colossians 2:9 ("In Him all the fulness of Deity dwells in bodily form"), 2 Thessalonians 1:12 ("according to the grace of our God and Lord, Jesus Christ"[9]), and Titus 2:13 ("our great God and Savior, Christ Jesus"[10]).[11]

There are more reasons why the first rendering is preferred.[12] *First,* "the form of doxology in the LXX and the New Testament does not

---

[6]Though Dodd calls upon this "chief argument" (see above note), Murray states that Dodd admits that Paul elsewhere ascribes to Christ "functions and dignities" that belong to God (ibid.).

[7]Heb. and LXX 3:5.

[8]I am here assuming that Paul authored Romans through Philemon.

[9]My translation of *kata tēn charin tou theou hēmōn kai kuriou Iēsou Christou* (κατὰ τὴν χάριν τοῦ θεοῦ ἡμῶν καὶ κυρίου Ἰησοῦ Χριστοῦ). Here the one definite article "the" (*tou*) governs both the nouns "God" and "Lord" (*theou* and *kuriou*).

[10]Again, in the phrase *tou megalou theou kai sōtēros hēmōn Iēsou Christou* (τοῦ μεγάλου θεοῦ καὶ σωτῆρος ἡμῶν Ἰησοῦ Χριστοῦ), the one article (*tou*) governs the two nouns (*theou* and *sōtēros*).

[11]Taken from Murray's *The Epistle to the Romans,* 2:247.

[12]Excellent arguments for this rendering are found in Murray's *The Epistle to the Romans,* 2:245-48, Everett F. Harrison, *Romans,* in Frank E. Gaebelein, ed., *The Expositor's Bible Commentary,* 12 vols. (Grand Rapids, Mich.: Zondervan Publishing House, 1976), 10:103, and William Sanday and Arthur C. Headlam, *A Critical and Exegetical Commentary on the Epistle to the Romans* (Edinburgh: T. & T. Clark, reprinted, 1977), 233-38. I thank all of these scholars for the following observations.

follow the pattern we find in Rom. 9:5."[13] *Second,* and in my opinion most important, the phrase "the one who is"[14] refers back to "Christ."[15] It is therefore most natural[16] to take it as "Christ..., the one [*or* He] who is over all, God blessed forever, Amen." *Third,* the fact that Paul would call Christ the one who is "over all"[17] should not be disputed on the basis of Paul calling the Father the same (see, for example, Eph. 4:6), for Paul ascribes to Jesus the phrase "Lord of all"[18] (Rom. 10:12; Acts 10:36 cf. Eph. 1:20-23).[19] I therefore conclude that Romans 9:5 is a clear declaration of the incarnate deity of Christ.

---

[13]Murray, *The Epistle to the Romans,* 2:245. This, then, renders the second translation unlikely. If Paul wanted to say "blessed be God" or "may God be blessed," he would have placed "blessed" (*eulogētos*) first in word order. In our text it is not first. See, for example, LXX Ps. 67:20. This formula is "very frequent," according to Murray. In 67:19, where *eulogētos* is not first in word order, it is disputable whether or not it is doxological. Ps. 112:2, 3 Kingdoms 10:9, 2 Chron. 9:8, and Job 1:21 are not exceptions for syntactical reasons (see Murray, *The Epistle to the Romans,* 2:245-46.) With the New Testament there are many examples of doxologies where *eulogetos* precedes, such as Matt. 21:9; 23:39; Mark 11:9, 10; Luke 1:42, 68; 13:35; 19:38; John 12:13; 2 Cor. 1:3; Eph. 1:3; 1 Pet. 1:3. I agree with Murray when he states that "this preponderant usage of both Testaments constitutes a potent argument against the supposition that Rom. 9:5b should be regarded as doxology to God" (2:246). See also Harrison, *Romans,* 103.

[14]Gr. *ho ōn.*

[15]Gr. *ho Christos.*

[16]Robert Reymond writes, "This natural, straightforward rendering of Romans 9:5—which every Greek scholar would unhesitatingly adopt if no question of doctrine were involved..." (*Jesus, Divine Messiah* [Phillipsburg, N.J.: Presbyterian and Reformed Publishing Co., 1990], 273). No one to my knowledge would dispute that it is most natural to view 2 Corinthians 11:31 (which has the same syntactical relationship as Rom. 9:5: *ho theos kai patēr tou kuriou Iēsou oiden, ho ōn eulogētos eis tous aiōnas,* ὁ θεὸς καὶ πατὴρ τοῦ κυρίου Ἰησοῦ οἶδεν, ὁ ὢν εὐλογητὸς εἰς τοὺς αἰῶνας ["the God and Father of the Lord Jesus, He who is blessed forever, knows"]) as having *ho ōn* ("He who is") refer back to God (*ho theos*)!

[17]Gr. *epi pantōn.*

[18]Gr. *kurios pantōn.*

[19]See Murray J. Harris, *Jesus as God: The New Testament Use of Theos in Reference to Jesus* (Grand Rapids, Mich.: Baker Book House, 1992), 160.

Romans 10:9, 13

"That if you confess with your mouth Jesus as Lord, and believe in your heart that God raised Him from the dead, you shall be saved.... for 'whoever will call upon the name of the Lord will be saved.'" Here Paul continues to call Christ God the Son. He equates Jesus, whom he calls "Lord," with Yahweh in Joel 2:32.[20]

Paul states in verse 9 that in order to have eternal life, one must confess Jesus as Lord (*kurios*). He then quotes Joel 2:32: "everyone who calls upon the name of *Yahweh* will be saved." Here Paul places "Lord" (*kurios*) in place of *Yahweh* in his Old Testament quotation of Joel. What grabs one's attention is not necessarily Paul's usage *per se* of *kurios* for the Hebrew *Yahweh*,[21] but that Paul, in such close proximity to his labeling of Jesus as Lord in verse 9, would then proceed to quote an Old Testament text where *Yahweh* is used. The parallel of "confessing" of Christ as Lord in verse 9, and "calling upon" the name of Yahweh in verse 13 shows Paul's high Christology: Christ is Yahweh.[22]

---

[20]Heb. and LXX 3:5.

[21]This is not surprising at all, given the LXX's rendering of *Yahweh* as *kurios*. According to Murray J. Harris, *Yahweh* is found "some 6,823 times in the Hebrew Bible" (he cites BDB, 217b). The LXX renders *Yahweh* as *kurios* 6,156 times, and as *theos* only 353 times (Harris, *Jesus as God*, 24-25). Because in Paul's theology Jesus is God the Son, he finds no problem with his applying the LXX translation of *Yahweh* (which is *kurios*) to Christ.

[22]In his epistles, Paul uses the title *kurios* to refer to the Son in the Yahwistic sense. The fact that Paul has no difficulty at all with this evidences that he esteems Christ in equal honor with the Father (see also the previous note). This, of course, is what Jesus Himself taught (John 5:23). Consider for example the string of texts in 1 Corinthians: "yet for us there is but one God the Father... and one Lord, Jesus Christ" (8:6); "no one can say, 'Jesus is Lord,' except by the Holy Spirit" (12:3b); "In the Law it is written, 'by men of strange tongues and by the lips of strangers I will speak to this people, and even so they will not listen to Me,' says the Lord" (14:21). Though Paul distinguishes in one place God the Father and the Lord Jesus, he finds no difficulty in expressing that no one can confess Christ as the Lord except by the Spirit, while at the same time calling the Yahweh who speaks in the Law (see Isa. 28:11, 12; Deut. 28:49) "Lord" (see also 1 Cor. 10:26).

Another example of Paul using "Lord" in the Yahwistic sense and applying it to Christ is found in Ephesians. All through the epistle, Paul *specifically*

1 Corinthians 1:8; 1 Thessalonians 5:2

"Who shall also confirm you to the end, blameless in the day of our Lord Jesus Christ." "The day of the Lord"[23] is the consummation of the ages, when the Lord of Glory, Jesus Christ, shall come on the clouds to judge the living and the dead. But Paul must be familiar with the Old Testament's teaching of "the day of Yahweh,"[24] which is prophetic of this consummation. Isaiah 13:6 tells of this great day of Yahweh: "Wail, for the day of the LORD[25] is near! It will come as destruction from the Almighty." In telling of the judgment of Christ to come, and by his use

---

names Jesus as "Lord" (see 1:2, 3, 15, 17; 3:11, 14; 5:20; 6:23, 24). Many times he simply uses "Lord" without specifically naming either person of the Trinity (2:21; 4:1, 5, 17; 5:8, 10, 17, 19; 6:1, 4, 7, 8, 10, 21). But in Eph. 6:4 we read, "And, fathers, do not provoke your children to anger; but bring them up in the discipline and instruction of the Lord." Clearly this is a reference to Gen. 18:19 and Deut. 6:7, where Yahweh's people are to teach their children the way of the LORD (*Yahweh*). (In Gen. 18:19 the command is to Abraham; in Deut 6:7 the command is to the covenant people in general.) Certainly Paul, if Christ were *not* Yahweh, would take the time to make the distinction in how he uses the title "Lord." But he does not. He uses the title so freely (see also Acts 1:6, 24; 2:21, 25, 34-36 for an example of this phenomenon outside the Pauline corpus), without hesitation, as to communicate to his readers that Jesus must be the LORD (to see this the reader is encouraged to read all of Eph. 6).

Finally, in 2 Tim. 4:18 Paul states, "The Lord will deliver me from every evil deed, and will bring me safely to His heavenly kingdom; to Him be the glory forever and ever. Amen." That Paul is ascribing glory to the risen Christ is without question, for in close proximity preceding this verse he calls Jesus "Lord" (see 4:1 cf. 4:8 and the theme of "judge"; see also the opening of the letter [1:2], where Paul distinguishes between "God the Father and Christ Jesus our Lord"). Certainly with this ascription of glory to Christ, Paul is affording the highest praise that can only be given to Yahweh.

[23]Gr. *tē hēmera tou kuriou*, τῇ ἡμμέρᾳ τοῦ κυρίου.

[24]Heb. *yom Yahweh*, יְהוָה יוֹם

[25]Heb. *Yahweh*, LXX *hē hēmera kuriou* (ἡ ἡμέρα κυρίου, "the day of the Lord").

of the stock phrase "the day of the LORD" applying to Christ,[26] Paul no doubt sees the incarnate Lord of glory as Yahweh the Son.[27]

1 Thessalonians 5:2

Paul again mentions "the day of the Lord." In encouragement and admonition, Paul begins to close his first letter to the Thessalonians, stating, *"For you yourselves know full well that the day of the Lord will come like a thief in the night."*
But it is verse 3 that firmly sets this reference to Christ[28] directly into the contexts of Isaiah and Jeremiah. Paul states in 1 Thessalonians 5:3: "While they are saying, 'Peace and safety!' then destruction will come upon them suddenly like birth pangs upon a woman with child; and they shall not escape." Isaiah 13:6-9 speaks of "the day of the LORD" (vv. 6, 9) with the nuance of the judged "writhing like a woman in labor" (v. 8). Isaiah 26:17, 18 also tells of Yahweh's eschatological judgment (see v. 19, 21), and the reaction of the judged as one writhing in labor pains. This will all take place, as Isaiah states, "In that day" (27:1, 2, 12, 13[29]). In Jeremiah 6:14 the theme of people speaking falsely with the words "Peace, peace," when in reality there is no peace,[30] is reminiscent of Paul's statement in 1 Thessalonians 5:3.

---

[26]See also Phil. 1:6; 2:16. As the reader familiar with Greek can tell, the phrase used by Paul in 1 Cor. 1:8 (see Phil. 1:6, 10) is that of the LXX's translation of the Hebrew *yom Yahweh* in Isa. 13:6, the only difference being that of case.

[27]See also 2 Pet. 3:10.

[28]"Lord" in 5:2 refers to Christ because only a few verses earlier Paul speaks of the "Lord Himself" descending from heaven (4:16, a clear reference to the Son). Moreover, 2 Thess. 1:7 mentions "the Lord Jesus" being "revealed from heaven with His mighty angels." Paul then states that these events will occur "on that day." These observations, coupled with the fact that in the Pauline corpus "the Lord Jesus" is certainly distinguished from "God our Father" or "God the Father," lend weight to the conclusion that "Lord" in 1 Thess. 5:2 is a reference to Christ.

[29]The context here is one of deliverance. In the same way, Paul speaks of deliverance of the Lord's people on "the day of the Lord" (see 1 Thess. 4:17; 5:9, 10).

[30]See also Jer. 8:11.

Moreover, in Jeremiah 6:24 the nuance of birth pains once again arises in the context of *Yahweh's* judgment.[31]

I conclude that once again Paul applies to Christ what our three Old Testament passages apply to Yahweh. For Paul, Jesus is the Yahweh who will judge.

2 Corinthians 5:10

"For we must all appear before the judgment seat of Christ, that each one may be recompensed for his deeds in the body, according to what he has done, whether good or bad." As we have seen so vividly in the Gospels, the performing of divine functions by Christ implicitly, though strongly, points to His deity. It is no different here.

Paul, who in Romans 14:10 stated that "we shall all stand before the judgment seat of God,"[32] now states that we shall stand before the judgment seat of Christ. The two are interchangeable: God's judgment seat is Christ's judgment seat. And the "recompensing" done by Christ is a divine function of God in the Old Testament (Ps. 62:12; see Matt. 16:27).

Immediately following verse 10, Paul connects the judgment seat motif with "the fear of the Lord" (v. 11), no doubt referring to Christ because of this immediacy (v. 10). "The fear of the Lord" (*Yahweh*) is itself a motif that may be found throughout the Old Testament, and Paul makes use of this phrase in application to Christ (see also Eph. 5:21, "the fear of Christ"). This should not surprise us. If Paul can use the title "Lord" interchangeably for Jesus and God the Father (see note 22

---

[31]See also Jer. 4:31; 22:23; 30:6 and their surrounding contexts. In the two Isaiah passages and the Jeremiah passage discussed above, there is, of course, the reality of the judgment (and deliverance, see Isaiah 27) of the nation of Israel; thus an immediate and not eschatological judgment. Yet, there is in these texts (Paul uses the Jeremiah passage to refer to eschatological judgment) the *ultimate fulfillment* of that immediate judgment, the eschatological judgment. Thus, the *pre*fillment in the immediate judgmental sense points to the ultimate *ful*fillment at the consummation of the ages.

[32]Some manuscripts have "Christ" instead of "God." By far the most reliable read "God." Note also Paul's immediate reference to Isa. 49:18 and 45:23 in Rom. 14:11. All shall give an account to Yahweh, for before Him "every knee shall bow, and every tongue shall give praise to God" (see Phil. 2:10-11).

and 2 Cor. 5:11 cf. 7:1), and use "Lord" in reference to Christ from Old Testament passages where *Yahweh* is used, he certainly can with ease refer to both "the judgment seat of God" and "the judgment seat of Christ," and in that usage ascribe to Christ divine functions that only Yahweh can perform (recompensing, i.e., eschatological judge).

Galatians 1:1

In the introduction to Galatians, the apostle Paul states, *"Paul, an apostle (not sent from men, nor through the agency of man, but through Jesus Christ, and God the Father, who raised Him from the dead)."*

Those who teach that Christ was merely a man[33] must face the obvious distinction[34] Paul draws between man and Jesus Christ (see also Gal. 1:12). Paul's calling as an apostle came not from men or through man (see Acts 9:3-9). Who from, then, if not man? The point is that Christ is more than a man. Fully human indeed, but more than that.

Paul was called to be an apostle through Jesus Christ and God the Father. The grouping of Jesus with the Father in the calling of Paul is interesting. *First*, the preposition "through"[35] alone is used for both Christ *and* God the Father.[36] Paul has not been called from men, but through Jesus and God the Father. This has the Father and Jesus both sharing in, on equal par, the calling of Paul; it is *through* both, not *by* the Father *through* Jesus Christ. *Second*, Jesus is mentioned in the same

---

[33]Unitarians and liberal Protestants, for example. The Jehovah's Witnesses, however, could argue that Jesus after His resurrection (not bodily) was an angel and therefore not man, since Paul's calling by Christ on the road to Damascus was after the resurrection (see Acts 9:3-9). Therefore they could claim that this text poses no threat to their Christology. Thus, with Jehovah's Witnesses, other texts clearly asserting Christ's deity should be used in place of Gal. 1:1, or in conjunction with it.

[34]"Not sent from men, nor through the agency of man, *but* [*alla,* ἀλλὰ, a strong adversative clearly marking the distinction] through Jesus Christ..."

[35]Gr. *dia,* διὰ.

[36]In context there could be reason to apply the preposition *ap',* ἀπ' ("from") to the second half of the verse, since it is mentioned in the negative regarding men. Even if this be the case, the preposition *dia* and the implied preposition *ap'* must refer equally to Jesus and the Father (the *kai* ["and"] connects the Father and the Son acting together). This is to say, the calling of Paul is both *from* and *through* Jesus Christ and God the Father, not *from* the Father *through* Jesus.

breath as the Father (Jesus being mentioned first!), implying equality with the Father, an implicit claim to Christ's deity.[37]

Ephesians 4:8

"Therefore it says, 'When He ascended on high, He led captive a host of captives, and He gave gifts to men.'" Here is yet another example of an Old Testament text (Ps. 68:18[38]) where *Yahweh* is applied to Christ.

A few observations at the outset are necessary. Psalm 68:18, referring to Yahweh, reads, "Thou hast ascended on high, Thou hast led captive thy captives; Thou hast received gifts among men, even among the rebellious also, that the LORD God may dwell there." *First,* the psalmist addresses Yahweh[39] in the second person (LXX and Heb.), whereas Paul turns the quotation into the third person. This could very easily be viewed as a "footnote" usage of the Psalm by Paul.[40] *Second,* the curious change from the second person to the third *within the Psalm itself* (*"Thou* hast ascended on high... that the *LORD God* may dwell there") is, stylistically in Hebrew, referring to the same person,[41] and this is displayed throughout the Psalm (see vv. 7-8; 28-30, 31).[42]

In the Psalm it is Yahweh who ascended on high, leading His captives captive. This is a reference to Mount Sinai (vv. 16, 17; see v. 8), where Yahweh *ascended* after His great act of deliverance of His people from the land of Egypt. The exodus event, the deliverance out of the hand of the Egyptians, out of the bond of slavery, is the event that the Israelites claimed in their identification as the people of Yahweh.

---

[37]See Robert Reymond, *Jesus, Divine Messiah,* 238: "Paul's apostolic calling, which he declared he received 'not from men [ἀπ' ἀνθρώπον, *ap' anthrōpon*] nor through man [δι' ἀνθρώπου, *di' anthrōpou*], but through Jesus Christ and God the Father' (Gal. 1:1)—an expression that many New Testament scholars suggest, because of the contrast Paul draws between 'men' and 'man' on the one hand and 'Jesus Christ and God the Father' on the other, contains an implicit assertion of Christ's divine character."

[38]LXX 67:19; Heb. 68:19.

[39]That "Thou" refers to Yahweh is evidenced in vv. 4, 16.

[40]See chap. 2, nn. 26, 27, and the body text under Zechariah 12:10.

[41]See chap. 2, n. 25.

[42]Paul further differs from the LXX rendering, "You have received gifts among men." Paul writes, "He gave gifts to men."

This was their salvation, and it is this event that is paradigmatic of the salvation of which Paul speaks. The "gift" of Ephesians 4:7 is the "gift" of salvation (Eph. 2:8).

Some see Mount Zion as the mountain to which Yahweh ascended (in Ps. 68:18).

> On the victorious completion of the Exodus, the Wilderness Wanderings, and the Conquest, the Lord returned as it were to heaven ("on high") to celebrate his kingship on earth (cf. [Ps.] 47:5-7).... In commemoration of his mighty acts, he chose Jerusalem among the mountains to establish his abode "where the LORD himself will dwell forever" (v. 16).[43]

But whether Sinai or Zion (I favor the former), Paul applies Psalm 68:18 to Christ,[44] communicating that Christ is Yahweh the Son (in v. 7 the mention of "Christ's gift" provides the antecedent to which the phrase "He gave gifts to men" refers [v. 8]). Paul parallels Christ's acts of salvation and ascension with Yahweh's acts of salvation and ascension in the Psalm.[45]

Philippians 2:6-11

This passage is one of the great christological hymns[46] of Paul witnessing the deity of Christ.[47]

> Christ Jesus, (6) who, although He existed[48] in the form[49] of God, did not regard equality[50] with God a thing to be grasped, (7) but emptied[51]

---

[43]Willem A. VanGemeren, *Psalms,* in Frank E. Gaebelein, ed., *The Expositor's Bible Commentary,* 12 vols. (Grand Rapids, Mich.: Zondervan Publishing House, 1984), 5:449.

[44]Murray J. Harris (*Jesus as God,* 316-17) and Robert Reymond (*Jesus, Divine Messiah,* 241) concur.

[45]See Reymond, *Jesus, Divine Messiah,* 266-67 and 216.

[46]Robert Reymond suggests the possibility of Phil. 2:6-11 comprising two hymns to Christ (*Jesus, Divine Messiah,* 252).

[47]And the humanity of Christ.

[48]Gr. *huparchōn,* ὑπάρχων.

[49]Gr. *morphē,* μορφῇ.

[50]Gr. *isa,* ἴσα.

[51]Gr. *ekenōsen,* ἐκένωσεν.

Himself, taking[52] the form[53] of a bond-servant, and being made in the likeness of men. (8) And being found in appearance as a man, He humbled Himself by becoming obedient to the point of death, even death on a cross. (9) Therefore also God highly exalted Him, and bestowed on Him the name which is above every name, (10) that at the name of Jesus every knee should bow, of those who are in heaven, and on earth, and under the earth, (11) and that every tongue should confess that Jesus Christ is Lord, to the glory of God the Father.

Issues

The classical Christian interpretation of this passage is to view it as teaching that Christ existed as God *prior* to the incarnation (v. 6), then emptied Himself by coming *from* His preincarnate state to His incarnate state (v.7). After this He went to the cross (v. 8) which resulted in His exaltation (v. 9). With the latter points taken from verses 8 and 9 I by all means agree, but wish to point out that verses 6 and 7 may be interpreted another way and in another context.[54] The alternative interpretation is that verse 6 does not speak of Christ's existence as God *prior* to the incarnation (though, as my previous exegesis of several biblical passages shows, I certainly believe Christ existed eternally as God prior to the incarnation), but as God *in His incarnate state.*

Problems

Before heading into the text itself, a few observations are in order. Robert Reymond points out the implications arising from the classical view mentioned above. *First,* if the phrase "[Christ] did not regard equality with God a thing to be grasped" is taken as either "a thing to be held onto" *or* "a thing to be seized," it is theologically problematic. If the former, that would mean that Jesus "emptied" Himself of equality with God when He became man (took the form of a servant). The meaning here is that He had equality with God, *but*[55] since He did not

---

[52]Gr. *labōn,* λαβών.

[53] Gr. *morphēn,* μορφὴν.

[54]For much of the following I thank Robert Reymond. In his exegesis of this passage in *Jesus, Divine Messiah* (pp. 251-66), he challenges the classical Christian interpretation of vv. 6-7. I will echo his conclusion in the text above.

[55]Verse 7 begins with the strong adversative *alla* (ἀλλὰ, "but").

deem that equality a thing to be held onto, He emptied Himself, taking the form of a servant. But if He emptied Himself of equality with God, then it logically follows in the flow of thought that Christ divested Himself of deity. If the latter, that is, if Christ did not consider equality with God a thing to be seized, that would imply that Christ did not already possess equality with God.[56] A third option is to see "something to be grasped [or seized]" as "something to be *asserted*." I hold this interpretation (as we will see later) but, in *this* context (preincarnate) it poses problems. For example, with *whom* potentially was He to make this assertion? With the Father? With the Spirit? Such a view raises implications regarding the unity of the Godhead.

Second, if verse 6 is teaching that Christ existed as God prior to the incarnation, then Reymond is right in asking, "what can His later exaltation [v. 9] possibly have meant to Him?"[57] That is to say, "if exaltation is to have any meaning at all, it must involve elevation to a state not in one's prior possession."[58] Thus, if the passage in verse 6 is speaking of Christ as God in His preincarnate state, then the Son as God in His preincarnate state certainly possesses the highest of exaltation due Him as God. What, then, can the exaltation mean in verse 9? Reymond continues:

> But, if the evangelical scholar insists that the exaltation was still indeed the exaltation of the preexistent Son of God *per se,* then he makes the Son's former state [v. 6] lower in dignity than His latter state [v. 9] and elevates the Son's latter state above that which He enjoyed when "existing in the form of God" prior to His incarnation. But Scripture and right reason simply will not permit such a conclusion.[59]

A *third* difficulty in seeing the passage in the classical sense is that it results in semantic gymnastics[60] on the part of Christians in order to avoid a full-blown kenotic Christology. A kenotic (this word is derived from *ekenōsen*, "He emptied"] in v. 7) Christology in its most blatant form is heretical in that it ascribes to Christ an "emptying" of deity ("equality with God") just prior to the incarnation. This, of course,

---

[56]See *Jesus, Divine Messiah,* 259-60.
[57]Ibid., 261.
[58]Ibid.
[59]Ibid.
[60]Reymond calls it "hermeneutical gymnastics." See ibid., 260.

results in Jesus not being God in His incarnate state.[61] Christians, while holding to the classical interpretation, do not want to become kenotic to this degree in their Christology (and this to their credit). Thus, they have resorted to getting around the problems of a full-blown kenotic Christology through philosophical speculations that find no warrant in the Scripture itself. Reymond states,

> For example, it is said, "He did not divest Himself of His divine attributes, but only the independent use of His attributes." But when did the Son ever exercise His attributes independently? Or, "He did not divest Himself of His deity, but only the glory of His deity." But is not the "divine glory" just the sum and substance of the deity? And how does one square this interpretation with John 1:14 and 2:11 et al.?[62]

Seeing the passage another way (and I believe this other way is faithful to the intent of Paul) completely avoids all the theological problems we have discussed.

Interpretation

The passage should be interpreted as pertaining to "Christ Jesus" (v. 5) *solely in His incarnate state.*[63] It was this Christ Jesus in His incarnate state who "existed in the form of God" (v. 6).[64] What does "form of God" mean?[65] It refers to the very essence or nature of the God-man Jesus. He is in His very nature God.[66] This is an explicit

---

[61]See Millard Erickson, *Christian Theology* (Grand Rapids, Mich.: Baker Book House, 1985), 732-33.

[62]*Jesus, Divine Messiah,* 260-61.

[63]See ibid., 262. Reymond makes mention, however, of the title "Christ Jesus" in Paul's writings where it refers to His preincarnate state as well (1 Tim. 1:15).

[64]The present active participle *huparchōn* conveys the meaning of *continually existing* in the form of God. True, we have here an affirmation of the pre-existent deity of Christ, but that does not exclude the possibility that Paul could mention this *in reference to the God-man* Christ Jesus. In other words, Paul says that *this God-man* Jesus Christ always existed as God.

[65]See G. E. Ladd, *A Theology of the New Testament* (Grand Rapids, Mich.: Wm. B. Eerdmans Publishing Co., 1974), 419-21, for various views.

[66]See Reymond, *Jesus, Divine Messiah,* 257-58, David Wells, *The Person of Christ* (Westchester, Ill.: Crossway Books, 1984), 64, Homer A. Kent, Jr.,

affirmation of the full deity of the Son.[67] As God the Son He did not regard equality with God (which He possessed in His incarnate state, see John 5:18; 10:30) something to be seized. That is to say, Christ's equality with God *was not something He asserted.* When this phrase is put in the context of His temptation in Matthew 4,[68] we see that He chose to continue in His ministry as the Servant of God (Isaiah 52:13-53:12) and not step outside the already ordained plan of God. Christ did not act outside the Father's will (in autonomous fashion, which was the sin of Adam), and take hold of "all the kingdoms of this world" (Matt. 4:8; this is keeping with Paul's exhortation to Christians in vv. 3-5!).[69] Giving into the temptation of Satan, Adam chose autonomy, but Jesus as "the second man," "the last Adam," steadfastly resisted this.

Instead of succumbing to temptation by asserting His already possessed equality with God, Jesus resisted and later "emptied Himself, having taken[70] the form of a servant." The phrase "He emptied Himself" refers back to the description of the servant in Isaiah 53:12. Reymond points out that this phrase ("He emptied Himself"), keeping with the conclusion of some scholars,[71] "is the nonliteral Greek

---

Philippians, in Frank E. Gaebelein, ed., *The Expositor's Bible Commentary,* 12 vols. (Grand Rapids, Mich.: Zondervan Publishing House, 1976), 11:126, and J. B. Lightfoot, *St. Paul's Epistle to the Philippians* (Lynn, Mass.: Hendrickson Publishers, Inc., reprinted, 1982), 133.

[67]*Morphē* is said by some to be a synonym for *doxa* ($\delta\acute{o}\xi\alpha$, "glory"), but this may be rejected because "this identification is not feasible linguistically" (Wells, *The Person of Christ,* 63). Wells mentions that "the form of God is itself full of *doxa* [here transliterated]" (ibid., 63-64).

[68]If the phrase "did not regard equality with God a thing to be grasped [i.e., asserted]" is taken in the context of the temptation in Matt. 4, the theological flow of thought is smooth. In the context of the *already* incarnate Christ, this does not lead to the problems mentioned earlier for the preincarnate framework.

[69]See Reymond, *Jesus, Divine Messiah,* 262-63.

[70] It is important to note, lest some find fault in this conclusion because the text seems to suggest that the "emptying" took place *before* taking a servant's form, that the action of the aorist participle *labōn* ("taking" the form of a servant) may be viewed as *occurring before* the "emptying." Thus, "*after* taking" (or "having taken") a servant's form (*morphē* denoting a full human essence in the person of God the Son; see also Isaiah 52:13-14; 53:2), He emptied Himself (went to the cross). See *Jesus, Divine Messiah,* 264.

[71]Reymond (ibid., 263) mentions several scholars who concur with the view to follow: "H. Wheeler Robinson, *The Cross of the Servant* (London:

dynamic equivalent to the Isaianic phrase, 'He poured His soul out [which means, 'He poured Himself out'] unto death' (which means, 'He voluntarily died') in Isaiah 53:12."[72]

But what of the phrases, "being made in the likeness of men," and "being found in appearance as a man" (vv. 7b-8a)? Some argue that even if the phrase "He emptied Himself" refers to the cross event and not to the event of the incarnation, these phrases certainly do refer to the incarnation.[73] But for two reasons this is questionable. *First,* by putting verses 6 and 7a together, then placing 7b and 8 together, we see that they comprise two strophes[74]:

(6) Who, although He existed in the form of God, did not regard equality with God a thing to be grasped, (7a) but emptied Himself, taking the form of a bond-servant.

(7b) Being made in the likeness of men, (8) and being found in appearance as a man, He humbled Himself by becoming obedient to the point of death, even death on a cross.

The first strophe I take as speaking of the God-man Jesus, but emphasizing His deity. Although He is God in flesh, He suffered on the cross. The second I take as speaking of the God-man Jesus, but the emphasis is on His humanity. As man as well He suffered on the cross.

Second (and I think this makes it decisive), the phrases "being made in the likeness of men" and "being found in appearance as a man" also (just as "He emptied Himself" and "taking the form of a servant") point us back to Isaiah 52:14 (in part, "So His appearance was marred more than any man") and 53:2 (in part, "He has no stately form or majesty, that we should look upon Him, nor appearance that we should be attracted to Him"), where the emphasis is not on Christ's preincarnate state and coming into flesh, but on the *already* (though prophetically)

SCM Press, 1926), pp. 72-74; Jeremias, in *Studia Paulina,* p. 154 n. 3, and his article, *'pais'* [here transliterated], in *Theological Dictionary of the New Testament,* vol. 5, pp. 711-12." Reymond mentions others who concur, such as C. H. Dodd, *According to the Scriptures* (London: Nisbet and Company, 1952), 93. For a brief summary of other views on this issue in this passage, see G. E. Ladd, *A Theology of the New Testament,* 419-21.

[72]*Jesus, Divine Messiah,* 263, brackets and parentheses original.
[73]See Lightfoot, *St. Paul's Epistle to the Philippians,* 132.
[74]See Reymond, *Jesus, Divine Messiah,* 256.

human suffering servant! Thus, if we take Isaiah as the background for the two strophes it becomes clear that Paul is referring to the already incarnate Christ.

Verse 9a refers to Isaiah 52:13 ("Behold, My servant will prosper, He will be high and lifted up, and greatly exalted") and 53:12a ("therefore, I will allot Him a portion with the great"), making it clear that Paul has in mind the already incarnate suffering servant of Isaiah.

Verses 10 and 11a shout the deity of Christ. "That at the name of Jesus every knee should bow... and that every tongue should confess that Jesus is Lord" is a direct allusion to Isaiah 45:23b, where *Yahweh* states, "That to Me every knee will bow, every tongue will swear." Christ's exaltation, and the confessing of Him as Yahweh, is the *result*[75] of His work on the cross. Yet, in the economy of the Trinity, this confession of Christ as Yahweh ("Lord," i.e., God the Son) will bring glory to God the Father (v. 11b)!

To summarize, I take Philippians 2:6a to refer to the *already incarnate* Christ Jesus. This verse states that He is God the Son. Those who disagree with this setting and wish to see 2:6a as referring to the *preincarnate* Christ as God the Son are, of course, in the company of able Christian scholars. It is important to note, however, that whether the reader holds the classical view or the alternate view, there is still agreement among Christians that Paul calls Jesus God (whether in His preincarnate state or in His incarnate state).

Philippians 3:8, 10

Paul states: *"(8a) More than that, I count all things to be loss in view of the surpassing value of knowing Christ Jesus my Lord.... (10a) that I may know Him, and the power of His resurrection..."* Against their Old Testament background, the phrases "knowing Christ Jesus my Lord" and "that I may know Him" are rich with implication that the incarnate Christ is Yahweh.

But the focal point is not "Lord," for that has already been discussed. Rather, our focus is on Paul's *knowing* of Christ Jesus. Interesting is the context in which this "knowing" occurs. Paul mentions those who are "of the false circumcision" and those of "the true circumcision" (Phil. 3:2-3). Paul then mentions his "zeal," his

---

[75]Verse 9 begins with "therefore" (Gr. *dio,* διὸ).

being "found blameless" pertaining to "righteousness which is in the Law" (v. 6). To Paul these things are nothing at all (of no value). Paul now knows Christ (vv. 7-10). If Paul is to boast about what really counts, he will boast in knowing Christ the Lord (see also 2 Cor. 10:17).

These phenomena in our context (the false and true circumcision, boasting, what really counts is knowing Christ the Lord) point us to Jeremiah 9:23-26:

> (23) Thus says the LORD [*Yahweh*], "Let not a wise man boast of his wisdom, and let not the mighty man boast of his might, let not a rich man boast of his riches; (24) but let him who boasts boast of this, that he understands and knows Me, that I am the LORD who exercises lovingkindness, justice, and righteousness on earth, for I delight in these things," declares the LORD. (25) "Behold, the days are coming," declares the LORD, "that I will punish all who are circumcised and yet uncircumcised... (26b) for all the nations are uncircumcised, and all the house of Israel are uncircumcised of heart."

Key to our discussion once again is the use of *Yahweh* in the Jeremiah passage. It is Yahweh who states that anyone boasting ought to boast that he understands and *knows Him*. The tie between the two contexts (Paul's and Jeremiah's), that of true and false circumcision, boasting, and "knowing" the Lord, is no mere coincidence. I believe Paul is once again utilizing an Old Testament theme and applying it to Christ. Yahweh calls His covenant people to *know Him*, as the Jeremiah passage indicates (see also Jer. 24:7). Paul boasts that he *knows Christ Jesus* as *his* Lord. That Paul had a more than adequate understanding of the Old Testament is evidenced in this passage (3:5-6). Indeed, he was "circumcised the eighth day, of the nation of Israel" (v. 5; another mention of circumcision, not to mention "the nation of Israel"; these point us back to the Jeremiah passage ["house of Israel" in the context of circumcision]). Paul was of course fully aware of the implications of the statement, "*knowing* Christ Jesus my Lord," when all the while *Yahweh's* call to His people is to *know Him!* Yahweh calls His people to "know Him" and be circumcised of heart; Paul has done this by knowing Yahweh the Son as his Lord.

Colossians 1:15, 16

"And He is the image of the invisible God, the first-born of all creation. For by Him all things were created, both in the heavens and on earth, visible and invisible, whether thrones or dominions or rulers or authorities—all things have been created by Him and for Him." Ironically, the very description of Jesus that the Jehovah's Witnesses use to *deny* His deity ("firstborn"[76]) actually ends up *affirming* that Jesus is deity! Paul, in using "firstborn" and "image of the invisible God" to describe Jesus, is expressing that Jesus is God the Son.

It is possible that incipient Gnosticism was the reason Paul wrote to the Colossian church. Apparently there were some heretics teaching the existence of angelic intermediaries (or aeons) between God (called the *plērōma* [πλήρωμα], "fullness") and the material creation.[77] Jesus was therefore viewed as one of these intermediaries, and, as Reymond states, "It was to oppose this christological representation that Paul incorporated this hymn [Col. 1:15-20] to Christ in his letter to the Colossians."[78]

Paul, then, calls Christ "the image (Gr. *eikōn,* εἰκὼν) of the invisible God." In the person of Christ we have deity stamped in the flesh. Paul uses the phrase in description of Christ elsewhere in his corpus (2 Cor. 4:4),[79] for we see in the face of Christ what God truly is (2 Cor. 4:6). In another context, Paul calls Jesus the "Lord of glory" (1 Cor. 2:8; cf. Zech. 2:5). Since Jesus is the image of the invisible God and the Lord of glory, He may, of course, "reveal" the Father to us (John 14:7, 9). Indeed, no one has seen the Father, but Christ has

---

[76]But see n. 82. They also appeal to Rev. 3:14, where Christ is called "the beginning (Gr. *archē,* ἀρχὴ) of the creation by God" (*New World Translation*). "Thus," they say, "Jesus had a beginning." But this is far-fetched when we consider that in the Book of Revelation Christ is described as Jehovah! Christ is "the first and the last" (1:17; 2:8; 22:13; cf. Isa. 44:6). *Archē* may be translated "source" or, as the NIV has it, "ruler." Another orthodox interpretation of the phrase is that Jesus in His glorified humanity is the "beginning" of the "new creation" in Christ (cf. 2 Cor. 5:17). That is to say, Christ is the prototype of the new humanity we as believers will one day be (cf. 1 John 3:2).

[77]See Reymond, *Jesus, Divine Messiah*, 243-44.

[78]Ibid., 244.

[79]The writer of Hebrews incorporates a similar phrase to Christ, calling Him "the radiance of His [God's] glory and the exact representation of His nature" (1:3).

explained Him (John 1:18). Thus, in the person of Christ the invisible God is seen and made known. God (the Son) alone can reveal God (the Father), and by this phrase in our text Paul means to communicate not merely an outward manifestation of God, but truly that Christ in the very depths of His being[80] is God.[81]

"Firstborn" (Gr. *prōtotokos,* πρωτότοκος) should not be taken as "first-created," as the Jehovah's Witnesses believe.[82] On their part, this evidences a simplistic exegesis. Rather, it means *preeminent.* In the Old Testament sense "firstborn" carried with it a "priority of rank."[83] Here this is the stress of meaning.[84] Christ is the one who is preeminent over[85] all creation.

---

[80]"Thus *eikōn* [here transliterated] does not imply a weakening or a feeble copy of something. It implies the illumination of its inner core and essence" (G. Kittel, ed., *Theological Dictionary of the New Testament,* 10 vols. [Grand Rapids, Mich.: Wm. B. Eerdmans Publishing Co., 1964], 2:389).

[81]We should not think that the phrase "image of God" in Colossians 1:15, in its application to Christ, *is limited* because of its application to humanity (Gen. 1:26-27). The Gr. *hoti* (ὅτι, "because") of Colossians 1:16 prohibits this, for the *grounds* or *reasons* are given by Paul as to why he calls Christ "the image of God" and the "firstborn." See further above as the exposition continues.

[82]They see the Greek genitive phrase *pasēs ktiseōs* (πάσης κτίσεως, "*of* all creation") in the partitive sense (but note the NIV "the firstborn *over* all creation"). In other words, Jesus is part of the creation. But the Gr. *hoti* ("because") of v. 16 renders this inconceivable: "*because* all things have been created by Him." If He is a created being, as the Jehovah's Witnesses believe, then *how* could He have created *all* things? Even granting (for the moment) their understanding that "firstborn" means "first-created," was Israel the first nation created by Jehovah? No, for they only began to be a nation at the calling of Abraham in Gen. 12. There were, of course, other nations that were created before them. How, then, is it that Jehovah calls Israel His firstborn (Exod. 4:22)? Bruce Metzger writes: "If Paul wished to express [that He was made or created], he had available a Greek word to do so, the word *prōtoktistos* [here transliterated], meaning 'first created'" ("The Jehovah's Witnesses and Jesus Christ," *Theology Today* [April 1953]: 77).

[83]Reymond, *Jesus, Divine Messiah,* 247. See R. Laird Harris, Gleason L. Archer, Jr., and Bruce K. Waltke, *Theological Wordbook of the Old Testament,* 2 vols. (Chicago, Ill.: Moody Press, 1980), 1:109-110.

[84]The word is not limited to that meaning alone. It has other nuances of meaning, as we shall soon see.

[85]See the NIV. I take *pasēs ktiseōs* as a genitive of subordination (see

"Firstborn" also carries the meaning of "enthronement." In the ancient Near East, the firstborn was, *metaphorically*, the enthroned one. Psalm 89:27a[86] states, "I shall make him My firstborn, the highest of the kings of the earth." The immediate context is the enthronement of David as king, and thus he is called the firstborn. But note that in David's biography (1 Sam. 16:1-13), David is *literally* neither the firstborn son of Yahweh, nor of his actual father, Jesse! Finally, the synonymous parallelism of 89:27b describes the firstborn as "the highest,"[87] furthering the meaning of enthronement (and preeminence).

Carried in this sense over to Christ, we have in His incarnate state His exaltation (enthronement) as the God-man. This is something He never had before in His preincarnate glory with the Father, for at that point He was yet to become the obedient servant of the Lord and become our exalted Lord and high priest (see the exposition of Phil. 2:6-11). By virtue of all that Christ is, and by virtue of all that He has accomplished by His life, death, and resurrection, He has truly been enthroned; He is the Father's heir (Heb. 1:2), and the preeminent one over all creation!

Most important to further buttress the above is the "because"[88] (signifying grounds or reasons) clause of verse 16. Simply put, He is the preeminent one *over* all creation *because* all things were created "by"[89] Him, "through" Him, and "for" Him. These three prepositions

Daniel B. Wallace, *Greek Grammar Beyond the Basics: An Exegetical Syntax of the New Testament* [Grand Rapids, Mich.: Zondervan Publishing House, 1996], 103-104). This places the genitive phrase under the headship of the noun ("firstborn"). *Over* all creation better keeps with the context of the passage.

[86]Heb. v. 28.

[87]The Heb. *elyon* (עֶלְיוֹן) may be translated "most exalted," thus meaning "enthroned." For a thorough treatment of "firstborn," see throughout Jon D. Levenson, *The Death and Resurrection of the Beloved Son* (New Haven, Conn. and London: Yale University Press, 1993). See also David Noel Freedman, ed., *The Anchor Bible Dictionary*, 6 vols. (New York: Doubleday, 1992), 4:45: "The claim is advanced in a number of royal psalms and other texts that the king was the 'son' or 'first-born' of Yahweh, while Yahweh was the 'father' of the king (Pss. 2:7; 89:27; 2 Sam. 7:14; cf. Isa. 9:6). This is clearly an important ideological claim which underlies the right of the occupant of the throne to rule on behalf of the deity of the state."

[88]Gr. *hoti.*

[89]Gr. *en, ἐν.* I take this as a dative of means or instrument. Certainly another option is to render the preposition *en* as a dative of sphere. Here the

teach us that Christ is, respectively, creator, mediating agent, and goal of all things. Only God may be described in this way.

With the probable Colossian heresy in view, Paul in this verse wages war against the Christology that sees Christ merely as an angelic intermediary between the "Pleroma" (God) and the material creation. The heretics used the words "thrones or dominions or rulers or authorities" to describe these intermediaries, and applied these designations to the Son of God Himself. Paul refutes this by stating that Christ created *them* (granting for the moment their erroneous cosmology). Moreover, Paul states that all these things are under the lordship of Christ, and that all things have Christ as their goal. How, then, can Christ be numbered with these intermediaries? The irony of this is that the Jehovah's Witnesses believe that Christ is the angelic intermediary between Jehovah God and the material creation; and they use Colossians 1:15 as their reason for believing it. Though the situation of the Jehovah's Witnesses does not match entirely that of the Colossian heresy, it does in some points. Thus, as stated earlier, the very passage the Jehovah's Witnesses use to deny Christ as God and creator actually ends up affirming that Christ is God and creator.

Colossians 2:9

Speaking of Christ, Paul writes, *"For in Him all the fulness of the Deity dwells in bodily form."* Paul once again asserts that the incarnate and glorified Son of God is God in the ontological sense.

Against the incipient gnostic heresy challenging the Colossians (mentioned in the previous section), Paul with one statement affirms Christ's deity and at the same time blasts the Colossian heretics' view of God, to them known as the "Fulness" (Gr. *plērōma*, πλήρωμα). He uses their own designation ("Fulness") to refute them. This was already mentioned by Paul in 1:19 ("For it was the Father's good pleasure for all the fulness to dwell in Him [Christ Jesus]"). These heretics did not see Jesus as the "Fulness" (in their estimation the true God), but rather as a mere intermediary between the material creation and the true God.

---

meaning would be that all creation has taken place within the sphere of Christ's person and power (see Curtis Vaughan, in Frank E. Gaebelein, ed., *The Expositor's Bible Commentary,* 12 vols. [Grand Rapids, Mich.: Zondervan Publishing House, 1978], 11:182). In this sense, all creation is "in" Christ (though Christ is not in all creation).

Further, they could not fathom the deity dwelling in the base, defiled material creation. As a result, Paul commands his readers not to be taken captive through vain philosophies of men (2:8), "For[90] in Him all the *fulness* of Deity dwells *in bodily form.*"[91]

The fulness of deity is said to dwell permanently[92] in the glorified and risen Savior. "Deity" translates the Greek *theotētos* (θεότητος), a word that means "Godness," that is, "the state of being God."[93] Thus, in the person of Jesus we have all the fulness of essential deity[94] dwelling bodily (i.e., His now glorified body of flesh and bones [see Luke 24:39]). In the person of Jesus we have nothing less than true deity in bodily form.

---

[90]Gr. *hoti* (ὅτι, "because").

[91]Paul not only calls Jesus deity, but places that deity in permanent (the force of the present tense *katoikei,* κατοικεῖ) residence in the now glorified *flesh* of Christ! The "in Him" is placed just after the *hoti* for emphasis. The heretics saw Jesus as a mere intermediary and therefore de-emphasized what He truly was. Paul places "in Him" first because of this, and is communicating that in Christ *alone* the fulness of deity dwells.

[92]Gr. *katoikei* is in the present tense, denoting continuous action. See the previous note.

[93]See J. H. Thayer, *A Greek-English Lexicon of the New Testament* (Grand Rapids, Mich.: Zondervan, n.d.), 288. I think the lack of the definite article (which *would* have read *tou theou,* τοῦ θεοῦ) emphasizes the ontological. With the use of *theotētos,* Paul is without doubt referring to the essence of Christ, which is "deity" that dwells bodily.

[94]The Jehovah's Witnesses attempt to soften the force of *theotēlos.* They render *theotētos* as "divine quality," which is more akin to *theiotētos* rather than *theotētos* (see Thayer, *A Greek-English Lexicon of the New Testament,* 288; BAG, 354, 358; see also Kittel, *Theological Dictionary of the New Testament,* 3:123, though perhaps here the argument may be made that there is no difference between the two terms because the functional *qualities* [in *theiotētos*] imply the ontological [thus, *theotētos*]). The former emphasizes divine qualities or attributes. The latter emphasizes essential nature (see Harris, *Jesus as God: The New Testament Use of Theos in Reference to Jesus,* 287, n. 48, where he cites Nash's findings supporting this distinction, i.e., that early Christians found limitations with *theiotētos* and favored *theotētos*). Of course, with the use of "quality," the Jehovah's Witnesses emphasize Jesus being "like" God, but not God. Also, with the translation "divine quality," they use the translation of a different Greek word (*theiotētos*) than that which is in the text itself (*theotētos*), thus differing from the more accepted (and lexically proper) "Deity" (for example, NASB) or "Godhead" (for example, NKJV).

1 Thessalonians 1:1; 3:11

"Paul and Silvanus and Timothy to the church of the Thessalonians in God the Father and the Lord Jesus Christ: Grace to you and peace."

With this simple yet conventional salutation Paul implies the deity of Christ.[95] He links the Father and the Lord Jesus Christ with one preposition ("in,"[96]), thus implying that the church is in union with, equally, both the Father and[97] the Son. The ease with which Paul makes the statement is characteristic of someone who had no difficulty at all with the equality of the Father and the Son.

Another instance of Christ being placed alongside the Father, and thus an implicit claim to His deity, is found in 1 Thessalonians 3:11.[98] Paul states, *"Now may our God and Father Himself and Jesus our Lord direct our way to you."* He gives equal honor to the Father and the Son (see John 5:23), mentioning both the Father and the Son in the context of prayer (also interesting is Paul's placement of Father before Son, but his reversal of that order in another context of prayer in 2 Thess. 2:16). Only to God is prayer directed. Paul considers Christ as God the Son, for he prays that Christ may direct their (Paul, Silvanus and Timothy) way to the Thessalonians (for other examples of prayer directed to Jesus, see Rom. 10:12-14 cf. 10:9, 2 Cor. 12:8-9, 2 Thess. 3:16, 2 Tim. 2:22, Stephen's prayer in Acts 7:59, and other statements in Acts 9:14, 21 and 22:16).

What follows in verses 12 and 13 is equally interesting. Paul additionally prays, "and may the Lord cause you to increase and abound in love..., so that He may establish your hearts unblamable before our God and Father at the coming of our Lord Jesus with all

---

[95] See Robert L. Thomas, *1 Thessalonians*, in *The Expositor's Bible Commentary*, 11:238, and Reymond, *Jesus, Divine Messiah*, 241.

[96] Gr. *en*, ἐν.

[97] Gr. *kai*, καὶ, the coordinating conjunction. Other examples are found in Rom. 1:7; 1 Cor. 1:3; 2 Cor. 1:2; Gal. 1:3; Eph. 1:2; Phil. 1:2; 2 Thess. 1:2; 1 Tim. 1:2; 2 Tim. 1:2; Titus 1:4; Philem. 3. In the non-Pauline epistles this occurs in 2 Pet. 1:2; 1 John 1:3 (one preposition [*meth*, μεθ', "with"], though repeated), 2 John 3 (one preposition [*para*, παρὰ, "from"], though repeated), and Rev. 1:4-5 (one preposition [*apo*, ἀπὸ, "from"], though repeated).

[98] See Thomas, *1 Thessalonians*, 11:267, and the various scholars he cites to support this.

His[99] saints." Here the petition is to Jesus alone. The implications are still as above, with the addition theologically that Christ is the Lord of the Church; He is its Sovereign Lord. As such He is the one who causes Christians to increase and abound in love. As such He is the one who establishes the heart unblamable. With the shift of focus (in prayer) from both the Father and the Son in verse 11 to the Son alone in verses 12-13, Paul by no means degrades the Father (it is "before our God and Father" that we must be "unblamable"). Rather, because he does not even think twice about granting equal honor to the Son (and thus acknowledging Him as God), he may at one time pray to both the Father and the Son (v. 11), or to the Son alone (vv. 12-13).[100] Paul without doubt views the risen Christ as God the Son, the Sovereign of the Church.

1 Thessalonians 4:6

Paul in this verse states that *"the Lord [Jesus, see 4:1, 2] is the avenger*[101] *in all these things"* (pertaining to sin). In its immediate context Paul is talking about those who profess Christ. They must know that the Lord will punish sins. They must know that God will avenge all sin, more especially at the consummation of the ages.

Paul's statement that "the Lord" will punish sin is yet another example of Jesus "being" (or "acting") God. That is to say, in teaching that the Lord will avenge, Paul is applying to Christ that which pertains to Yahweh in the Old Testament. In Deuteronomy 32:35, it is Yahweh

---

[99]The phenomenon of "ownership" (i.e., "Yahweh owns") has been discussed earlier in this book. See chap. 4 under Matthew 1:21-23. To reiterate, the covenant people of God are the *His* saints, and here Paul states they belong to Christ. This brief remark by Paul at the end of 1 Thess. 3:13 carries with it full implications that Christ is Yahweh the Son.

[100]I must register caution at this point. Though I fully adhere to the distinction of the three persons of the Trinity (see Appendix 2), I also adhere to their unity. Thus, when the Son is prayed to, the Spirit and the Father hear the prayer; and when the Son answers He does so in union with the Father and the Spirit. Thus, as is seen in my exposition above, when I state that the Son alone is prayed to, I mean to draw attention to Paul's *emphasis* of the Son, *not* his exclusion of the Father.

[101]Gr. *ekdikos,* ἔκδικος.

who states, "Vengeance is Mine."[102] Another example is found in Psalm 94:1, where the psalmist pleads, "O LORD, God of vengeance, God of vengeance, shine forth!"[103]

In both Old Testament contexts, as well as in Paul, the eschatological judgment is in view.[104] Yahweh is the eschatological judge who will punish sinners; for Paul it is the Lord Christ who will punish sinners. It is unmistakable that for Paul, the risen and glorified Jesus is Yahweh the Son.

Titus 1:4

"To Titus, my true child in a common faith: Grace and peace from God the Father and Christ Jesus our Savior." What is significant is that Paul calls Jesus "our Savior," while in the preceding verse (3) he calls God (the Father) "our Savior." Commentators have pointed out the significance of this in the sense that both the Father and the Son bring about salvation: "both are involved in bestowing the same salvation."[105] In addition to this observation, I suggest[106] that in light of the many Old Testament passages where Yahweh is the *only* Savior (Isa. 43:3, 11; 45:21; 49:26; 60:16; Hos. 13:4; cf. 1 Sam. 10:19; 14:39; 2 Sam. 22:3; Pss. 7:10; 17:7; 106:21; Isa. 45:15; 63:8; Jer. 14:8),[107] Paul's mention of

---

[102]LXX reads, "In the day of vengeance (Gr. *ekdikēseōs,* ἐκδικήσεως) I will recompense."

[103]LXX 93:1, "The Lord is the God of vengeance (Gr. *ekdikēseōn,* ἐκδικήσεων)."

[104]Though I would not dismiss entirely from Deut. 32 and Ps. 94 an immediate judgment as well.

[105]For example, D. Edmond Hiebert, in Frank E. Gaebelein, ed., *The Expositor's Bible Commentary,* 11:428. See also Gordon D. Fee, *1 and 2 Timothy, Titus* in the *New International Biblical Commentary* (Peabody, Mass.: Hendrickson Publishers, 1988), 170, and Homer A. Kent, Jr., *The Pastoral Epistles* (Chicago, Ill.: Moody Press, 1958), 217.

[106]With Robert Reymond (see *Jesus, Divine Messiah,* 130). Though here Reymond brings in a slightly different nuance. Reymond (rightly so) mentions the fact that both the Father and the Son are called Savior in this passage. He then mentions many Old Testament verses teaching that Yahweh alone is Savior. Reymond's emphasis is that it is no wonder that "Jesus" means "Yahweh saves."

[107]Thanks to Robert Reymond (ibid.) for this list of citations.

Christ as Savior (immediately after calling the Father Savior) is indicative of Jesus' identification as Yahweh the Son.[108]

How is it that Paul, obviously familiar with the Old Testament, can so easily ascribe the title of "Savior" to both the Father and the Son? Is not Isaiah 43:11 clear in its claim, "I, even I, am the LORD; and there is no savior besides Me" (see 45:21; Hos. 13:4)? Yet, throughout the Epistle to Titus, Paul uses the title for the Father (1:3; 2:10; 3:4) *and* the Son (1:4; 2:13; 3:6). If there is only one Savior, and the Father and the Son are both called Savior, the inevitable conclusion is that Trinitarian theology (gleaned, of course, from the Scriptures) alone can make sense of this text. That is to say, with regard to the *oneness of essence* of the Father and the Son, in order for the Father and the Son to bring about salvation (a natural conclusion arising out of this passage) while maintaining the scriptural teaching that there is only one Savior, the Father and the Son must share the same nature and act in unity.[109] With regard to the *distinction of the persons* of the Father and the Son, if Yahweh alone is Savior, and Jesus is called Savior, then Jesus must be Yahweh *the Son*.[110]

Titus 2:13

In this verse Paul not only calls Jesus Savior, he calls Him God: *"Looking for the blessed hope and the appearing of the glory of our great God and Savior, Christ Jesus."*

The debate among scholars as to whether or not this text identifies Christ as God (Gr. *theos*, θεός) has been long-standing ever since Granville Sharp (1735-1813) published his short volume with a characteristically (for that time period) long title: *Remarks on the Definitive Article in the Greek Text of the New Testament, Containing Many New Proofs of the Divinity of Christ, from Passages Which Are*

---

[108]Walter Lock, in his *The Pastoral Epistles* (Edinburgh: T. & T. Clark, 1978) states (probably on the evidence that Paul mentions the Father and the Son, as I have pointed out, "in one breath") that "Christ is placed on the same level as God" (p. 128).

[109]The application of sameness of nature from this theological argument is *implicit* from the Isa. 43:11, 45:21, and Hos. 13:4 passages. It is *Yahweh* alone who is the Savior.

[110]As Reymond points out, "Jesus" means "Yahweh saves" (see *Jesus, Divine Messiah*, 130).

Wrongly Translated in the Common English Version [KJV]. Sharp, in his thorough reading of the Greek text of the New Testament, listed six rules concerning the definite article (*kai,* καί, "the"). Our discussion of Titus 2:13 concerns his first rule, which I will in due time quote. But before I do, it should be noted that two hundred years of testing by competent scholars have failed to disprove Sharp's thesis. Sharp's rule is said "to have the highest degree of validity within the N[ew] T[estament]."[111]

The debate centers on the two basic ways of translating, and thus understanding, Titus 2:13. Should it be translated, "Looking for that blessed hope, and the glorious appearing of the great God and our Saviour Jesus Christ" (KJV), or as, "Looking for the blessed hope and the appearing of the glory of our great God and Savior, Christ Jesus" (NASB)?[112] If one takes the first translation, Paul would be referring to two persons, the Father and the Son. Thus "the appearing of the glory of the great God [the Father] *and* our Savior Jesus Christ" would be the meaning. If the second, Paul would be referring only to the Son: "the appearing of the glory of our great God and Savior, Jesus Christ." Here Jesus is called "our great God and Savior."

Titus 2:13 should be understood to refer to Christ alone. Reasons for this are grammatical and contextual/theological. As for *grammar,* Granville Sharp's first rule renders the view that Titus 2:13 refers to Jesus as *our great God and Savior* "as secure as any in the canon when it comes to identifying Christ as *theos* [God]."[113] Sharp's first rule states,

---

[111]Daniel B. Wallace, *Greek Grammar Beyond the Basics: An Exegetical Syntax of the New Testament,* 290.

[112]Gr. *prosdechomenoi tēn makarian elpida kai epiphaneian tēs doxēs tou megalou theou kai sōtēros hēmōn Iēsou Christou,* προσδεχόμενοι τὴν μακαρίαν ἐλπίδα καὶ ἐπιφάνειαν τῆς δόξης τοῦ μεγάλου θεοῦ καὶ σωτῆρος ἡμῶν Ἰησοῦ Χριστοῦ. For an excellent presentation of both sides of the argument, and for the conclusion that *theos* is a reference to Christ, see Murray J. Harris, *Jesus as God,* 173-85.

[113]Wallace, *Greek Grammar,* 290. Greek transliterated.

When the copulative *kai* ["and"] connects two nouns of the same case, if the article ὁ [*ho,* "the"], or any of its cases, precedes the first of the said nouns or participles, and is not repeated before the second noun or participle, the latter always relates to the same person that is expressed or described by the first noun or participle: i.e. it denotes a farther description of the first-named person.[114]

Sharp's rule states that when two nouns of the same case[115] are governed by one definite article, the phrase refers to one person. The two nouns are "God"[116] and "Savior,"[117] and are of the same case (the genitive case). In the Greek text there is only one definite article ("the") in this clause (also in the genitive case[118]). Thus the one article governs both nouns. Sharp's rule states that "Savior" relates to the first-named person ("God"), and is a *further description* of that first-named person.[119] With the phrase ending with "Jesus Christ," there can be no

---

[114]Taken from ibid., 271.

[115]Wallace cautions that the two nouns, if Sharp's work is interpreted in its context, *must* be personal, singular, and non-proper names. Many have tried to refute (or have misunderstood) Sharp by putting his rule to the test using impersonal nouns, plural nouns, and proper names (*Greek Grammar,* 271-72). In other words, because some have tested Sharp's first rule with plurals and impersonals, they have not viewed Sharp's rule as absolute. Thus, as Wallace states, "the exceptions they find to the rule are *actually outside the scope of the rule* and are thus not exceptions at all" (p. 273, emphases mine). In a note pertaining to this point, Wallace lists some notable scholars who have misunderstood the rule, such as J. H. Moulton (who said of the translation of Titus 2:13: "we must, as grammarians, leave the matter open" [*Grammar of New Testament Greek* {Edinburgh: T. & T. Clark, 1985}, 1:84]), A. T. Robertson, Dana-Mantey, M. J. Harris, F. F. Bruce, and C. F. D. Moule.

[116]Gr. *theou.*

[117]Gr. *sōtēros.*

[118]Gr. *tou.*

[119]See, for example, the phrase *ho theos kai patēr tou kuriou hēmōn Iēsou Christou,* ὁ θεὸς καὶ πατὴρ τοῦ κυρίου ἡμῶν Ἰησοῦ Χριστοῦ (1 Pet. 1:3; "*the God and Father* of our Lord Jesus Christ"). Here the one definite article governs both *theos* and *patēr.* Wallace states, "Not counting the christologically significant passages, there are 80 constructions in the NT which fit the requirements for Sharp's rule. But do they all fit the *semantics* of the rule—that is, do the substantives always refer to one and the same person? In a word, yes. Even Sharp's opponents could not find any exceptions; all had to admit that the rule was valid in the NT" (*Greek Grammar,* 273).

question at all that Paul has been careful to name the recipient of the phrase "our great God and Savior."[120]

Regarding the *contextual/theological*, the passage is best understood as referring to Christ. *First*, in Paul's time, the phrase "God and Savior" was used to refer to *one deity* in pagan religions.[121] Murray J. Harris states that

> it is difficult to avoid the conclusion that, whatever the date of Titus, one impulse behind this particular verse was the desire to combat the extravagant titular endowment that had been accorded to human rulers such as Antiochus Epiphanes (*theos epiphanēs*[122]) [glorious God], Ptolemy I (*sōtēr kai theos*) [Savior and God], or Julius Caesar (*theos kai sōtēr*) [God and Savior], or to claim exclusively for the Christians' Lord the divine honors freely granted to goddesses such as Aphrodite and Artemis or to gods such as Asclepius and Zeus.[123]

It is quite probable, then, that Paul was using this phraseology as a polemic against pagan cults. If so, his intent was to confess Jesus Christ as "our great God and Savior" over against anyone or any religion that would confess any other deity by that phrase.

---

[120]In agreement are D. Edmond Hiebert, *The Expositor's Bible Commentary*, 11:441, Gordon D. Fee, *1 and 2 Timothy, Titus*, 196, Homer A. Kent, Jr., *The Pastoral Epistles*, 236, Robert Reymond, *Jesus, Divine Messiah*, 275-77, and Murray J. Harris, *Jesus as God*, 185, to name a few.

[121]In addition to the following quotation, Harris states that the phrase *theos kai sōtēr* (θεὸς καὶ σωτήρ, "God and Savior") "never referred to two deities or persons" (*Jesus as God*, 180), and that the phrase "was (apparently) used by both Diaspora and Palestinian Jews in reference to Yahweh, and invariably denoted one deity, not two" (p. 179). Fee further mentions that *theos kai sōtēr* is stereotypical of LXX phraseology (*1 and 2 Timothy, Titus*, 196).

[122]Greek here and following transliterated.

[123]*Jesus as God*, 179. Commentators have referenced this as well. See D. Edmond Hiebert, *The Expositor's Bible Commentary*, 11:441, Gordon D. Fee, *1 and 2 Timothy, Titus*, 196, Homer A. Kent, Jr., *The Pastoral Epistles*, 236, and Donald Guthrie, *The Pastoral Epistles* (Grand Rapids, Mich.: Wm. B. Eerdmans, 1978), 200. J. H. Moulton, in his *Grammar of New Testament Greek*, 1:84, writes, "A curious echo is found in the Ptolemaic formula applied to the deified kings: thus GH 15 (ii/B.C.), τοῦ μεγάλου θεοῦ εὐεργέτου καὶ σωτῆρος [ἐπιφανοῦς] εὐχαρίστου" (*tou megalou theou euergetou kai sōteros* [*epiphanous*] *eucharistou*). The phrase here is, of course, applied to one person."

Second, the word "appearing" is never used of the Father in the New Testament.[124]

Third, in the very next verse Paul ascribes to Christ that which the Old Testament ascribes to Yahweh. Verse 14 reads, "who [Jesus[125]] gave Himself for us, that He might redeem us from every lawless deed and purify for Himself a people for His own possession, zealous for good deeds." The phrase "redeem us from every lawless deed" is reminiscent of the language of Psalm 130:8[126] and Ezekiel 37:23.[127] Both these passages refer to *Yahweh.* Moreover, *Yahweh's* covenant people were "His very own possession." This is clear in Exodus 19:5, Deuteronomy 7:6, 14:2, 28:18, and Psalm 135:4 (cf. 1 Pet. 2:9). Yet, in Titus 2:14 the covenant people are Christ's possession.[128] Again, Christ is Yahweh the Son. If this were not so, Paul would never have applied such a precious covenantal theme to the Son.

Conclusion

Paul has in fact a high Christology. He has in the plainest sense ascribed deity to Christ both in the ontological and functional categories: Paul has plainly called Jesus God (for example, Rom. 9:5; Titus 2:13) and has ascribed to Jesus (1) only that which Yahweh can

---

[124]D. Edmond Hiebert, *The Expositor's Bible Commentary,* 11:441; Gordon D. Fee, *1 and 2 Timothy, Titus,* 196; Donald Guthrie, *The Pastoral Epistles,* 200. Harris writes, "nowhere in the NT is *epiphaneia* [Gr. transliterated] used of the Father (but five times of Christ)—or are two persons said to appear at the Last Day?" (*Jesus as God,* 176; see p. 184). Some object to this. If the verse is translated, "the appearing of the glory of our great God and our Savior Jesus Christ" (here *two* persons are involved), the Father does not have to appear, only His *glory* (see Luke 9:26). But the observation that the word *appearing* never is used of the Father still holds. Further, according to Hiebert, "In the Pastorals the coming epiphany is referred to Christ alone" (*The Expositor's Bible Commentary,* 11:441).

[125]The relative pronoun *hos* (ὃς, "who") that begins v. 14 refers to "Christ Jesus" at the end of v. 13.

[126]LXX 129:8.

[127]See Guthrie, *The Pastoral Epistles,* 201, and Fee, *1 and 2 Timothy, Titus,* 197.

[128]I take the phrase "that *He* might redeem us..." to refer to the nearest antecedent, which is "who" (*hos*) as it begins v. 14. In turn, "who" refers to Jesus Christ (latter part of v. 13).

do, and (2) Old Testament passages that apply to Yahweh. We turn now to the witness of the incarnate deity of Jesus in Acts and Hebrews.

Chapter 6

Acts and Hebrews: The Incarnate Deity of Christ

"For He said truth, 'before Abraham was, I am'.... He is God, above always."—Augustine, Sermon LXXI

"Jesus himself said that he was not God."—Elijah Muhammad, Our Savior Has Arrived

Within the four Gospels and the writings of Paul we have found a high Christology. We will find in Acts and Hebrews the high Christology that characterized Matthew, Mark, Luke, John, and Paul; a Christology that lifts up Jesus Christ as God the Son.

Acts 1:8b

"And you shall be My witnesses[1] both in Jerusalem, and in all Judea and Samaria, and even to the remotest part of the earth."

---

[1]Gr. *mou martures,* μου μάρτυρες. Instead of translating this phrase as "My witnesses," the Jehovah's Witnesses choose "witnesses of me." This

In stating that the disciples will be *His* witnesses, Jesus is applying to Himself something that Yahweh alone can claim. Key to our understanding that Jesus is claiming to be Yahweh is Isaiah 43. In verse 1 Yahweh states of Israel, "I have redeemed you; I have called you by name; you are Mine!" (see also vv. 7, 21). Israel was called to be Yahweh's people. He chose them (see Acts 1:2, where Jesus chose the disciples!), possessed them, and they were to be *His* witnesses (vv. 10, 12 [see also Isa. 44:8: "you are My witnesses"]).[2] In the midst of these commands by Yahweh, He also declares Himself to be the only Savior (v. 11), and God (v. 12). How strange it would be (and blasphemous[3]) for Christ to make the declaration that the disciples are *His* witnesses if He were not Yahweh the Son. In Acts 1:8 Christ is claiming to *own* the disciples. As Yahweh declared of Israel, "you are Mine," Christ declares the same of His disciples. As Yahweh said of Israel, "You are my witnesses," so does Christ say "you are My witnesses."

In the disciples' proclamation of Christ throughout Acts, are they proclaiming an archangel or a mere man? Such a view is far removed from the Old Testament. By its very emphasis on Yahweh *alone* being declared, the Old Testament bans this practice. Christ is Yahweh the Son, and His covenant people throughout the Book of Acts declare *Him*. Seeing the Old Testament in the New Testament, a very powerful parallel is drawn. In the Old Testament *Yahweh* was to be declared among the nations (Ps. 96:3); in the New Testament Christ was to be declared among the nations (see Acts 2:5, 21-22).

With this in mind, a word should be said of the alternate ways of translating the phrase. Whether taken as "witnesses *of* me," "witnesses *unto* [to] me," or "witnesses *for* me," the force of Christ as Yahweh the Son is not eliminated. In all these alternative translations what is said of

---

translation takes the genitive pronoun as objective rather than possessive. Other possibilities include "witnesses unto [to] me" and "witnesses for me." I shall comment briefly on these alternative translations at the end of this section.

[2]The Hebrew in both verses is *atem eday* (אַתֶּם עֵדַי) and is most naturally translated "you are my witnesses." The LXX has two different translations: v. 10, *genesthe moi martures,* γένεσθέ μοι μάρτυρες; v. 12, *humeis emoi martures,* ὑμεῖς ἐμοὶ μάρτυρες. The Greek of Acts (*esesthe mou martures,* ἔσεσθε μου μάρτυρες) better follows the Hebrew than it does the LXX.

[3]See Robert L. Reymond, *Jesus, Divine Messiah* (Phillipsburg, N.J.: Presbyterian and Reformed Publishing Co., 1990), 215.

Christ is true of Yahweh alone, as we have seen above. Israel must be a witness *of* Yahweh alone, *unto* Yahweh alone, and *for* Yahweh alone.

Acts 1:24

"And they prayed, and said, 'Thou, Lord, who knowest the hearts of all men, show which one of these two Thou hast chosen." If taken in isolation from the rest of the chapter, it would be difficult to determine whether by "Lord" the apostles meant the Father or the Son. The context, however, shows that "Lord" refers to the Son, and that by this the apostles are addressing Jesus as Yahweh.

In Acts 1:2 Jesus had chosen (implying deity; see Isa. 43:10) the apostles ("He had by the Holy Spirit given orders to the apostles whom He had chosen"). Thus, when these apostles prayed that the Lord would show them the one He had chosen (v. 24), contextual considerations force us to conclude that Jesus is the "Lord" addressed in the prayer (which further implies His deity). Take into consideration as well the close proximity of "the Lord Jesus" in verse 21.[4] Here Peter specifically names Jesus as "Lord."

Since it is Jesus who is addressed in this prayer of the apostles, the statement that He "knows the hearts of all men" also confesses Him as deity.[5] In the Old Testament it is Yahweh who knows the hearts of all men (1 Sam. 16:7; 1 Kings 8:39; 1 Chron. 28:9). Parts of the New Testament claim that God knows the heart (Luke 16:15; Acts 15:8). The apostles therefore believed Jesus to be God the Son, He "who knows the hearts of all men."

Acts 2:21-36

In this passage Peter is preaching, and we have another example of "LORD" (Yahweh) in the Old Testament applying to Jesus.

Peter begins his sermon (2:17) with a quotation of Joel 2:28-32. In Acts 2:21 Peter closes his citation of Joel: "And it shall be, that every one who calls upon the name of the LORD[6] shall be saved."

---

[4]As pointed out by Reymond, *Jesus, Divine Messiah,* 216, in the notes.

[5]Acts 1:24 is not the only text that states that Jesus knows the hearts of men, for we find in John 2:24-25 that Jesus knows all men and knows what is in man.

[6]Heb. *Yahweh*, Joel 2:32.

Immediately in Acts 2:22 Peter begins to preach Christ: "Men of Israel, listen to these words: Jesus the Nazarene..." The immediacy of Peter in bringing Jesus to the attention of the Israelites *just after* quoting the prophet Joel's "every one who calls upon the name of the Lord (Yahweh) will be saved" is significant, for it is an example of Peter's high view of Jesus, identifying Him as the LORD of Joel.

Note also that throughout this passage we have a distinction of the persons of the Father, the Son, and the Holy Spirit. Since Peter distinguishes between "God" (the Father) and Jesus, it is even more likely that by "Lord" Peter means Jesus. Peter states that God (the *Father*[7]) raised Jesus from the dead (vv. 24, 32; see also vv. 22, 23, 30, 33, 36), and that *Jesus* received "the promise of the *Holy Spirit*" (v. 33). Who, then, is the "LORD" of verse 21? It is Jesus, for the reason given in the preceding paragraph (Peter in v. 22 immediately introduces Jesus after citing Joel's "LORD"), and because "God [the Father] has made[8] him both *Lord* and Christ—this Jesus whom you crucified" (v. 36). Peter's quotation of Joel 2:32 ("every one who calls on the name of the LORD shall be saved") refers in its Old Testament context to *Yahweh* as the object of one's confession unto salvation, while *Jesus* is the object of confession unto salvation in Peter's sermon (v. 38; see also 4:12).[9]

In previous chapters we learned that the apostles did not at all hesitate to call Jesus "Lord," especially with reference to Old Testament contexts where the designation is ascribed to Yahweh. As F. F. Bruce writes,

---

[7]Throughout the New Testament, "God" is often used as a synonym for "the Father." See chap. 4, nn. 55, 56, and the body text.

[8]Gr. *epoiēsen,* ἐποίησεν. Rather than teaching adoptionism (the heretical view that Jesus *became* God's Son, most often claimed to have occurred at His baptism), this verb may be taken to mean "appointed." Richard N. Longenecker states that "in functional contexts, *epoiēsen* has the sense of 'appointed' (cf. 1 Kingdoms 12:6 LXX; 1 Kingdoms 12:31 LXX; Mark 3:14; Heb. 3:2), and it is in just such a context that Peter uses it here" (Frank E. Gaebelein, ed., *The Expositor's Bible Commentary,* 12 vols. [Grand Rapids, Mich.: Zondervan Publishing House, 1981], 9:280-81). Thus Peter is not teaching that Jesus became the Son of God, but is proclaiming that Jesus *as the already Son of God* was exalted in His role as Messiah to the right hand of the Father (see vv. 33, 34).

[9]See Robert Reymond, *Jesus, Divine Messiah,* 230.

The first apostolic sermon [this sermon by Peter] leads up to the first apostolic creed: "Jesus is Lord" (cf. Rom. 10:9; 1 Cor. 12:3; Phil. 2:11)—"Lord" not only as the bearer of a courtesy title, but as bearer of "the name which is above every name" (Phil. 2:9). To a Jew, there was only one name "above every name"—the Ineffable Name of the God of Israel, represented in the synagogue reading and in the LXX text by the title "Lord." And that the apostles meant to give Jesus the title "Lord" in this highest sense of all is indicated by the way in which they do not hesitate on occasion to apply to Him passages of OT scripture referring to Jehovah.[10] Indeed, in this very context it may well be that the promise "that whosoever shall call on the name of Jehovah shall be delivered" (Joel 2:32) is viewed as being fulfilled in those members of Peter's audience who repentantly invoke Jesus as Lord.[11]

Further examination of this passage leads one to conclude that Jesus is God the Son, on at least two accounts. *First,* Jesus' position at "the right hand of God" (vv. 33, 34) means His exercising of divine authority. Robert Reymond rightly points out, "He who would sit as 'Lord over all' [see Acts 10:36!] the nations on the throne of God must be God Himself."[12] Put another way, the *rights held* by the Son of God and the *actions performed* by the Son of God in His position at the right hand of God the Father testify to His deity. *Lord of all* (rights held) and *eschatological judge* (actions performed) are but two examples.

Second is the parallel between verses 17 and 33. In verse 17 it is God who pours out His Spirit ("God says, That I will pour forth of My Spirit..."; note the deliberate insertion, "God says" by Peter into the quotation of Joel[13]), while in verse 33 Jesus has the divine prerogative

---

[10]Or Yahweh. I add here that if we take Acts 2:39 ("For the promise is for you and your children, and for all who are far off, as many as the Lord our God shall call to Himself") and the phrase "Lord our God" to apply to the Father, the apostles' not hesitating to call Jesus "Lord" offers more evidence that they had the highest view of Christ possible.

[11]F. F. Bruce, *Commentary on The Book of The Acts* (Grand Rapids, Mich.: Wm. B. Eerdmans Publishing Co., reprinted, 1980), 73-74.

[12]*Jesus, Divine Messiah,* 229. See also B. B. Warfield, *The Lord of Glory* (New York: American Tract Society, 1907), 211. Speaking of the phrase "Lord of all" in Acts 10:36, Warfield states, "that is to say, universal sovereign, a phrase which recalls the great declaration of Rom. 9:5 to the effect that He is 'God over all,' as indeed He who sits on the throne of God must be."

[13]As pointed out by Reymond, *Jesus, Divine Messiah,* 230. Reymond then states that this could not have been unintentional on Peter's part.

of pouring forth the Spirit ("He [Jesus] has poured forth this which you both see and hear").[14] Thus, when we arrive at verse 33, we can come to no other conclusion than to say that Peter had the highest view of Christ.

Acts 7:59

"And they went on stoning Stephen as he called upon the Lord and said, 'Lord Jesus, receive my spirit!'" By praying to Jesus, Stephen was acknowledging Jesus as God the Son. Two observations evidence this.

First is the parallelism between Jesus' prayer to the Father at His death in Luke 23:46 ("Father, into Thy hands I commit My spirit"), and Stephen's in this verse. F. F. Bruce states, "whereas Jesus commended His spirit to the Father, Stephen commended his to Jesus. This is surely an early, if tacit, testimony to the Christian belief in our Lord's essential deity."[15] Another parallelism is our Lord's prayer in Luke 23:34 ("Father, forgive them; for they do not know what they are doing"), and Stephen's in Acts 7:60 ("Lord, do not hold this sin against them"). This is another testimony to the essential deity of Christ.[16]

Second is Jesus' promise to His disciples that He would answer their prayers. In John 14:14 Jesus promises, "If you ask Me anything in My name, that will I do, that the Father may be glorified in the Son." Thus, prayers may be addressed to both the Father and the Son.[17] As Reymond points out, the prayers of the disciples (here and in Acts 1:24; 2 Cor. 12:9, among others) "bear out the literalness with which the disciples understood Jesus' promise and show also their immediate recognition of His divinity."[18]

---

[14]Bruce, *Commentary on The Book of The Acts*, 72.

[15]*Commentary on The Book of The Acts*, 171.

[16]Perhaps we should consider that both Jesus and Stephen were well aware of Ecclesiastes 12:7 ("the spirit returns to God who gave it") and were praying accordingly!

[17]Jesus, of course, is the one mediator between us and the Father, and as such prayers may be addressed to the Father *through* or *in* the Son. But here Jesus asks us to pray directly to Him. See Leon Morris, *The Gospel According to John* (Grand Rapids, Mich.: Wm. B. Eerdmans Publishing Co., 1971), 647.

[18]*Jesus, Divine Messiah*, 119.

Acts 9:4

Paul's calling was of divine origin. Before his conversion, this persecutor of the followers of Christ was traveling on the Damascus road when "suddenly a light from heaven flashed around him" (v. 3). *"And he fell to the ground, and heard a voice saying to him, 'Saul, Saul, why are you persecuting Me?'"* (v. 4).

The repetition of one's name in an address "was common in antiquity,"[19] but it was common for God as well when He addressed His subjects (see Gen. 22:11; 46:2; Exod. 3:4; 1 Sam. 3:10; see also the address in 2 Bar. 22:2).[20] In which category are we to place Jesus' address to Paul? Is it simple common address, or is it an address from God?

The phenomena of "light from heaven," the voice from heaven ("both of which signaled the divine presence"[21]), and Paul's reaction of falling to the ground, when placed in the context of Rabbinic tradition (of which Paul was a part!), make a strong case that the resurrected and already ascended Lord of glory is Yahweh the Son appearing to Paul.[22] Richard N. Longenecker puts it succinctly:

> Of more significance is the fact that Saul understood the voice to be a message from God himself, for in rabbinism to hear a voice from heaven (a *bath qol,* lit., "a daughter of the voice" of God) never meant either a lower deity in the pantheon of gods speaking, as in Greek speculations, or some psychological disturbance, as many would presume today. On the contrary, it always connoted a rebuke or a word of instruction from God.[23]

For all these reasons Paul's words, "Who art Thou, Lord?" should be understood as the humble, fearful, and worshipful address[24] that characterized all who came into the presence of God, here in the person of the Son.

---

[19]Richard N. Longenecker, *The Expositor's Bible Commentary,* 9:370.

[20]Ibid. See also F. F. Bruce, *Commentary on The Book of The Acts,* 195.

[21]Ibid., 371.

[22]These phenomena make Paul's use of "Lord" different from that of the angel's appearance to Cornelius, whom he addressed as "Lord" (see Acts 10:3-4).

[23]*The Expositor's Bible Commentary,* 9:370-71.

[24]See ibid., 371.

128   *Knowing Christ in the Challenge of Heresy*

Acts 9:15

Closely connected to the above are the Lord's words to Ananias concerning Paul: *"Go, for he is a chosen instrument of Mine, to bear My name before the Gentiles."*

As was discussed in the exposition of Acts 1:8, by these words Jesus is claiming deity, for Paul is *His* chosen instrument (see Isa. 43:10; see also vv. 1, 7, 21). Here Jesus claims for Himself the divine prerogative of choosing His own vessels (see Rom. 9:21-23). Jesus' words point to Himself, and thus His servants point to Him in their proclamation of the good news throughout Acts (it is no coincidence that *Yahweh* says in Isa. 43:21, "The people whom I formed for Myself, will declare My praise"). *He* is the central figure in their preaching (5:42; 8:35; 9:27; 11:20; 17:18; etc.). It is *His* name that is called upon (9:14 cf. Joel 2:32). Sinners "turn"[25] to *Him* (9:35). It is *His* name that Paul must bear to the Gentiles (9:15). It is for *His* name that Paul must suffer (9:16). And what are we to make of "Name"? Is Luke applying this designation to Christ in such a flippant manner that it should condemn him as a blasphemer, or is he communicating in no uncertain theological terms that Jesus is God the Son? B. B. Warfield comments,

> A side-light is thrown upon the high estimate which was placed among these early Christians on Jesus' person by the usurpation by it of the Old Testament pregnant use of the term "Name." As in the Old Testament we read continually of "the Name of Jehovah" as the designation of His manifested majesty,[26] and even of simply "the Name" used absolutely with the same high connotation, so in Acts we read of the Name of Jesus Christ, to the exclusion of the old phrase, and

---

[25]After Jesus heals a paralyzed man through Peter (v. 34), "all who lived in Lydda and Sharon... turned (Gr. *epestrepsan,* ἐπέστρεψαν) to the Lord." Here "Lord" refers to Jesus (see 9:27, 28). In the Old Testament, people are to turn to *Yahweh alone* (see Isa. 6:10b, LXX *epistrepsōsin,* ἐπιστρέψωσιν).

[26]Here Warfield states that "Name" means the "manifested majesty" of God. See Walther Eichrodt, *Theology of the Old Testament,* trans. J. A. Baker, 2 vols. (Philadelphia, Pa.: The Westminster Press, 1967), 2:40-45. Eichrodt not only gives to "Name" what Warfield has stated, but goes on to write, "it is in the person of Jesus that the function of the Name of Yahweh as a form of the divine self-manifestation finds its fulfillment" (2:45).

again of simply "the name" ([Acts] 5:41, cf. 3 John 7) used absolutely[27] of Jesus. Those that were persecuted for His sake we are told rejoiced "that they were counted worthy to suffer dishonor for the Name" (5:41, cf. 3 John 7). In the Old Testament this would have meant the Name of Jehovah: here it means the Name of Jesus. "The Name," as it has been truly remarked, "had become a watchword of the faith, and is consequently used alone to express the name of Jesus, as it stood in former days for the Name of Jehovah (Lev. 24:11)."[28] Nothing could more convincingly bear in upon us the position to which Jesus had been exalted in men's thoughts than this constant tendency to substitute Him in their religious outlook for Jehovah.[29]

Hebrews 1:3a

"And He is the radiance of His glory and the exact representation of His nature, and upholds all things by the word of His power." Written to persecuted Christians, this epistle seeks to comfort these persecuted believers with the all-sufficiency of the person of Christ and His work on the cross for sins. Christ is the final and perfect revealing of God to the remnant, not only because of who He is but also because of what He did.

For now it concerns us to find out *who* He is. He is the radiance[30] of

---

[27]By this Warfield means there is no predicate phrase to complete the meaning (i.e., the name *of Jesus* or the name *of Paul*) and thus there can be no doubt that the term is used here of Jesus in the sense that it is used for Yahweh in the Old Testament. In the Old Testament "the Name" meant Yahweh, as it does here in reference to the Son of God.

[28]Quoting Rashdall, *in loc.*

[29]B. B. Warfield, *The Lord of Glory* (New York: American Tract Society, 1907), 218-19. This theme, either ignored or missed by the cults, tells of the essential deity of the Lord Jesus Christ. The ease with which Luke applies "the Name" to both God the Father and God the Son must result either in Luke's utter theological perversity or his infinitely high view of Christ. Consider Acts 15:13-18, where James states, "God first concerned Himself about taking from among the Gentiles a people for His name" (v. 14). James then alludes to Amos 9:11, 12 and quotes Yahweh: "all the Gentiles who are called by My name" (v. 17b). How is it that Christ can state, "he [Paul] is a chosen instrument of Mine, *to bear My name before the Gentiles...*" (Acts 9:15)? The answer is that Jesus is Yahweh the Son.

[30]Gr. *apaugasma*, ἀπαύγασμα.

God's glory.[31] In Him is manifested the very presence of God. Moreover, the Son is *forever*[32] the radiance of the Father's glory. This phrase (lit. "the radiance of *the glory*") is reminiscent of the presence of God proclaimed in the Old Testament. It therefore is not surprising to have the coming of Jesus described elsewhere as God "tenting" with us, having His glory seen, and being "full of grace and truth" (John 1:14).

The next phrase speaks of the ontological oneness of the Father and the Son. He is the exact representation[33] of His [God's] nature.[34] The language here is stronger than that used in 2 Corinthians 4:4 and Colossians 1:15 ("image"[35]of God).[36] The Greek word *charaktēr* ("exact representation"), used nowhere else in the New Testament, is used in other literature of the time to describe the impression left on a coin from an imprint device.[37] Thus Christ is "deity stamped in flesh" because He is the exact representation of the nature (Gr. *hupostasis*, ὑπόστασις) of God. F. F. Bruce states, "Just as the glory is really in the effulgence [radiance], so the substance (Gk. *hypostasis* [or *hupostasis*]) of God is really in Christ, who is its impress, its exact representation and embodiment."[38] Christ is essentially, or as to substance, one with the Father.

---

[31]See F. F. Bruce, *The Epistle to the Hebrews* (Grand Rapids, Mich.: Wm. B. Eerdmans Publishing Co., 1964), 5. Bruce states that the writer of Hebrews may have been familiar with the Alexandrian Book of Wisdom. Here "Wisdom" is seen as an attribute of the Almighty: "... a breath of the power of God, and a clear effulgence of the glory of the Almighty;... an effulgence from everlasting light, and an unspotted mirror of the working of God, and an image of His goodness" (Wisd. 7:25-26). Philo also used the word to describe the image of God in man (see Bruce, ibid.). But, as Bruce rightly observes, "For them [Wisdom and Philo] the Logos or Wisdom is the personification of a divine attribute; for him [author of Hebrews] the language is descriptive of a man who had lived and died..., but who nonetheless was the eternal Son and supreme revelation of God" (ibid.).

[32]Gr. *ōn, ὤν*. The present tense signifies continuous action.

[33]Gr. *charaktēr*, χαρακτὴρ.

[34] Gr. *hupostaseōs*, ὑποστάσεως.

[35] Gr. *eikōn*, εἰκών.

[36]See Bruce, *The Epistle to the Hebrews*, 6.

[37]Ibid.

[38]Ibid.

It is precisely because of who He is that "He (continually[39]) upholds all things by the word of His power." Here the Son is the focus. The universe was made *through* Him (v. 2), and He actively sustains it (see also Col. 1:17). When we begin to think of the vastness of the universe, everything in it that is held steadfastly into place while maintaining course, and the people and events that are under the sovereign rule of Christ, we consequently can only *begin* to conceive of the infinite power of God the Son.

Hebrews 1:8 [Psalm 45:6]

Psalm 45:6 ("Thy throne, O God, is forever and ever; A scepter of uprightness is the scepter of Thy kingdom") and its citation in Hebrews 1:8 ("But of the Son *He* [God] *says,* 'Thy throne, O God, is forever and ever, and the righteous scepter is the scepter of His kingdom'") bear testimony to the deity of Christ. The Psalm tells of the divine Messiah to come.[40] The writer of Hebrews applies the Psalm's confession to Jesus, the Son of God, and thus testifies to the incarnate deity of the Son of God.[41]

---

[39]Gr. present tense participle (*pherōn*, φέρων) denoting continuous action. It is partly for this reason that deists err. Deism affirms that God created the universe, but takes no active part in sustaining it. Often the illustration of a clock maker is used: the clock is made, then wound and allowed to sustain itself.

[40]The Psalm in its *immediate* intent is addressed to a king. Who this king is has been a matter of debate (see Bruce, *Epistle to the Hebrews*, 18-19). Since the writer of Hebrews sets the Psalm as addressing the Messiah (and thus its ultimate object of point), it is highly probable that the king addressed is in the line of David. The writer applies this psalmic verse to "when God brings His firstborn into the world" (1:6). It is not clear that the writer of Hebrews is referring to (1) the incarnation, or (2) the second coming (mainly because the Gr. *palin*, πάλιν ["again," v. 6] suggests this). The writer may not have any time period in mind, and thus could easily refer to Christ's "exaltation and enthronement as sovereign over the inhabited universe" (ibid., 17). Interesting as well are the commands in the LXX (though missing in the Hebrew text) to angels to worship Yahweh (see Deut. 32:43 and Ps. 96:7). Here they are applied to the Son!

[41]This would perfectly be in step with the confession contained in 1:2-3.

"Thy throne, O God,"[42] however, is not read in all translations, though "the overwhelming majority" of translations and scholars prefer it.[43] "Thy throne is God" or "God is thy throne" are options.[44] For both grammatical and contextual reasons, I prefer "Thy throne, O God"[45] over "Thy throne is God"[46] or "God is thy throne."[47]

Regarding grammar,[48] *first,* the Greek word order favors the translation as an address to the Son by the Father ("Thy throne, O God"). This word order is not uncommon in the New Testament. As A. T. Robertson points out, there are some 60 examples of this in the New Testament.[49] *Second,* the optional translation, "thy throne is God," has been viewed as "only just conceivable."[50] *Third,* the other option, "God is thy throne," is unlikely, given the word order in the Greek.[51]

Contextually, there are strong arguments for "Thy throne, O God." *First,* as Robert Reymond points out, Psalm 44:4, 6 *in the LXX* (45:3 in

---

[42]Gr. *ho thronos sou ho theos,* ὁ θρόνος σου ὁ θεὸς.

[43]"[T]he overwhelming majority of grammarians, commentators, authors of general studies, and English translations construe *ho theos* [here transliterated] as vocative [thus, "Thy throne, O God"]" (Murray J. Harris, *Jesus as God: The New Testament Use of Theos in Reference to Jesus* (Grand Rapids, Mich.: Baker Book House, 1992), 217-18.

[44]Daniel B. Wallace, in his *Greek Grammar Beyond the Basics: An Exegetical Syntax of the New Testament* (Grand Rapids, Mich.: Zondervan Publishing House, 1996), 59, points out that in Harris' "excellent study [*Jesus as God*] of Heb. 1:8, Harris could only find Hort and Nairne among the commentators to hold this view [i.e., "your throne is God"]." As for "God is your throne," Wallace lists Wescott, Moffatt, RSV margin, NEB margin (ibid.).

[45]Gr. *theos* understood in the vocative (direct address) sense.

[46]Gr. *ho theos* as the predicative nominative.

[47]Gr. *ho theos* as nominative, indicating subject.

[48]Some of the following observations in this paragraph are taken from Robert Reymond's *Jesus, Divine Messiah,* 296-97.

[49]A. T. Robertson, *A Grammar of the Greek New Testament In the Light of Historical Research* (Nashville, Tenn.: Broadman Press, 1934), 465. Robertson admits the uncertainty regarding the phrase.

[50]See Nigel Turner, *A Grammar of New Testament Greek* (Edinburgh: T. & T. Clark, 1963), 3:34. Moreover, if the phrase in question had no definite article before *theos* and its word order was *ho thronos sou theos,* "thy throne is God" would be the proper translation. It, however, has the article, making the vocative sense much more natural in the dynamic equivalent translation.

[51]Regarding this translation, the word order would more likely be *ho theos ho thronos sou.* But again, this is not the case. See Harris, *Jesus as God,* 215.

English) have the address, "O Mighty One."⁵² When we arrive at 44:7
(45:6 in the English), the natural understanding should also be to take it
as address ("Thy throne, *O God*").⁵³ In the Hebrew text we have "O
Mighty One"⁵⁴ in 45:4 (verse 3 in English): "Gird Thy sword on *Thy*
thigh, O Mighty One [or "O Warrior"]." This makes strong the
possibility of the Hebrew *elohim* ("God") in verse 7 (verse 6 in
English) being understood as address as well.⁵⁵ *Second,* Hebrews 1:10
has the address to the Son continuing.⁵⁶ This, as well, makes the case
for address in 1:8 all the more stronger.⁵⁷ *Finally,* concerning the Son it

---

⁵²Gr. *dunate,* δυνατέ. See Reymond, *Jesus, Divine Messiah,* 297.

⁵³Interesting is Aquila's version of the LXX, where he uses the
unquestionable vocative: "*ho thronos sou thee* (θεέ)..."

⁵⁴The vocative *gibbor,* גִּבּוֹר.

⁵⁵In the immediate context of the Psalm addressing a king, the word *elohim*
may be used to refer to authorities that are not the true and living God (see
Exod. 21:6; and Ps. 82:6). This possibility is strengthened by verse 7, where we
read, "Therefore God, Thy God, has anointed thee." In the immediate context
the writer of this Psalm makes it clear that this king is surpassed in glory by
God. This, however, does not weaken the force of Hebrews applying this to the
Son of God, for (1) the Psalm's immediate context is *heightened* by Hebrews'
application of this passage to God the Son (see Bruce, *Epistle to the Hebrews,*
19-20), and (2) in the Son's eternal relationship with the Father we may view
the phrase "Therefore God, Thy God" without difficulty because of the eternal
triune nature of God.

⁵⁶As the *kai* [καί, "and"] signals at the beginning of the verse. "And, Thou,
Lord (*kurie,* κύριε)..." Here the indisputable vocative (form of address) *kurie* is
used.

⁵⁷See Reymond, *Jesus, Divine Messiah,* 297. In keeping with the vocative
sense throughout the passage, it may be well to translate 1:9b as "Therefore, O
God, your God has anointed you..." Though Murray J. Harris deems the
vocative sense in 1:9b improbable but not impossible, he nonetheless states
concerning Heb. 1:8 (Heb. and Gr. transliterated): "Two general conclusions
may now be stated. First, although some slight degree of uncertainty remains as
to whether *elohim* in Psalm 45:7 (MT [Heb. text]) is a vocative [thus the
translation, "Thy throne, *O God*"], there can be little doubt that the LXX
translator construed it so... *and that the author of Hebrews,* whose quotations of
the OT generally follow the LXX, *assumed that the Septuagintal ho theos in
Psalm 44:7 was a vocative and incorporated it in this sense into his argument
in chapter 1,* an argument that was designed to establish the superiority of the
Son over the angels. The appellation *ho theos* that was figurative and
hyperbolic when applied to a mortal king was applied to the immortal Son in a

is clear from the language used in Hebrews 1:3a that He is ontologically deity, that He is of the same substance as the Father: "He is the radiance of His [the Father's] glory and the exact representation of His nature, and upholds all things by the word of His power." In short, the Son (1) forever is the radiance of deity, (2) forever is the Father's exact representation as to His very nature (being, essence), and (3) continues to hold in place by the word of His power all things in the universe, an attribute that is exercised only by God. These attributes would *never* apply to angels (therefore see v. 5). They do, however, apply to the Son, and thus the writer accords to the Son worship that is due only to God (1:6[58]).

---

literal and true sense. *Jesus is not merely superior to the angels. Equally with the Father he shares in the divine nature* (ho theos, ["O God," referring to Jesus], v. 8) while remaining distinct from him (ho theos sou ["your God"], v. 9). The author places Jesus far above any angel with respect to nature and function [see vv. 5-7], and on par with God with regard to nature but subordinate to God with regard to function. There is an 'essential' unity but a functional subordination. Second, given the vocative *ho theos* in 1:8, it cannot be deemed impossible for the comparable *ho theos* in 1:9 to be translated 'O God,' but this interpretation seems improbable" (Murray J. Harris, *Jesus as God*, 227, emphases added. See his thorough treatment of Psalm 45:7 and Hebrews 1:8 on pp. 187-227).

[58] Anti-trinitarian cults sometimes argue that Heb. 1:6 calls the Son the "firstborn" (*prōtotokon*, πρωτότοκον). Specifically, Jehovah's Witnesses interpret this word to mean "first-created." But this is a stretched interpretation. When interpreted in light of the Old Testament usage of the term as it applied to king David, a usage we should not ignore since theologically Christ is the fulfillment of the Davidic throne, it means enthronement. Psalm 89:27 reads, "I also shall make him My firstborn (LXX 88:28, *prōtotokon*), the highest of the kings of the earth." In its immediate context this applies to David, but prophetically it refers to the enthronement/exaltation of the Son of God "after He made purification of sins" (Heb. 1:3). It denotes the heirship of the Son of God (Heb. 1:2), His ruling over all creation, and has nothing to do with coming into existence as a created being. (Taken to its logical conclusion, according to the Jehovah's Witness interpretation of the word, David was the first creature created! This, of course, they would never admit.) Taking Psalm 89:27 as it stands, phrase A ("I also shall make him My firstborn") and phrase B ("the highest of the kings of the earth") are in synonymous parallelism: "firstborn" *means* "highest of the kings of the earth." Again, this applies to both David (immediate sense) and Christ (ultimate fulfillment).

Hebrews 1:10-12 [Psalm 102:25-27]

Chapter one of Hebrews continues its witness to the deity and supremacy of the Son by quoting Psalm 102:25-27, which refers to Yahweh ("Of old Thou didst found the earth; and the heavens are the work of Thy hands. Even they will perish, but Thou dost endure; and all of them will wear out like a garment; like clothing Thou wilt change them, and they will be changed. But Thou art the same, and Thy years will not come to an end"), and applying it to the Son:

> *(10) And[59] "Thou, Lord, in the beginning didst lay the foundation of the earth, and the heavens are the works of Thy hands; (11) they will perish, but Thou remainest, and they will all become old as a garment, (12) and as a mantle Thou wilt roll them up; as a garment they will also be changed. But Thou art the same, and Thy years will not come to an end."*

For the writer of Hebrews, Christ is the LORD of Psalm 102[60] (see LORD, Heb. *Yahweh,* in Ps. 102:1, 12, 15, 16, 18, 19, 22). In the Psalm *Yahweh* in the beginning laid the foundations of the earth. He is the creator, and in contrast to the creation, which will perish, He remains forever the same in His eternal deity. In Hebrews, all this applies to Christ. Further, we must not forget that in these verses it is the Father who is addressing the Son! The Father addresses the Son as "Lord," then goes on to state that the Son laid the foundation of the earth, that the heavens are the works of His hands (v. 10), and that He is eternal (v. 12). Here the Father acknowledges the Son's ontological oneness *and functional equality* with Himself.[61]

---

[59]The Gr. *kai* (καί, "and") beginning v. 10 leaves no doubt that the writer of Hebrews is continuing the Father's address to the Son, which began in v. 8.

[60]Contrary to the Jehovah's Witnesses, who view Jesus as a created angel, the writer of Hebrews sets Christ apart from the angels. Note the Gr. adversative *de* (δέ, "but") starting vv. 8, 13.

[61]Though Christian scholars see in this chapter, and generally in christological study, the continual functional subordination of the Son to the Father (while maintaining the Son's ontological oneness with the Father), these words spoken to the Son by the Father raise a question of doubt. Rather than continual subordination of the Son, would a functional "deference" of the three persons of the Trinity (sometimes the Son and the Spirit defer to the Father, sometimes the Father to the Son, sometimes the Father and the Son to the

Finally, the writer of Hebrews takes great pains to closely link statements about Christ's ontological deity (1:8, for example) to His enthronement and exaltation. The words "firstborn" and "begotten" (Heb. 1:5, 6) are not to be understood in the sense of coming into existence in time, as the Jehovah's Witnesses and the Mormons understand these terms. Rather, they should be understood in enthronement contexts (see Pss. 2:6-9; 89:27; and the previous section), which is the point of Hebrews 1:13 ("But to which of the angels has He ever said, 'Sit at My right hand, until I make Thine enemies a footstool for Thy feet'"). Here the "sitting" of the Son at the Father's "right hand"[62] points to the Son's supreme authority and enthronement[63] (see Ps. 110:1 as it refers immediately to David's authority and kingship). Christ is the same yesterday, today, and forever (Heb. 13:8). He is the Son of God, the Yahweh of Psalm 102, the enthroned King. It is to Him, therefore, that we are to ascribe glory (Heb. 13:21[64]), just as the covenant people ascribed glory to Yahweh in the Old Testament.

Spirit) be more on target? See Royce G. Gruenler's *The Trinity in the Gospel of John* (Grand Rapids, Mich.: Baker Book House, 1986) for this view.

[62]The Mormons wrongly view verses like Hebrews 1:13 as teaching that God the Father has body parts like a man (in this case hands). The phrase "right hand" refers to one who sits in a place of authority and honor (see David Noel Freedman, ed., *The Anchor Bible Dictionary*, 6 vols. [New York: Doubleday, 1992], 5:724).

[63]See Bruce, *Epistle to the Hebrews*, 23.

[64]Hebrews 13:20-21 reads, "Now the *God of peace*, who brought up from the dead the great Shepherd of the sheep through the blood of the eternal covenant, even Jesus our Lord, equip you in every good thing to do His will, working in us that which is pleasing in His sight, through *Jesus Christ*, to whom be the glory forever. Amen." To whom is the glory ascribed? Is it the Father ("God of peace") or the Son ("Jesus Christ")? There is a difference of opinion among commentators. Harris states there is ambiguity (*Jesus as God*, 235). Bruce states that the phrase "is probably to be taken as an ascription of the glory to God [the Father], the subject of the sentence." He then cites v. 15, wherein it is stated that glory is to be given to God through Christ (*Epistle to the Hebrews*, 412). Warfield argues that "there is no reason why this author [of Hebrews] should not have ascribed "eternal glory" to the Being he had described as in His very nature "the effulgence of the divine glory." Warfield then comments that, given this, "it may be a matter of indifference to us whether he has done so or not" (*Lord of Glory*, 281). Morris admits the syntax of these two verses "poses a problem," stating that those who take it to refer to the Father cite as evidence the fact that "the God of peace" is the subject of the

sentence, while those who see Christ as the referent appeal to Him being the nearest antecedent (Frank E. Gaebelein, ed., *The Expositor's Bible Commentary*, 12 vols. [Grand Rapids, Mich.: Zondervan Publishing House, 1981], 12:156). Reymond appeals to just this, and writes that Jesus "is the subject of the doxology in 13:21.... Certainly, the collocation of the relative pronoun and the title 'Jesus Christ' in 13:21 favors such an interpretation" (*Jesus, Divine Messiah*, 299). Warfield, in his *Lord of Glory,* cites in a note Riehm, who states, "'Still how can it occasion surprise that the author in 13:21 praises Jesus Christ with the doxology ᾧ ἡ δόξα εἰς τοὺς αἰῶνας [*hō hē doxa eis tous aiōnas*], which, according to O. T. notions, is due to Jehovah only, but in the N. T. passages is also transferred to Christ? It is recognized by all recent [early twentieth century] commentators that the relative ᾧ [*hō*] refers to Christ and not to God [the Father].' So also Bleek, Lunemann, Maier, Kurtz, Lowrie: contra, Delitzsch: *non liquet,* Davidson" (p. 281, n. 11).

The arguments that it should refer to God because He is the subject of the statement, and because v. 15 states we are to give praise to God through Christ, are convincing. However, I think it should refer to Christ. I appeal to (1) the early ascription by the writer to Christ as ontologically deity (Heb. 1), (2) the relative pronoun *hō* ("to whom") occurring *immediately* after "Jesus Christ," (3) the writer certainly having the right to place the relative pronoun clause directly after or sometime after *theos* ("God," v. 20) and before "Jesus Christ," and (4) the subject-object relationship of the sentence being *completed* before the mention of "Jesus Christ." Concerning this last point, in v. 20 "the God of peace" is the subject, and "equip you in every..." functions to finish the thought. Then, "through Jesus Christ" is introduced, and the relative pronoun ("to whom") occurs immediately after this. For this reason the flow of thought is awkward if the relative pronoun refers to the Father.

Chapter 7

The General Epistles and Revelation: The Incarnate Deity of Christ

"For in all these letters, too, as in those which have already claimed our attention, Jesus appears fundamentally as the divine object of the reverential service of all Christians.... Christ is our Redeemer; Christ is God."—B. B Warfield, The Lord of Glory

"I dip my forefinger in the watery blood of your impotent mad redeemer, and write over his thorn-torn brow: The TRUE prince of evil—the king of the slaves!"—Anton Szandor LaVey, The Satanic Bible

James opens our study of the General Epistles.[1]

James 1:1a

"James, a bond-servant of God and of the Lord Jesus Christ." In his salutation, James refers to his being a servant of God (the Father)

---

[1]The General Epistles include James through Jude.

and of Christ. In doing so, he places Christ on equal par with God the Father.

The Old Testament theme of Yahweh's covenant people being His servants (Gen. 32:10; Judg. 2:8; Ps. 89:3; Isa. 41:8; 43:10) comes before us once again.[2] On the lips of a monotheist (see James 2:19), the mention of serving two masters (God the Father and the Lord Jesus Christ; see also Paul's statement in Titus 1:1) seems odd (Matt. 6:24), unless of course James believes in the co-equality, the ontological oneness, of the Father and the Son.[3] D. Edmond Hiebert states,

> For a strong monotheist like James (2:19), it would have been unthinkable thus to name Jesus Christ as equal with God if he rejected His true deity. While James distinguishes the Persons of the Trinity, for him They are one in nature and essence.[4]

Further, we should consider James' use of the title "Lord," here and throughout the epistle (1:1, 7; 2:1; 3:9; 4:10, 15; 5:4, 7, 8, 10, 11, 14, 15).[5] The ease with which he uses the term for the Father (for example, 3:9 cf. 1:27[6]) and the Son (for example 1:1) demonstrates his view of equality of the Son with the Father.[7] James has the highest view of Christ a monotheist could have, especially in light of the Old Testament

---

[2]See D. Edmond Hiebert, *The Epistle of James: Tests of a Living Faith* (Chicago, Ill.: Moody Press, 1979), 61: "In the Old Testament the expression 'servant of the Lord' was used as a term of honor and authority, of those who served God in a special way. It was used of Moses as well as the Old Testament prophets generally as God's authorized spokesmen."

[3]See ibid.

[4]Ibid. See also A. T. Robertson, *Word Pictures in the New Testament*, 6 vols. (Grand Rapids, Mich.: Baker Book House, reprinted, n.d.), 6:10, B. B. Warfield, *The Lord of Glory* (New York: American Tract Society, 1907), 264, and Robert L. Reymond, *Jesus, Divine Messiah* (Phillipsburg, N.J.: Presbyterian and Reformed Publishing Co., 1990), 282.

[5]My opinion is that 1:7; 3:9; 4:10, 15; 5:4, 10, 11 refer to the Father, while 1:1; 2:1; 5:7, 8, 14, 15 refer to the Son.

[6]In both verses the one article governs two nouns, referring to the same person. In 1:27 the Greek reads *tō theō kai patri,* τῷ θεῷ καὶ πατρὶ ("God and Father"). In 3:9 it reads *ton kurion kai patera,* τὸν κύριον καὶ πατέρα ("Lord and Father." Some manuscripts have "God" instead of "Lord" here, but this variant has less text support [see Hiebert, 222, n. 50]. "Lord" is supported by P70, Aleph, A and B).

[7]See Reymond, *Jesus, Divine Messiah,* 282.

confession of *one* LORD (Deut. 4:35, 39; 6:4; Isa. 45:21-24; Zech. 14:9).

James 2:1

In this verse James praises his Lord, to whom he belongs as a servant: *"My brethren, do not hold your faith in our glorious[8] Lord Jesus Christ with an attitude of personal favoritism. "*
Our focus is on the translation and subsequent meaning of the phrase "our glorious Lord Jesus Christ."[9] Should we translate the phrase as above, namely, "our glorious Lord Jesus Christ,"[10] as "our Lord of glory, Jesus Christ,"[11] as "our Lord Jesus Christ, *the Lord* of Glory (here the italicized words are repeated to smooth out the meaning), or as "our Lord Jesus Christ, the Glory"?[12] I believe it should be translated and understood in the latter sense.[13] Though it is the string of genitives that lends to the ambiguity, it is more natural to render the phrase this way.[14]
What, then, is the *meaning* of "our Lord Jesus Christ, the Glory"? Most certainly James has the highest view of his Lord because "the Glory" refers back to the Old Testament concept of the presence of

---

[8]Gr. *tēs doxēs*, τῆς δόξης.

[9]Gr. *tou kuriou hēmōn Iēsou Christou tēs doxēs*, τοῦ κυρίου ἡμῶν ᾽Ιησοῦ Χριστοῦ (all in the genitive case).

[10]*Tēs doxēs* functions adjectivally, thus "glorious."

[11] *Tēs doxēs* modifying "Lord."

[12]Another view is to relate *tēs doxēs* to *tēn pistin* (τὴν πίστιν) thus "the faith in the glory of our Lord Jesus Christ" or "the glorious faith." In the Greek, *tēn pistin* immediately precedes our phrase quoted above.

[13]See Hiebert (pp. 148-49), who lists Mayor, Osterley, Lenski, Moffat, and others (Bengel, Hort, Laws, Ramsey) who concur. See also Reymond (p. 282) and Robertson (6:27). All these scholars note that *tēs doxēs* is in apposition to "Lord." Some have therefore translated the phrase as "Jesus Christ, who is the glory" (Weymouth). This rightly conveys the apposition. Some of those on the side of "our glorious Lord Jesus Christ" are Dibelius, Cantinant, Ropes, Mussner, Davids (though he admits this is "awkward"), the NIV and the NASB.

[14]Mayor says Bengel's suggestion of "Jesus Christ, the Glory" is "perfectly natural and easy" (J. B. Mayor, *The Epistle of St. James* [Minneapolis, Minn.: Klock & Klock, reprinted, 1977], notes, 80-81). See also Hiebert, 149, who cites Ramsey saying that this rendering "fits the Greek better than the others."

Yahweh.[15] In the person of God the Son we have Yahweh's glory manifested. Jesus is "God with us" (Matt. 1:23); those who have seen Him "beheld His glory" (John 1:14); He is the radiance of the Father's glory and the exact representation of the His very being (Heb. 1:3). James calls the incarnate and glorified Christ "the Glory," and firmly believes that in God the Son, Yahweh, who manifested His glory to His covenant people (Exod. 16:7, 10; 40:34; Num. 14:10; 16:19, 42; 20:6; 1 Kings 8:11;[16] Zech. 2:5; etc.), is with the people of the new covenant. Hiebert, speaking of the Old Testament theme of Yahweh's glory, states, "New Testament Christology associates this glory of God with the person of Jesus Christ, and James here thinks of Christ as Himself 'the glory' in the midst of His people."[17]

This statement of James, when interpreted in light of the Old Testament, its proper background, is a confession of Jesus in the highest christological sense. Those who have been redeemed by Christ view Him as "the Glory," God manifested and tenting among His people by His presence, which He promised would always be with them (Matt. 28:20).

1 Peter 2:3

"If you have tasted the kindness of the Lord." In First Peter, this is the first of three texts that apply to Christ various Old Testament citations referring to Yahweh.

Psalm 34:8a states, "O taste and see that the LORD [*Yahweh*] is good."[18] In the Psalm we are commanded to taste and see that the Lord is good. Peter's "Lord" is Jesus Christ, proven by the following verse. We are "to come to *Him* [2:4, referring back to "Lord" in v. 3] as to a

---

[15]See my expositions of Matt. 1:21-23 and John 1:14.

[16]Cf. Jesus' words in John 2:19, wherein He points to *Himself* being the embodiment of the glory of the Lord (cf. further John 1:14). Jesus is the temple!

[17]*The Epistle of James,* 149. See also 1 Pet. 4:13.

[18]Peter follows for the most part the LXX of the Psalm (33:9). In the LXX the verb "to taste" is used as a command, "Taste [*geusasthe,* γεύσασθε, aorist imperative] and see that the Lord is good," but by Peter to communicate a conditional clause (*if* you have tasted [*ei egeusasthe,* εἰ ἐγεύσασθε] that the Lord is good [v. 3], you will grow in respect to salvation [v. 2]). Peter also matches the LXX for "good" (*chrēstos,* χρηστὸς).

living stone, rejected by men, but choice and precious in the sight of God [the Father[19]]." There can be no doubt that for Peter, Jesus is "the Lord,"[20] the *Yahweh* of Psalm 34:8.[21]

1 Peter 2:6-8a

"(6) For this is contained in Scripture: 'Behold I lay in Zion a choice stone, a precious corner stone, and he who believes in Him shall not be disappointed.' (7) This precious value, then, is for you who believe, but for those who disbelieve, 'The stone which the builders rejected, this became the very corner stone,' (8) and, 'A stone of stumbling and a rock of offense.'" As mentioned in the previous section, we are discussing a string of Old Testament texts that refer to Yahweh and are applied by Peter to Christ.

In 1 Peter 2:6-7[22] the Old Testament passages cited refer to the coming Messiah, with no connotation *at this point* that this coming Messiah is Yahweh. First Peter 2:6 is a quotation of Isaiah 28:16, and 1 Peter 2:7 of Psalm 118:22. Peter means to teach that the Lord Jesus is this coming One, this "stone" of Isaiah and the Psalm. *But what Peter does next in 2:8 confirms the coming Messiah's deity.*[23] Here he quotes

---

[19]This is further proof that the "living stone" is Christ, for Peter distinguishes between this living stone and the Father.

[20]Interesting as well is Peter's substitution of "Lord" (*kurios*) in 1:25 for "God" in both the Hebrew (*elohim*) and the LXX (*theos*) of Isa. 40:8, which he quotes (see Reymond, *Jesus, Divine Messiah,* 287). Perhaps Peter is preparing his readers to see Christ as the Yahweh of the Psalm cited above, especially in light of 1 Pet. 1:3, where he clearly designates Jesus as the Lord! Peter's designation of Jesus as "the Lord" carries with it the meaning shared by the New Testament writers already examined in our study: Jesus is God the Son.

[21]See Reymond, *Jesus, Divine Messiah,* 287, who cites several scholars that agree.

[22]See also Eph. 2:20; Matt. 21:42; Luke 20:18. In Luke, Jesus, who is this stone rejected (v. 17), alludes to Isa. 8:13, 14, where the "stone" is identified as "The LORD of Hosts." Isaiah 8:15 then tells of people who will "fall and be broken," Yahweh being the stone over which they will fall and be broken. In Luke 20:18 it is Jesus!

[23]For this I am indebted to Robert Reymond (*Jesus, Divine Messiah,* 287).

Isaiah 8:14b,[24] which reads, "A stone of stumbling and a rock of offense."[25] But to whom does this refer? The LORD of Hosts[26] of Isaiah 8:13. Peter's line of thought is consistent to point to the Messiah *all through* 2:6-8. This is to say, there can be no discontinuity of persons between 2:6-7 and 2:8.[27] Jesus is "the LORD of Hosts" of Isaiah 8:13-14.

1 Peter 3:14b-15a

Our final Old Testament citation involving Yahweh which Peter in his first epistle applies to Jesus occurs in 3:14b-15a: *"And do not fear their intimidation, and do not be troubled, but sanctify Christ as Lord in your hearts."*

This is a quotation of Isaiah 8:12b-13a,[28] which reads, "And you are not to fear what they fear or be in dread of it. It is the LORD of Hosts[29] whom you should regard as holy." This last sentence may be translated, "The LORD of Hosts, Him you shall sanctify."[30] The reference is unquestionable, and Peter has no difficulty whatsoever in applying this Old Testament text, which speaks of Yahweh of Hosts, to the Lord Jesus Christ, who will one day be revealed in all His glory[31] (1 Pet. 4:13).

---

[24]Ibid., and Edwin A Blum, in Frank E. Gaebelein, ed., *The Expositor's Bible Commentary,* 12 vols. (Grand Rapids, Mich.: Zondervan Publishing House, 1981), 12:230.

[25]My translation. Peter follows the Heb. here (*le eben negeph u le tsur mikshol,* לְאֶבֶן נֶגֶף וּלְצוּר מִכְשׁוֹל) rather than the LXX.

[26]Heb. *Yahweh Tsebaoth,* יְהוָה צְבָאוֹת.

[27]The connecting *kai* (καὶ) that begins verse eight is a coordinating conjunction, linking the two independent clauses (quotations) of v. 7 and v. 8 (see Daniel B. Wallace, *Greek Grammar Beyond the Basics: An Exegetical Syntax of the New Testament* [Grand Rapids, Mich.: Zondervan Publishing House, 1996], 667-68).

[28]Peter follows closely the LXX.

[29]Heb. *Yahweh Tsebaoth.* See Heb. in n. 26.

[30]See Keil and Delitzsch, *Commentary on the Old Testament,* 10 vols. (Grand Rapids, Mich.: Eerdmans Publishing Co., reprinted, 1983), 7:236, and John N. Oswalt, *The Book of Isaiah: Chapters 1:39* (Grand Rapids, Mich.: Eerdmans Publishing Co., 1986), 229.

[31]For what this means, see under James 2:1 in this chapter.

Further, in the Isaiah passage just quoted the remnant of Israel is exhorted to place its confidence in the person and promise of Yahweh, although devastating physical trial awaits them. He holds them in the hollow of His hand, and a remnant will indeed return from captivity (see Isa. 10:21[32]). Likewise Peter seeks to comfort the persecuted Christians, the true remnant of God, and he could not have chosen a more emotive theme than that of Isaiah's words of comfort and exhortation regarding the fate of the exiled. In both the Isaiah and Peter texts, the remnant is to look to God as the center of their lives, and make that vision the ground for godly living.[33]

1 Peter 1:11 cf. 4:14

"[The prophets], seeking to know what person or time the Spirit of Christ within them was indicating as He predicted the sufferings of Christ and the glories to follow." Isaiah is surely one of these prophets who spoke of the coming of the Messiah, who is the "Mighty God" (Isa. 9:6; 10:21) and the "Lord of Hosts," whom we are to sanctify in our hearts (Isa. 8:13 cf. 1 Pet. 3:15).

Note the ease with which Peter speaks of "the [Holy] Spirit of Christ"[34] in 1:11 *and* "the [Holy] Spirit of God" in 4:14. He equates the two, strongly implying the equality of both the Father and the Son.[35]

---

[32]Isa. 10:21 states that a remnant will return *"to el gibbor"* (אֶל־אֵל גִּבּוֹר, "to mighty God" or "to the mighty God"). The true and living God, Yahweh, is meant here. Note that Isaiah speaks of the coming Messiah as *"el gibbor"* (גִּבּוֹר אֵל, "mighty God" or "the mighty God") in 9:6. In order to substantiate their denial of the deity of Christ, Jehovah's Witnesses attempt to make a distinction between *a* mighty God (9:6) and *the al*mighty God (10:21). Such a distinction, however, is not sustained by the Hebrew text. *El gibbor* in both 9:6 and 10:21 are anarthrous (without the definite article). Therefore *no* distinction is made in the Hebrew. If context rules, both instances of *el gibbor* refer to Christ.

[33]Bringing this to our situation today, in the face of persecution we should remember that Jesus, our LORD of Hosts of Isaiah, is with us. This is to characterize all our actions, and provide the ground for hope in the midst that persecution.

[34]Which, by the way, speaks of the pre-existence of Christ. If the Spirit of Christ was speaking through the prophets, then that presupposes Christ's pre-existence.

[35]Paul refers to the "Spirit of God" (or "His Spirit") 16 times and to the "Spirit of Christ" 3 times (see Gordon D. Fee, *God's Empowering Presence:*

This speaks of the deity of Christ in another way. In the Old Testament "The Spirit of the LORD [*Yahweh*]" is the only one who could have spoken through the prophets of old (see Ezek. 11:5). Thus, "the Spirit of the LORD" is equated with Peter's "the Spirit of Christ." And again, note the ease with which Peter takes this Old Testament theological theme and applies it to Christ. Peter's Jesus is Yahweh the Son, and this confession is echoed in his second epistle, to which we now turn.

2 Peter 1:1

In the opening of his second epistle, Peter describes Jesus in the highest sense possible: *"Simon Peter, a bond-servant and apostle of Jesus Christ,*[36] *to those who have received a faith of the same kind as ours, by the righteousness of our God and Savior, Jesus Christ."*

The question that arises is this: In the phrase "our God and Savior," are there two persons spoken of (God the Father and Jesus) or one person (Jesus alone)?[37] We encountered this issue in the interpretation of Titus 2:13, and found that the one definite article ("the") governed both nouns ("great God" and "Savior"). In chapter 5 (under Titus 2:13) I quoted Granville Sharp's first rule concerning the definite article. Here it is again:

> When the copulative *kai* ["and"] connects two nouns of the same case, if the article ὁ [*ho,* "the"] or any of its cases, precedes the first of the said nouns or participles, and is not repeated before the second noun or participle, the latter always relates to the same person that is expressed or described by the first noun or participle: i.e. it denotes a farther description of the first-named person.[38]

In 2 Peter 1:1 we have the definite article preceding the first noun, *not* repeated after the second noun, and connected by *kai* ("and").[39]

The Holy Spirit in the Letters of Paul [Peabody, Mass.: Hendrickson Publishers, 1994], 14-15).

[36]For the theological implications of "a servant of Jesus Christ," see chap. 5 under Romans 1:1.

[37]See Reymond, *Jesus, Divine Messiah,* 288.

[38]Taken from Daniel B. Wallace, *Greek Grammar Beyond the Basics: An Exegetical Syntax of the New Testament,* 271.

[39]Gr. *tou theou hēmōn kai sōtēros Iēsou Christou,* τοῦ θεοῦ ἡμῶν καὶ σωτῆρος Ἰησοῦ Χριστοῦ. Note that there is one definite article (*tou*) before

According to Sharp's rule, the phrase "God and Savior" refers to one person. And, just as in Titus 2:13, that person is expressly named ("Jesus Christ").

Those who object to this number more than a few, but they nevertheless must answer why it is that they translate 2 Peter 1:11 as "our Lord and Savior Jesus Christ,"[40] where the same *one article/two noun relationship* occurs. Here "Lord" and "Savior" refer to the same person. They should also answer why it would be theologically outside Peter to refer to Christ as God and Savior, especially in light of the doxology of 2 Peter 3:18: "... Jesus Christ. To Him be the glory, both now and to the day of eternity. Amen."[41] Further, Peter in the very next verse (1:2[42]) *without question* separates the Father and the Son ("of God and of Jesus our Lord"[43]). The point is that in 1:1 he had within his grasp the grammatical ability to make "God" refer to the Father and

---

the first noun (*theou*) that is not repeated before the second noun (*sōteros*), and that the two nouns are connected by *kai*.

[40]Gr. *tou kuriou hēmōn kai sōteros Iesou Christou*, τοῦ κυρίου ἡμῶν καὶ σωτῆρος ᾿Ιησοῦ Χριστοῦ. See also 2 Pet. 2:20 ("knowledge of the Lord and Savior Jesus Christ"), 3:2 ("the commandment of the Lord and Savior"), and 3:18 ("knowledge of our Lord and Savior Jesus Christ"). Here all acknowledge that Christ is the sole referent. This same syntactical relationship occurs in 1 Pet. 1:3, this time concerning the Father: *ho theos kai patēr* (ὁ θεὸς καὶ πατήρ, "the God and Father..."). All translations here acknowledge one person, namely the Father, as the referent. See A. T. Robertson, *A Grammar of the Greek New Testament in the Light of Historical Research* (Nashville, Tenn.: Broadman Press, 1934), 785-86, and Wallace, *Greek Grammar*, 276-77. See also Robertson's article, "The Greek Article and the Deity of Christ," *The Expositor*, 8th series, 21 (1921): 185. Moreover, the KJV, RV, RSV, NASB, NEB, NIV, and the NKJV translate 2 Pet. 1:1 as referring to Christ (see Reymond, *Jesus, Divine Messiah*, 288).

[41]See Reymond, *Jesus, Divine Messiah*, 288-89.

[42]Incidentally, but not less importantly, Peter in this verse places Christ on equal par with the Father as the object of a Christian's knowledge. This strongly implies the ontological oneness, the equality, of the Father and the Son.

[43]Gr. *tou theou kai Iēsou tou kuriou hēmōn*, τοῦ θεοῦ καὶ ᾿Ιησοῦ τοῦ κυρίου ἡμῶν. Notice *two* definite articles, one before *theou,* and one before *kuriou.* One definite article for each noun relates two separate persons.

"Savior" to the Son, as in 1:2, but he did not.[44] As 2 Peter 1:1 stands, Peter acknowledges the deity of Christ.

2 Peter 3:18

"But grow in the grace and knowledge of our Lord and Savior Jesus Christ. To Him be the glory, both now and to the day of eternity. Amen." Second Peter begins with a recognition of the deity of Christ, and ends with a confession that is only fitting for Him.

First, grace is given by Christ to His covenant people. It is His grace to give by His divine prerogative, since it is Yahweh Himself who is full of grace and truth (see Exod. 34:6 cf. John 1:14[45]). *Second,* believers are to grow in the knowledge of Christ. *He* is the object of knowledge. With the Old Testament command given by Yahweh to know *Him* (Jeremiah 9:23-24), this admonition by Peter places the Son in the position of deity.[46] *Third* is the ascription of *eternal* glory to Jesus Christ. These words of praise can only be given to Yahweh, for He alone is worthy to be glorified for all eternity (Ps. 86:12).

Christology of 1 John

In all probability John wrote this letter as a polemic against Cerinthus.[47] The letter's emphasis concerning the physical manifestation of the Son (1 John 1:1-2), the reality of sin (1:8, 10), a warning against separating Jesus and the Christ[48] (2:22), and the fact that Jesus came by both water *and* blood (5:6),[49] make Cerinthianism,

---

[44]He could have done so simply by placing "our Savior" *after* "Jesus Christ," as he did with "our Lord" in 1:2, or by placing a definite article in front of "Savior" (thus rendering Granville Sharp's first rule inapplicable and referring to two persons). See Reymond, *Jesus, Divine Messiah,* 288.

[45]See chap. 4 under John 1:14.

[46]See chap. 5 under Philippians 3:8, 10.

[47]See Introduction, n. 12, and chap. 1 under Christian Science, for summaries of the teachings of Cerinthus.

[48]Thus viewing Jesus and Christ as two separate beings.

[49]1 John 5:6 states that *Jesus Christ* (note "Jesus Christ," not just "Jesus" or "Christ") "came by water and blood... not with the water only, but with the water and with the blood." Cerinthus taught that the heavenly "Christ" rested upon Jesus at His baptism, but left Him at His crucifixion. In this verse John

or at the very least incipient Gnosticism, the most likely target for John's anathemas.

In 1 John there are a few christological themes strongly implying the deity of Christ that have already been examined from other New Testament writings. For this reason they do not have to be repeated in detail, only mentioned.

First John 1:3b tells of the fellowship that believers have "with the Father, and with His Son Jesus Christ." John writes that Jesus is the Father's Son (see also 1:7; 2:22, 23, 24; 3:8, 23; 4:9, 10, 14, 15; 5:5, 9, 10, 11, 12, 13, 20). As in his Gospel, John's designation of Christ as the Son of God implies ontological oneness and equality with the Father.[50]

John here places the Son on equal par with the Father, for we have fellowship not only with the Father, but also with the Son.[51] In 1 John 2:13 John writes, "I am writing to you, fathers, because you know Him who has been from the beginning. I am writing to you, young men, because you have overcome the evil one. I have written to you, children, because you know the Father." In the introduction it is Christ who is "from the beginning" (1:1).[52] Christ therefore is "Him" who is known by Christians, a common Old Testament theme where *Yahweh* is the one who is known by His covenant people.[53] Yet at the same time the Father must also be known. Knowledge of the Father, however, can only come through the knowledge of the Son (John 17:3), and by believers being "in" the Son (1 John 5:20[54]). This further implies the

---

refutes this heresy by stating that Jesus came with water (baptism) *and* blood (crucifixion).

[50]See chap. 2 under John 1:1, and chap. 4 under John 1:14, 1:18, 5:18, and 10:30.

[51]See chap. 5 under 1 Thessalonians 1:1.

[52]Some take this phrase in 1 John 2:13 to refer to the Father. This is possible, as 2:13a may be synonymous with 2:13b ("because you know the Father"). But because "from the beginning" has already referred to the Son, there is good reason to view "you know Him who has been from the beginning" as referring to Christ, and "because you know the Father" as referring to the Father. If this is the case, this is further proof of the equality of the Son with the Father, for *both* are the object of one's knowledge.

[53]See chap. 5 under Philippians 3:8, 10.

[54]"And we know that the Son of God has come, and has given us understanding, in order that we might know Him who is true, and we are in Him who is true, in His Son Jesus Christ. This [Gr. *houtos*, οὗτός] is the true God and eternal life." Debate exists over whether this last phrase refers to the

ontological oneness and equality of the Father and the Son, for to know the Son is to know the Father. All this is evidence that the Christology of 1 John is as high as any other New Testament book.

Father or the Son. Proponents of the former suggest that *houtos* ("this one," or "He") refers back to "Him who is true" (*ton alēthinon*, τὸν ἀληθινόν), namely the Father. Proponents of the latter suggest that *houtos* refers back to its nearest antecedent, namely "Jesus Christ." I prefer the latter, though with caution.

The first question is, "what is the nearest antecedent to *houtos*?" Without doubt it is "Jesus Christ." Robert Reymond makes the point that "it is an exegetically sound principle to find the antecedent of demonstrative pronouns in the nearest possible noun unless there are compelling reasons for not doing so. There are no such reasons here, as there are in the oft-cited counter examples of 1 John 2:22 or 2 John 7..." (*Jesus, Divine Messiah,* 311). Thus, there are no grammatical reasons why Jesus Christ should *not* be the referent of *houtos*.

This leads to the next logical step, that being to determine whether or not there is a theological problem with *houtos* referring back to Jesus Christ. *First,* in the *overall* context of the New Testament (including 1 John) there should be no problem with calling Jesus God. *Second,* the Gospel of John in no uncertain terms calls Jesus God. It thus is no surprise to find this very same apostle giving to Jesus the title "the true God." (Some cite as evidence to the contrary the fact that in John 17:3 the apostle calls the Father "the only true God." Consider though the fact that John applies to Christ the phrase "the true one" [Rev. 3:7, 14; 19:11], a phrase used to describe God [Rev. 6:10]).

Finally, further grammatical considerations *and* the context of 1 John show at least the plausibility of the view that the last phrase refers to Christ. Grammatically "God" and "eternal life" stand under one definite article. This makes the title "the true God and eternal life" refer to one person (pointed out by Reymond, *Jesus, Divine Messiah,* 311). With the nearest antecedent being "Jesus Christ," the title is therefore applied to Him. Contextually, Jesus is called *"the eternal life* which was with the Father" (1:2). In a way reminiscent of his Gospel, which begins and ends with the assertion that Christ is God (John 1:1; 20:28), John in his first letter begins and ends with the assertion that Jesus is the "eternal life." This being the case, and since the one definite article governs both "God" and "eternal life," Jesus is here called God. Murray J. Harris, however, reaches the conclusion that the last sentence of 1 John 5:20 refers to the Father. His discussion of the issues is excellent. See his *Jesus as God* (Grand Rapids, Baker Book House, 1992), 239-53.

Revelation 1:5b-6 [Revelation 5:12]

We come now to the Revelation of Jesus Christ. Here we shall find a fresh set of Old Testament designations of Yahweh that are ascribed to Christ, testifying to His incarnate deity. We also find recurring theological themes already found in the previous books. We begin with just that, as Revelation 1:5b-6 gives to us another ascription of glory to the Son of God,[55] an ascription that rightly belongs to one who is God! *"To Him who loves us, and released us from our sins by His blood, and He has made us to be a kingdom, priests to His God and Father; to Him be the glory and the dominion forever and ever. Amen."* In addition we shall examine Revelation 5:12: *"Worthy is the Lamb that was slain to receive power and riches and wisdom and might and honor and glory and blessing."*

John's adoration for his risen Savior is evident in his words in 1:5a. Christ is "the faithful witness, the first-born from the dead, and the ruler of the kings of the earth." This last designation implies Christ's deity, for John not only alludes to the terminology of Daniel 2:47 (Daniel's God is "Lord of kings"), but sets Christ over those Roman kings who would claim the designation of (or be designated by others as) "Lord and God." G. E. Ladd comments:

> The emperors were beginning to use the titles of deity. Julius Caesar, Augustus, Claudius, Vespasian, and Titus had been officially declared divine after their death by the Roman Senate, and the last three had used the term *DIVUS* (divine) on their coins. Domitian, the emperor when John wrote, had advanced this tendency by requesting that he be addressed as *Dominus et Deus* (Lord and God).[56]

"To Him [Christ] be the glory and the dominion forever and ever." Here the Son of God is singled out as the one to whom all glory and dominion is given. Only the LORD is worthy of such praise. First Chronicles 29:11 reads, "Thine, O LORD (*Yahweh*), is the greatness

---

[55]Agreeing are Harris (*Jesus as God*, 146, n. 6), Robertson (*Word Pictures in the New Testament*, 287), G. E. Ladd (*A Commentary on the Revelation of John* [Grand Rapids, Mich.: Wm. B. Eerdmans Publishing Co., 1972], 26), and Alan F. Johnson (in Frank E. Gaebelein, ed., *The Expositor's Bible Commentary*, 12 vols. [Grand Rapids, Mich.: Zondervan Publishing House, 1981], 12:421-22), to name a few.

[56]*Commentary on the Revelation of John*, 25-26.

and the power and the glory and the victory and the majesty, indeed
everything that is in the heavens and the earth; Thine is the dominion,
O LORD, and Thou dost exalt Thyself as head over all." In both
Revelation 1:6 and Revelation 5:12 all praise due to Yahweh is given to
the Son.[57] To give Him glory is to testify to His mighty works, which
are mentioned in verses 5-7. Verses 5 and 6 were mentioned above, and
verse 7 has Jesus once again riding on the clouds (a designation of
deity; see Isa. 19:1; Dan. 7:13[58]) at His second coming. Moreover,

---

[57]In Rev. 5:13 both the Father and the Son are placed on an equality, as
they both are given "blessing and honor and glory and dominion forever and
ever." Whatever praise the Father is to receive is to be given to the Son as well.
In Revelation 5:14 we are told that "the elders fell down and worshipped." In
light of v. 13 there is every reason to think that the Son is here worshipped
along with the Father!

[58]Verse 7 reads: "Behold, He is coming with the clouds, and every eye will
see Him, even those who pierced Him; and all the tribes of the earth will mourn
over Him." Both Dan. 7:13 and Zech. 12:10 are used here by John. In Dan.
7:13 we read of a "Son of Man" who comes with the clouds of heaven. The
glory of Yahweh was always associated with His presence in the cloud. This
Son of Man then approaches the "Ancient of Days" and is presented before
Him. The scenario is one where Yahweh the Son receives what is rightfully His
as heir of all creation. In Daniel 7:14, as in John, dominion and glory belong to
the Son, for the express purpose "that all the peoples, nations, and men of every
language might serve Him" (and obey Him; cf. 7:27). In Zech. 12:10 it is
Yahweh who is pierced ("They will look on Me, whom they have pierced"); in
Rev. 1:7 it is the Son who was pierced.

Some object to calling Jesus Yahweh on the basis of Daniel 7:13-14. The
objection results from two points in the text. *First* is that the Son of Man *comes
up* to the Ancient of Days, implying therefore that He is not Yahweh. *Second* is
that glory and dominion are *given* to the Son, implying that He did not have it
previously and that therefore the Son cannot be Yahweh. But there are several
problems with such an objection. The fact that the Son comes up to the Ancient
of Days does not *of necessity* imply that the Son is not of the same essence as
the Ancient of Days, for the Son can Himself be deity and be distinct from the
Ancient of Days. Indeed the Bible teaches that there is one divine essence that
is three distinct persons. By the Son being "given" dominion and glory, Daniel
does not intend to teach that the Son is not deity. Rather, the intent here is in
the context of the eschaton, the second coming. Did not Christ have glory with
the Father "before the world was"? Surely He did (John 17:5), and in light of
Yahweh stating that He would not give His glory to another (Isa. 42:8; 48:11),
we must believe that the Son *eternally* had glory with the Father. So what shall
we make of the fact that at the eschaton the Son is given glory? The answer lies

Jesus exercises "dominion" over all things, and as such He is Yahweh (see 1 Chron. 29:11), Sovereign of the universe (see 1 Chron. 29:12). All this renders inescapable the conclusion that the Son is true deity. Were such language to be used for someone other than God, it would not *border* on blasphemy, it would most certainly *be* blasphemy.

Revelation 1:17

Before verse 17 the risen and glorified Son of God appears to John. "In words drawn almost entirely from imagery used in Daniel, Ezekiel, and Isaiah of God's majesty and power,"[59] Jesus is described as "one like a son of man" (v. 13), "His head and His hair white like wool, like snow; and His eyes like a flame of fire" (v. 14), "His feet like burning bronze... and His voice like the sound of many waters" (v. 15). In verse 17, John, overtaken by Christ's glorified majesty, falls *"at His feet as a dead man. And He laid His right hand upon me, saying, 'Do not be afraid; I am the first and the last.'"*

"One like a son of man" (v. 13) comes from both Ezekiel 1:26 and Daniel 7:13 (Ezekiel uses the phrase "appearance of a man" as does Dan. 8:18). Though the phrase "Son of Man" may mean simply "a man,"[60] we should not limit the phrase to that meaning, for the biblical authors associated deity with this phrase as well.[61] As mentioned, several of the descriptive phrases used in Revelation 1:13-16 to describe Christ are used in the Old Testament to describe God. John describes this Son of Man in the same way as the Ancient of Days

---

in the death and resurrection of the *incarnate* Son. This is to say, as the eternal Son of God *before the incarnation,* He always had glory and dominion with the Father. But *His incarnate state* brings with it glory and dominion for the *God-Man* Jesus in an existence never before experienced by Him (see Phil. 2:5-11 in chap. 5). The "giving" of glory and dominion to the Son therefore has to do with the *exalted God-Man,* as heir of all creation, receiving glory and dominion by virtue of His life, death, and resurrection (see Matt. 28:18), *not* with His "not having these" beforehand as the eternal Word who was God.

[59]Alan F. Johnson, *The Expositor's Bible Commentary,* 12:426.
[60]See Robert Reymond, *Jesus, Divine Messiah,* 313.
[61]See the many statements in the Gospels where Jesus uses the phrase as the pronoun "I" (for example, Matt. 24:30). This being true, it is the Son, *both God and man,* who makes such use of the phrase. Moreover, in the example here given, the Son of Man will be coming on the clouds of the sky. As has been discussed, this is an attribute of Yahweh (see Isa. 19:1).

(Rev. 1:14 cf. Dan. 7:9). Note as well that in Ezekiel the phrase "appearance of a man" is associated with deity, as the "appearance" (1:26) is synonymous with "the glory of the LORD" (1:28).

G. E. Ladd states that the phrase "His head and His hair were white like wool, like snow" (v. 14) represents Christ's deity. "Christ," Ladd says, "shares this feature with God the Father himself (Dan. 7:9)."[62] In this same verse Christ is also said to have "eyes like a flame of fire," not taken from Daniel 7 but from Daniel 10:6[63]: "His body also was like beryl, his face had the appearance of lightning, his eyes were like flaming torches, his arms and feet like the gleam of polished bronze, and the sound of his words like the sound of a tumult." Here as well the case is made for the deity of Christ.[64] Daniel 10:16 identifies the messenger as "Lord,"[65] and the phenomena that accompany the appearance of the messenger in Daniel 10:6 show Him to be God when interpreted in light of the theophany[66] of Ezekiel 1,[67] which describe "the glory of the LORD" (Ezek. 1:28)[68] as the shining of His body (cf. Ezek. 1:26; Rev. 1:14-16), His radiance (cf. Ezek. 1:26-28; Rev. 1:14-16), His flaming eyes (cf. Ezek. 1:27; Rev. 1:14[69]), His arms and feet as bronze (cf. Ezek. 1:7, 27; Rev. 1:15), and His voice like the sound of a tumult (cf. Ezek. 1:24; 43:2;[70] Rev. 1:15). Keil and Delitzsch offer "that

---

[62]*A Commentary on the Revelation of John,* 33. See also R. T. France, *Jesus and the Old Testament* (London: Tyndale Press, 1971), 203. France states that in Rev. 1:14 "the actual personal characteristics of the Ancient of Days [in Dan. 7:9-10] are used in describing the exalted Jesus."

[63]See also Ezek. 1:13. Both Old Testament contexts, and Revelation as well, have to do with judgment!

[64]See Keil and Delitzsch, *Commentary on the Old Testament,* 10 vols. (Grand Rapids, Mich.: Wm. B. Eerdmans Publishing Co., reprinted, July 1985), 9:410.

[65]Heb. *adoni,* אֲדֹנִי.

[66]Meaning "an appearance of God."

[67]See also Ezek. 8:2.

[68]See Keil and Delitzsch, *Commentary on the Old Testament,* 9:410. I am indebted to them for the following.

[69]See also Rev. 2:18, though here John calls Jesus "the Son of God." In this passage, as in the other messages to the churches of the Book of Revelation, it is Jesus who acts as divine judge, a theme suggested by "flaming eyes."

[70]See also 4 Ezra 6:17.

the man[71] seen by Daniel was no common angel-prince, but a manifestation of Jehovah, *i.e.* the Logos."[72]

What happens at the beginning of Revelation 1:17 also has its Old Testament parallels. John falls at Christ's feet as if dead, for He is in the presence of the glorious Lord. Ezekiel does the same when in the presence of "the appearance of the likeness of the glory of the LORD" (Ezek. 1:28, further tying the two contexts together). Thus it is no surprise to read Jesus' own words to describe Himself in Revelation 1:17: "I am the first and the last" (see also 2:8; 22:13). And here is a most explicit statement evidencing Christ's deity. In Isaiah 44:6 and 48:12 it is Yahweh who states these words![73] Jesus' connecting[74] words in verse 18 ("[I am] the living One;[75] and I was dead, and behold, I am alive forevermore") make it definite that He is the speaker of the words "the first and the last" and thus God in the truest sense.

Revelation 2:7b

Here Jesus states, *"To him who overcomes, I will grant to eat of the tree of life, which is in the paradise of God."*

W*hose* prerogative is it to grant such a thing? In the paradise of God it was Yahweh who was the sovereign of the tree of life, and it was His to grant to eat of it as He willed (Gen. 2:9, 16-17). In the same sense, when paradise is restored, Jesus will grant to whom He wills the right to eat of the tree of life.[76]

---

[71]Heb. *ish*, אִישׁ in original.

[72]*Commentary on the Old Testament*, 9:410.

[73]The phrase in Rev. 1:17 and in Rev. 22:13 follows the Hebrew entirely and the LXX in part.

[74]Verse 18 begins with *kai* (καὶ, "and").

[75]The present participle *zōn* (ζῶν) carries the sense of "living forever more." See Rev. 4:9 where "the Lord God, the Almighty" is given glory and honor (see 1:6) and is described as the One "who lives forever and ever." This designation is appropriate for the LORD (Deut. 32:40).

[76]The same occurs in Rev. 2:17. Here Jesus gives of "the hidden manna" that Yahweh promised to give His covenant people (Exod. 16:31-33; see also Ps. 78:24), and gives the overcomer "a new name," reminiscent of Yahweh's promise in Isa. 56:5, 62:2, and 65:15. Several other passages in Revelation witness the Son exercising His divine prerogative of "granting" or "giving" to overcomers what He wills (2:26, 28; 3:5 [cf. Exod. 32:32-33; Deut. 29:20; Pss. 9:5; 69:28]; 3:12, 21). In the economy of the Triune God, the Son is in these

Revelation 2:23

A string of attributes are here given to Christ, yet it is Yahweh alone who is able to sovereignly perform them. Jesus claims for Himself that which only the LORD has done, can do, and will do: *"And I will kill her children with pestilence; and all the churches will know that I am He who searches the minds and hearts; and I will give to each one of you according to your deeds."*

The three divine acts mentioned above have their Old Testament parallels. The killing of masses with pestilence by Yahweh (or the potential of such) is found in Exodus 5:3, 9:15, Leviticus 26:25, Numbers 14:12, Deuteronomy 28:21, 2 Samuel 24:15, and Ezekiel 33:27. The searching of the hearts and minds by Yahweh is found in Psalms 7:9, 26:2, 1 Samuel 16:7, and Jeremiah 11:20, 17:10. The rendering of judgment by Yahweh according to one's deeds is found in Job 34:11, Psalms 28:4, 62:12, and Proverbs 24:12. Christ, as divine judge and by His divine will, accomplishes all the above.

Revelation 3:19

"Those whom I love, I reprove and discipline; be zealous therefore, and repent." By this statement Christ claims to do that which Yahweh does.

Consider Proverbs 3:11-12:[77] "My son, do not reject the discipline of the LORD [*Yahweh*], or loathe His reproof, for whom the LORD loves He reproves, even as a father, the son in whom He delights." Interesting as well is that the writer of Hebrews applies this quotation of Proverbs 3:12 *to God.* Hebrews 12:6 contains the quote, which is then interpreted in 12:7: "It is for discipline that you endure; God deals with you as with sons..." Jesus must here again be viewed as ontologically equal to God the Father, for functionally He does that which God does (Heb. 12:6-7), and that which Yahweh is said to do in the Old Testament (Prov. 3:12).

---

passages "taking the lead," implying His Godness and essential equality with both the Father and the Spirit, while the Father and the Spirit defer to Him in this ministry (see chap. 4, nn. 68, 71).

[77]See LXX of Prov. 3:11-12, where the same Greek verbs (*elengchō,* ἐλέγχω and *paideuō,* παιδεύω) are used in Rev. 3:19.

Revelation 19:16 [17:14]

Revelation 19:11-19 describes the coming of Christ. Here He comes as eschatological judge, and His acts imply that He is *Yahweh* the Son. In righteousness He judges and wages war (v. 11 cf. Isa. 11:4), He will come with the hosts of heaven following Him (v. 14 cf. Zech. 14:5), and He will smite the nations with His mouth (v. 15 cf. Isa. 11:4). Jesus is also called "the Word of God" (v. 13), a phrase found in John's Gospel prologue meaning God the Son (John 1:1).

In Revelation 19:16, John ends his description of the glorified Son, calling Him *"King of kings, and Lord of lords"* (in Rev. 17:14 the order of the two phrases is reversed). John means to communicate Christ's absolute sovereignty.[78] The risen Son of God is King over all kings (see Zech. 14:9: *"Yahweh* will be king over all the earth"), and Lord over all lords. John has no difficulty at all with the phrase applying to Christ, even in light of Deuteronomy 10:17, where *Yahweh* is "God of gods and the Lord of lords" (see also Ps. 136:1, 3). How is it that John can apply this title to Christ, knowing full well the Old Testament restriction on such a practice if the recipient of the title is not Yahweh (cf. 1 Tim. 6:15, where the title is given to the Father)? It can only be because John's Christ is God the Son.

Revelation 22:12

"Behold, I am coming quickly, and My reward is with Me, to render to every man according to what he has done."

Jesus is the one "coming quickly" (see 22:20). Therefore He is the speaker in this verse. In His statement, "My reward is with Me, to render to every man according to what he has done," he speaks as

---

[78]See Ladd, *A Commentary on the Revelation of John,* 256. Additionally, at the consummation of the ages, the Son's absolute sovereignty is shared with the Father, once again showing the Son's equality with the Father. In Revelation 21:22 the new Jerusalem will have no temple, "for the Lord God, the Almighty, *and the Lamb,* are its temple." In Revelation 21:23 the city will be illumined by both the Father *and* the Son. Finally, in Revelation 21:24, 26 the kings of the earth will bring their glory and the glory and honor of the nations into the city under subjection to the Father and the Son, for the throne in heaven is "the throne of God *and* of the Lamb" (Rev. 22:1, 3, emphases added here and in the other citations).

Yahweh speaks. Isaiah 40:10 and 62:11 state that "His [*Yahweh's*] reward is with Him, and His recompense before Him." Psalm 28:4 is a plea to Yahweh to "Requite them according to their work and according to the evil of their practices; requite them according to the deeds of their hands; repay them their recompense." In Jeremiah 17:10 the LORD (*Yahweh*) "give[s] to each man according to his ways, according to the results of his deeds."

Revelation 22:13

Yahweh the Son now states, *"I am the Alpha and the Omega, the first and the last, the beginning and the end."*[79]

All three phrases confirm the deity of Christ. With "I am the Alpha and the Omega," Christ describes Himself in the very same way the Father does in Revelation 1:8[80] and 21:6. "The first and the last" are Yahweh's words in Isaiah 44:6 and 48:12 (see on Revelation 1:17). The last part of the verse ("the beginning and the end"), like the first, is used to describe God the Father in 21:6. Christ, like the Father, is God, the Alpha and the Omega, the beginning and the end. Again, the ease with which John applies to Christ the attributes that the Father possesses cannot be ignored. As the Son He shares in the nature of the Father. The Son is God, and accordingly the Book of Revelation ends with the prayer that *His* grace be with all (22:21).

---

[79]All three phrases may be viewed as synonymous.

[80]See William Hendricksen, *More than Conquerors* (Grand Rapids, Mich.: Baker Book House, 1982), 54-55, for the view that in Rev. 1:8 it is Christ, rather than the Father, who speaks. For the view that it is the Father who speaks in 1:8, see Ladd, *Commentary on the Revelation of John*, 29, Robertson, *Word Pictures in the New Testament*, 288, and Johnson, *The Expositor's Bible Commentary*, 12:423.

Chapter 8

Heresy and the Humanity and Work of Christ

"So he [Jesus] became identified with Christ, a man no longer, but at one with God. The man was an illusion..."—The "Voice," A Course In Miracles

"How may it be proved that Christ is really a man? He is called man.—1 Tim. ii. 5."—A. A. Hodge, Outlines of Theology

The Church affirms, because of the testimony of Scripture, that in the one person of Jesus of Nazareth are two natures, both human and deity. Over and over again Scripture reveals to us that Jesus Christ is God the Son. It also reveals the *absolute necessity* of believing that Jesus Christ is God the Son (John 8:24). In the following examples of cults, heretical expressions of the atonement, the virgin birth, salvation, Christ's mediatorial role, and His resurrection arise because of denials of His deity. Over and over again the Bible tells us something more of Christ. He is fully human. His full humanity is also an *absolute necessity* if His people are to be redeemed in every aspect of their humanity (Heb. 2:14-17[1]). In other words (and as is the case with His deity), it is imperative that Jesus be human in the fullest sense if His work (His birth, life, death, resurrection and ascension) is to apply to the elect of God, and His righteousness imputed to them.

Further, the testimony of Scripture is that Jesus was resurrected in the *same* body that died on the cross, and that He ascended to the right hand of the Father in this *same* body, though now glorified since the resurrection. The good news is that Christ is the only way of salvation and the great high priest and mediator between God and man. In order to be saved one must place faith in Christ alone, in His sacrifice on the cross for sin. But heresies abound that challenge the humanity and/or work of Christ, placing those who believe them outside the camp of Christianity.

Jehovah's Witnesses

The Humanity of Christ

Though the Witnesses state that Jesus was a perfect human, thus leading us to believe that Christ was fully human, there are some questions that to my knowledge remain unanswered. First, do the Witnesses believe Jesus to be *only* a man? In their doctrine of the incarnation, Michael the Archangel, the first creature created by Jehovah, ceased to be in the form of an archangel and his "life essence" was transferred into the womb of Mary. This produced "the perfect man, Jesus." But what of this "life essence"? What happened to it? Was it *mixed* with the humanness of Jesus, or do we have in the one person of Jesus two *distinct* natures, an archangel nature and a human nature?[2]

If the Witnesses state that the two natures are mixed, they really do not have a Jesus who is truly human. Rather, Jesus is an *angelized* man. And if so, could Jesus really represent *them* on the torture stake[3] and provide for them a "corresponding ransom" (to use their phrase)? If

---

[1]See the next chapter for an exposition of this passage.

[2]The Christian doctrine of Christ is that He possesses two natures, human and deity, in their fullest capacities. These two natures are neither mixed nor separated, but *united* in the one person of Christ. More on this in the next chapter.

[3]Jehovah's Witnesses do not believe Jesus was crucified on a cross. Rather, He was crucified on an upright pole, a torture stake.

they believe the two natures are distinct and joined in union with one another in the one person of Jesus, then their theology at least affords them the opportunity of having a true human being on the torture stake.

One question regarding Jesus' humanity, however, *has* been answered. That question is, "Is Jesus a man *now*?" No. Jehovah's Witnesses do not believe in Christ's perpetual humanity beginning from the incarnation. Concerning Christ's ascension following His resurrection, the Witnesses state, "After dematerializing his fleshly body, he ascends to heaven as a spirit person."[4] Further, "While Jesus began his ascent in a physical form, thus being visible to his watching disciples, there is no basis for assuming that he continued to retain a material form after the cloud[5] interposed itself."[6] Thus, in their denial of the present humanity of Christ, the Witnesses do not have a "faithful high priest" who is fully human (Heb. 2:14-17).

Salvation

Jehovah's Witnesses believe that Jesus was a perfect man (but see the previous section), thus living a perfect life. He then offered Himself on the "torture stake" as a "corresponding ransom" to wipe out inherited sin and death caused by Adam's disobedience. This "opens the way for mankind to gain eternal life."[7] Though the Witnesses are insistent that we can never *earn* eternal life,[8] their theology is suspect when phrases and words such as "opens the way" and "gains" are used.

---

[4]No authors given, *The Greatest Man Who Ever Lived* (New York: Watchtower Bible and Tract Society of New York, Inc., 1991), section 131.

[5]Rather than seeing the biblical intent of the cloud at the ascension in Acts 1:9, and His return in Rev. 1:7 (the cloud associated with the presence of God), the Witnesses interpret the cloud as meaning that Jesus' return will be invisible. "What is indicated by 'clouds'? Invisibility. When an airplane is in a thick cloud or above the clouds, people on the ground usually cannot see it, although they may hear the roar of the engines" (no authors given, *Reasoning from the Scriptures* [Watchtower Bible and Tract Society of New York, Inc., 1985], 343).

[6]*Reasoning from the Scriptures*, 343.

[7]This statement may be found on page 2 of every current *The Watchtower* magazine.

[8]See *Reasoning from the Scriptures*, 216.

The Resurrection and Ascension of Christ

They deny the bodily resurrection and ascension of Christ. After His death on the stake, say the Witnesses, Jesus' body was placed in the tomb. Sometime during the three days His body was disposed.[9] Jesus then "materialized" different bodies[10] (resembling the body He had before His death) in order to appear to His disciples and others during the forty days prior to His ascension. Then, as mentioned earlier, before His ascension He dematerialized His last fleshly body, ascending to the right hand of Jehovah as a spirit person.

The Mediatorship of Christ

Implicit in the above is a rejection of Christ's present humanity. This renders obsolete His great high priesthood and mediatorial role, since biblically both are predicated upon His humanity. This now leads to an interesting point in Witness theology, the "two classes."

The "heavenly class" numbers 144,000 (taken from Revelation 7:4-8; 14:1-3). They are the only ones who have been born again and are in heaven (or still living and going there) reigning with the spirit person Jesus. They as well are not human, but spirit persons. The remaining class of people, the "earthly class," comprise all the faithful, who, after proving themselves loyal to Jehovah,[11] will gain eternal life and live forever as humans in paradise on earth. Now the main point: *Jesus is not the mediator of the earthly class, but only of the 144,000 in heaven.*[12] Granting their denial of the present humanity of Christ, this would make sense, since a spirit cannot mediate between humanity and God.

---

[9]Ibid., 217.

[10]Ibid.

[11]Thus the charge of works salvation by critics of Jehovah's Witnesses' theology (see *The Watchtower,* April 15, 1981, p. 23). See also *The Watchtower,* December 15, 1972: "So, recognition of that governing body [a group of men leading all Jehovah's Witnesses] and its place in God's theocratic arrangement of things is necessary for submission to the headship of God's Son." It seems that there is something else beside God in which to place one's trust.

[12]See *The Watchtower* magazine, April 1, 1979, p. 31.

Mormonism

The Church of Jesus Christ of Latter-day Saints' christological formulations on the humanity and work of Christ are, sadly, unbiblical. We have seen in earlier chapters that the Mormon Jesus is the firstborn spirit child of Elohim and heavenly Mother, a god and goddess who were once mortal humans but now are resurrected deities with body parts. This spirit child Jesus then took a body of flesh on earth by the literal sexual act of God the Father and the virgin Mary. We now examine further the Mormon Jesus' "humanity."

The Humanity of Christ

From the Mormon doctrine of humanity we learn that we all, including Jesus, preexisted as spirit children before coming to this earth to take on flesh. According to Mormon theology, the spirit part of our makeup was pre-existent, and so it was with Jesus. But the key to recognizing that the Mormon Jesus is but *partially* human lies in noting what He was in His pre-existence as a spirit child. In differentiation with all other spirit children (who were *human* spirits), Jesus was a god[13] (His name was Jehovah[14]), and therefore was not a pre-existent *human* spirit. In a Mormon christological work, James E. Talmage states, "Throughout the period of retirement, He ate not, but chose to fast, that His mortal body might the more completely be subjected to His *divine* spirit."[15] Moreover, the Mormon Jesus is said to possess a

---

[13]*Doctrines of the Gospel: Student Manual* (Salt Lake City, Utah: The Church of Jesus Christ of Latter-day Saints, 1986), 10.

[14]See James E. Talmage, *Jesus the Christ* (Salt Lake City, Utah: The Church of Jesus Christ of Latter-day Saints, 1981), 32, and *Doctrines of the Gospel: Student Manual*, 9.

[15]Talmage, *Jesus the Christ*, 128, emphasis mine. This phrase is also used in Daniel H. Ludlow, ed., *Encyclopedia of Mormonism*, 4 vols. (New York: Macmillan, 1992), 2:725, s.v. "Mortal Jesus." The following quotations also indicate implicitly that Mormon Christology does not have a genuinely human Jesus: "The human family is unable to save itself. Divine law required the sacrifice of a sinless, infinite, and eternal being—a God—someone not dominated by the Fall, to redeem..." (ibid., 2:729, s.v. "Only Begotten in the Flesh"). "The Father [Mormon theology allows for Jesus the title of Father with certain qualifications] and the Son, the Spirit and the flesh, the God and the man—these titles, roles, and attributes are *blended* wondrously in one being,

single nature: "In His nature would be combined the powers of Godhood with the capacity and possibilities of mortality."[16] Though Talmage at other times refers to Christ as possessing a "dual nature,"[17] note that "nature" is in the singular. The consequence of this is that the Mormon Jesus is a divinized man. His divine pre-existent spirit takes the place of a human spirit. As such He is not fully human as we are.

The Virgin Birth

See chapter 3 under Mormonism.

Salvation and the Atonement

There are three kinds of salvation in Mormon theology, each resulting in habitation in one of three places in the afterlife (Celestial kingdom, Terrestrial kingdom, and Telestial kingdom).[18] First is *General* or *Unconditional,* and assures a place in either the Terrestrial or Telestial kingdoms by grace and no obedience requirements. Second is *Individual* or *Conditional,* which comes by grace and gospel obedience and results in a place in the Celestial kingdom to serve the gods and goddesses. Third is *Exaltation* or *Godhood* and is attained by grace, obedience, going to the Mormon temple to receive endowments (special spiritual blessings), and temple marriage.[19] The first

---

Jesus Christ" (ibid., 2:740, s.v. "Jesus Christ, Fatherhood and Sonship of," emphasis mine). "Like Jesus Christ, all mortals live in a state of humiliation....There is no ultimate disparity between the divine and human natures" (ibid., 1:272-73, s.v. "Christology").

[16]Talmage, *Jesus the Christ,* 81.

[17]Ibid., 129.

[18]The Celestial kingdom is where the gods and goddesses (most faithful Mormons) and their servants will dwell. The Terrestrial kingdom will be comprised of good people and lukewarm Mormons. The Telestial kingdom will contain the wicked of the world. None of these levels are hell, since hell is reserved only for the sons of perdition (see n. 20).

[19]See Bruce R. McConkie, *Mormon Doctrine* (Salt Lake City, Utah: Bookcraft, 1979), 669-72. The Celestial kingdom will be populated by the gods and goddesses (those faithful Mormons who have received the endowments in the Mormon temple and have been married in the temple). Those temple Mormons not married in the temple will also inhabit the Celestial kingdom, but only as servants of the gods and goddesses.

accomplishes a general resurrection (immortality) of all humanity with the exception of "the sons of perdition."[20] The second comes with works added and also results in immortality. The third is called "eternal life," attained by works as well, and as gods and goddesses these Mormons may procreate spirit children to populate their own planets.

For Mormons, Christ's atonement took place both on the cross and in the garden of Gethsemane.[21] His atonement, however, only guarantees the first type of salvation, that of General. The two remaining types of salvation, Individual and Godhood, require works on the part of the individual. Additionally, Christ's atonement provides merely *the basis* by which to attain one of these two states. Further, Christ had to *qualify* as the Redeemer[22] and atoned universally for the effects of Adam's sin only.[23] On this latter point, LeGrand Richards, a member of the Council of the Twelve Apostles of the Mormon Church, once stated: "Jesus Christ redeemed all from the fall; he paid the price; he offered himself as a ransom; he atoned for Adam's sin, leaving us responsible for our own sins."[24]

The Mormon view of Christ's atonement is compounded by the Mormon doctrine of "blood atonement." According to Joseph Fielding Smith's (tenth Prophet of the Mormon Church) three-volume work, *Doctrines of Salvation*, this doctrine was taught by Joseph Smith:

> Are you aware that there are certain sins[25] that man may commit for which the atoning blood of Christ does not avail? Do you know, too, that this doctrine is taught in the Book of Mormon?... Joseph Smith taught that there were certain sins so grievous that man may commit,

---

[20]Ibid., 669. This a modified version of universal salvation (see the above quotation from LeGrand Richards). The sons of perdition are Lucifer and his demons and "those in this life who gain a perfect knowledge of the divinity of the gospel cause...and who then link themselves with Lucifer and come out in open rebellion" (ibid.). I have heard it stated that these are Mormons who have participated in the temple ceremonies and have renounced Mormonism.
[21]See Ezra Taft Benson, *The Teachings of Ezra Taft Benson* (Salt Lake City, Utah: Bookcraft, 1988), 14.
[22]Ibid., 8.
[23]See McConkie, *Mormon Doctrine*, 62.
[24]LeGrand Richards, *A Marvelous Work and a Wonder* (Salt Lake City, Utah: Deseret Book Co., 1976), 98-99.
[25]In all the Mormon works I have consulted, I found that murder and adultery are at least two of these sins.

that they will place the transgressors beyond the power of the atonement of Christ. If these offenses are committed, then the blood of Christ will not cleanse them from their sins even though they repent. Therefore their only hope is to have their own blood shed to atone....This is scriptural doctrine, and is taught in all the standard works of the Church.[26]

Though for Mormons this is a "scriptural" doctrine, according to them it was never *practiced by the Mormon Church.*[27] But contrary to this, Brigham Young once stated, "I could refer you to plenty of instances where men have been righteously slain, in order to atone for their sins."[28]

Christian Science

Because of its pantheistic worldview,[29] Christian Science denies the true humanity of Jesus and His work of redemption.

---

[26]Joseph Fielding Smith, *Doctrines of Salvation,* 3 vols. (Salt Lake City, Utah: Bookcraft, 1954), 1:133, 135, emphases original.

[27]"There is not one historical instance of so-called blood atonement in this dispensation, nor has there been one event or occurrence whatever, of any nature, from which the slightest inference arises that any such practice either existed or was taught" (Bruce R. McConkie, *Mormon Doctrine,* 92). McConkie as well admits the doctrine is scriptural (92-93).

[28]Reported by G. D. Watt, et al., *Journals of Discourses,* 27 vols. (London: Latter-Day Saints Book Depot, 1857), 4:220. There is further proof that the Mormon view of Christ's atonement is unbiblical. Regarding the acceptance of Joseph Smith as a Prophet in order to have salvation, Joseph Fielding Smith stated that there is "no salvation without accepting Joseph Smith" (*Doctrines of Salvation,* 1:189). Brigham Young once stated "that no man or woman in this dispensation will ever enter into the celestial kingdom of God without the consent of Joseph Smith" (*Journals of Discourses,* 7:289).

[29]Oddly enough, Christian Science claims it is not pantheistic. A short work by Mary Baker Eddy, titled *Christian Science versus Pantheism* (Boston: The First Church of Christ, Scientist, 1926), tries in vain to support this claim.

The Humanity of Jesus[30]

The worldview of Christian Science, that of absolute pantheism, holds that absolutely all is God. As a result Christian Science must adhere to monism, which is the belief that there is only one reality, that being God. Mary Baker Eddy's "Scientific Statement of Being" is most revealing:

> There is no life, truth, intelligence, nor substance in matter. All is infinite Mind[31] and its infinite manifestation, for God is All-in-all. Spirit is real and eternal; matter is the unreal and temporal. Spirit is God, and man is His image and likeness. Therefore man is not material; he is spiritual.[32]

It may be difficult for the reader to understand what Christian Science means by this. Further statements by Eddy will help: "If God is Spirit, and God is All, surely there can be no matter..."[33] "Christian Science authorizes the logical conclusion drawn from the Scriptures, that there is in reality none besides the eternal, infinite God, good."[34] In other words, Christian Science reasoning is as follows: All is God; God is Spirit; therefore All is Spirit; if all is Spirit, the material is not real.

What, then, of the real, tangible humanity of Jesus? It does not exist.[35]

---

[30]For the Christian Science view of the virgin birth of Jesus, see chap. 3 under Christian Science, Unity School of Christianity, Religious Science.

[31]For Christian Scientists, "Mind" is a synonym for God (see Mary Baker Eddy, *Science and Health with Key to the Scriptures* [Boston: The First Church of Christ, Scientist, 1971], 587).

[32]*Science and Health*, 468.

[33]Mary Baker Eddy, *Unity of Good* (Boston: The First Church of Christ, Scientist, 1936), 31.

[34]Mary Baker Eddy, *Miscellaneous Writings* (Boston: The First Church of Christ, Scientist, 1924), 93.

[35]This is not new as a challenge to biblical Christology. The early Church addressed heretics who denied the real humanity of Christ. They were known as Docetists. They espoused the belief that Jesus only *seemed* (Docetists are so named from the Greek verb *dokeō*, δοκέω, "I seem") to have flesh. The wording in John 1:14, "the Word became flesh," is repugnant to Christian Scientists, just as it was to the early Docetists, if interpreted biblically.

The Mediatorship of Jesus

Without true and real humanity, the mediatorial role of Jesus stemming from a *real* incarnation is eliminated. Biblically, He must be true humanity if He is to mediate between God the Father and humanity.

The Atonement of Jesus and Salvation

Again, the absolute pantheistic worldview of Christian Science determines its view of the atonement. It wants nothing to do with an actual blood atonement, an actual shedding of *real* blood by the Son of God in order to atone for sin, because it wants nothing to do with a real incarnation. Mary Baker Eddy states that "the material blood of Jesus was no more efficacious to cleanse from sin when it was shed upon 'the accursed tree,' than when it was flowing in his veins as he went about his Father's business."[36] Eddy attacks the orthodox view "that God requires human blood to propitiate His justice and bring his mercy," calling it a "heathen conception."[37] For Eddy, Jesus' suffering "was not to appease the wrath of God, but to show the allness of Love[38] and the nothingness of hate, sin,[39] and death..."[40] Thus for Christian Science there is no real atonement.

It then follows that Christian Science's view of salvation is not biblical, since it denies the reality of sin. "Sin is a lie from the beginning,—an illusion," writes Eddy.[41] If there is in reality no sin, there is no need for salvation in the biblical sense. Eddy states plainly that one is not saved by grace through faith in Jesus' vicarious sacrifice:

---

[36]*Science and Health,* 25.

[37]Mary Baker Eddy, *No and Yes* (Boston: the First Church of Christ, Scientist, 1936), 34.

[38]Another synonym for God, according to Eddy (see *Science and Health,* 587).

[39]Eddy goes on to state, "Hence there is no sin" (*No and Yes,* 35).

[40]*No and Yes,* 35.

[41]Mary Baker Eddy, *Message to the Mother Church, 1901* (Boston: The First Church of Christ, Scientist, 1929), 13.

Final deliverance from error, whereby we rejoice in immortality, boundless freedom, and sinless sense, is not reached through paths of flowers nor by pinning one's faith without works to another's vicarious effort.[42]

Rather than salvation by grace through faith in the real atoning death of Jesus, Christian Science opts for a change in consciousness, a uniting of the mind with the Divine Mind (God). This, says Christian Science, is heaven.[43] Jesus "demonstrated" this for all humanity, and therefore is not the way, but the "Way-Shower."[44]

The Death of Jesus

Christian Science believes death to be an illusion; yet another doctrine arising from its absolute pantheistic and monistic worldview. From *Science and Health* we read, "DEATH. An illusion, the lie of life in matter; the unreal and untrue."[45] The death of Jesus, therefore, did not really take place: "The fleshly Jesus seemed to die, though he did not."[46]

The Resurrection of Jesus

Resurrection is redefined as "spiritualization of thought; a new and higher idea of immortality, or spiritual existence."[47] And since Christian Science denies the ultimate reality of flesh, it therefore denies the *bodily* resurrection of Jesus. When Christian Scientists claim that Jesus was raised from the dead, they mean that His mind, His way of thinking, was resurrected from erroneous thinking, thus becoming one with Infinite Mind (God).

---

[42]*Science and Health*, 22.
[43]Ibid., 587, 588.
[44]Eddy, *Miscellaneous Writings*, 162.
[45]Pg. 584.
[46]Eddy, *Unity of Good*, 62.
[47]*Science and Health*, 593.

Unity School of Christianity, Religious Science

These two offspring of Christian Science share much in common with it. There are, however, *nuances* of difference between Christian Science and these two groups. This is due, in part, to both Unity and Religious Science not sharing with Christian Science its absolute pantheism.[48]

The Atonement of Jesus

The Unity School of Christianity strips the atonement of its biblical meaning, then *redefines* it for its adherents:

> We have been taught by the church that Jesus died for us—as an atonement for our sins.... Herein sense consciousness has led the church astray.... Paul is responsible for a good share of this throwing of the whole burden upon the blood of Jesus—doubtless the result of an old mental tendency carried over from his Hebrew idea of the blood sacrifices of the priesthood.[49]

> **atonement**—Reconciliation between God and man through Christ;[50] *the uniting of our consciousness with the higher consciousness.* Jesus became the way by which all who accept him may "pass over"[51] to the higher consciousness. We have atonement through Him.[52]

Concerning the atonement, Religious Science states, "The sense in which we use it is that of complete harmony: at-one-ment."[53]

---

[48]For both Unity and Religious Science there is a degree of belief in the reality of the material world. For example, "To say that the body is unreal is a mistake" (Ernest Holmes, *The Science of Mind* [New York: Dodd, Mead and Co., 1938], 99).

[49]Charles Fillmore, *Jesus Christ's Atonement* (Unity Village, Mo.: Unity School of Christianity, n.d.), 5, 9-10.

[50]"Christ" is redefined to mean "the incarnating *principle*" (see Charles Fillmore, *The Revealing Word* [Unity Village, Mo.: Unity School of Christianity, 9th printing, 1985], 34, emphasis added). Much like Christian Science, the "Christ" is a divine principle rather than the historic person of Jesus.

[51]Notice the redefinition of the biblical and theological phrase, "Passover."

[52]Fillmore, *The Revealing Word,* 18, bold original, other emphases added.

[53]Holmes, *The Science of Mind,* 576.

Far from the biblical meaning of a covering and cleansing of sin, and a taking away of the divine wrath of God, these two Mind Science groups make the atonement a change of consciousness, a theme quite common in ancient gnostic cults as well.[54]

Salvation

For Unity, "Jesus is the Way-Shower."[55] Rather than He being *the way* (John 14:6), Unity views Jesus as someone who demonstrated divine consciousness and modeled it, that we may achieve oneness with the Divine Mind (God). But there is more. Unity states, "So we see that the church is not so far wrong in its call to 'follow Jesus.' The error lies in the belief that He was the *only* begotten Son of God, and that He overcame for us, and that by simply *believing* on Him we are saved."[56] Further, "Jesus Christ was not meant to be slain as a substitute for us; that is, to atone vicariously for us."[57] "The belief that Jesus in an outer way atoned for our sins is not salvation. Salvation is based solely on an inner overcoming, a change in consciousness."[58] This "inner overcoming" rescues one from "sin," for "through the Christ Mind, our sins (wrong thinking) are forgiven or pardoned (erased from consciousness)."[59] To summarize, Jesus is the "Way-Shower," showing us how we as well can erase "sin" from our consciousness and become one with the Divine Mind.

Concerning its doctrine of salvation, Religious Science is not at all different from Christian Science and Unity. Salvation is divine illumination, a raising of consciousness in recognition that "we cannot

---

[54]The ancient gnostic cults emphasized salvation by "knowledge" (Gr. *gnōsis*). True, with the Christian doctrine of salvation one must come to a *knowledge* of Christ for salvation, but with Gnosticism we have knowledge that ignores sin in the biblical sense. Gnosticism then emphasizes the elevation of the human consciousness for the purpose of becoming one with the divine consciousness of "God."

[55]Fillmore, *The Revealing Word,* 111. Jesus is called the Way-Shower in Christian Science, and, as we shall see, Religious Science.

[56]Charles Fillmore, *Talks on Truth* (Unity Village, Mo.: Unity School of Christianity, n.d.), 166-67.

[57]No author, *The Way to Salvation* (Unity Village, Mo.: Unity School of Christianity, n.d.), 6.

[58]Fillmore, *The Revealing Word,* 173.

[59]Ibid., 180, parentheses original.

come unto the Father Which art in Heaven except through our own nature. Right here, through our own nature, is the gateway and path which leads to illumination, to realization."[60] According to Religious Science, Jesus did this, and is "the great Wayshower to mankind."[61]

For both groups heaven and hell are states of mind, the former being reached in the here and now when attaining divine consciousness, and the latter the state of mind that has not reached this divine illumination.[62] When the state of heaven is attained, a person becomes the Christ himself. The first of what follows comes from Unity, the second from Religious Science:

> Spiritual perception reveals to us that we are not persons, but factors in the cosmic mind. Reveal yourself to yourself by affirming, *"I am the Christ, son of the living God."*[63]

> As the human gives way to the Divine in all people, they become the Christ.[64]

The Resurrection of Jesus

True to their gnostic roots, both Unity and Religious Science believe that resurrection is the rising of consciousness, an elevation of the mind:

> **Resurrection**—the restoring of mind and body to their original, undying state.... The resurrection takes place every time we rise to Jesus' realization of the perpetual indwelling life that is connecting us with the Father.[65]

> RESURRECTION—Rising from a belief in death.[66]

---

[60]Holmes, *The Science of Mind*, 358-59.

[61]Ibid., 631.

[62]For Unity, see Fillmore, *The Revealing Word*, 94, 95. For Religious Science, see Holmes, *The Science of Mind*, 598, 599.

[63]No author, but compiled from Charles Fillmore's teachings, *Metaphysical Bible Dictionary* (Unity Village, Mo.: Unity School of Christianity, n.d.), 150.

[64]Holmes, *The Science of Mind*, 359.

[65]Fillmore, *The Revealing Word*, 169, bold original.

[66]Holmes, *The Science of Mind*, 630.

Jesus, then, did not rise from the dead in the biblical sense. Rather, His *mind* was raised to become one with God.

The New Age Movement[67]/A Course in Miracles

Though quite vast and containing many different twists in its denial of the humanity and work of Jesus, the New Age Movement can nonetheless be represented generally by the popular book titled, *A Course in Miracles*. Given to Helen Schucman by "the Voice" in the 1960s into early 1970s, *A Course in Miracles* has since spawned thousands of study groups by that name.

Since its worldview is much like Christian Science, a few quotations from the book shall suffice in showing that the New Age Movement denies all the essential doctrines of Christianity. Regarding the humanity of Jesus, *A Course in Miracles* states: "The man [Jesus] was an illusion."[68] Speaking of the physical body in general, the book teaches that "the body is a dream."[69] Further, all are Sons of God and not sinners,[70] since sin is not real,[71] and "your resurrection is your reawakening."[72]

The crucifixion's "value," says the *Course,*

---

[67]In this chapter I shall not include sections on Hinduism and Buddhism. Much of New Age thought is gleaned from these two eastern movements and is colored by either non-religious or Christian terminology. One can see in the following section an exact representation of the beliefs of many forms of Hinduism and Buddhism. Since Both Hinduism and Buddhism in their many expressions deny the eternal, unique deity of Jesus Christ (see chap. 3), it follows that they deny the work of Christ for salvation. Further, if any of the sects of Hinduism or Buddhism hold to absolute pantheism, they will in turn deny Christ's real humanity.

[68]No authors listed, *A Course in Miracles* (Tibouron, Calif.: Foundation For Inner Peace, 1985), Manual for Teachers, 83.

[69]Ibid., Workbook for Students, 415.

[70]Ibid., Text, 87.

[71]Ibid., Workbook for Students, 391. On page 326 there is a prayer that begins with, "Forgive us our illusions, Father."

[72]Ibid., Text, 86.

lies solely in the kind of learning it facilitates.... The Apostles often misunderstood it. Their own imperfect love made them vulnerable to projection, and out of their own fear they spoke of the "wrath of God" as His retaliatory weapon.... These are some of the examples of upside-down thinking in the New Testament, although its gospel is really only the message of love.[73]

Finally, "Salvation is nothing more than 'right-mindedness'.... There is no hell. Hell is only what the ego has made of the present."[74]

Islam

Though Islam affirms the Torah, the Psalms and the Gospel, its denial of the deity of the Son of God leads to denials of the work of Christ in many areas, a few of which follow.

The Virgin Birth

It is often stated (even by Christians) that the Qur'ān (or Koran) and Muslims affirm the virgin birth of Christ (see Sūrah[75] 3:45-47). Though it is indeed *affirmed*, I nonetheless contend that neither Muslims nor the Qur'ān affirm the doctrine in the biblical sense. After all, the Qur'ān also states that Jesus is "the Word of God" (Sūrah 4:171), but pours a different meaning into the phrase, denying that the Word was God (John 1:1). It is the same with the virgin birth. Since in Christian theology there are inextricable links between doctrines, and in this sense error in one doctrine affects other doctrines, the Christian doctrine of the virgin birth by necessity carries with it the doctrine of the deity of Christ (which the Qur'ān denies). Further still, biblically the Son of God was born of the virgin by the agency of God the Holy Spirit. Islam denies that the Holy Spirit is God, the third person of the Trinity.

---

[73]Ibid., Text, 84, 87.
[74]Ibid., Text, 53, 281.
[75]The name for the chapters of the Qur'ān.

The Crucifixion and Resurrection of Christ

Sūrah 4:157 states: "That they said (in boast) 'We killed Jesus the Son of Mary, the Apostle of God';—But they killed him not, nor crucified him." Muslims also deny that Christ rose from the dead after three days.[76]

Salvation

It therefore follows that Muslims would reject the biblical doctrine of believing in Christ as the only way of salvation,[77] since His vicarious sacrifice is rejected. Rather, "If anyone desires a religion other than Islam (submission to God), never will it be accepted of him; and in the hereafter he will be in the ranks of those who have lost (all spiritual good)" (Sūrah 3:85). With the religion of Islam, one cannot be reconciled to God unless there is submission to God *as commanded by the Qur'ān.* And since the Qur'ān rejects Jesus' deity and vicarious sacrifice on the cross, it follows that this submission would necessarily include these rejections.

The Unification Church

Though Unification theology affirms that Jesus is truly human,[78] it does not affirm Christian orthodoxy regarding His work of redemption.

The Crucifixion and Salvation

According to Unificationists, "the kingdom of Heaven on earth *should* have been established by Jesus."[79] We must then accept that "Jesus' crucifixion was the result of the ignorance and disbelief of the

---

[76]See A. Yusaf Ali, *The Holy Qur'ān: Text, Translation and Commentary* (Brentwood, Md.: Amana Corp., 1983), 230, n. 663, and Cyril Glassé, *The Concise Encyclopedia of Islam* (San Francisco: HarperCollins, 1989), 209.

[77]Thus His unique mediatorial role between humanity and the Father is null and void.

[78]See (no author) *Outline of the Principle: Level 4* (New York: Holy Spirit Association for the Unification of World Christianity, 1980), 140.

[79]Ibid., 140, emphasis added.

Jewish people and was not God's predestination[80] to fulfill the whole purpose of Jesus' coming as the Messiah."[81] Continuing, we learn that "Jesus knew he could not fulfill the purpose of his advent as the Messiah through the cross,"[82] and that "redemption through the cross cannot completely liquidate our original sin."[83] In Unification thought, this means that Jesus only accomplished spiritual salvation, *not* physical salvation. His mission was to marry and have sinless, perfect offspring. His mission failed because of His crucifixion: "If Jesus had not been crucified, what would have happened? He would have accomplished the providence of salvation both spiritually and physically.... [H]e should have fulfilled the salvation of both spirit and body."[84] The Unification Church therefore denies the all-sufficiency of the cross of Christ.

Jesus' Uniqueness and Mediatorship

While Christian theology affirms that Jesus (as *uniquely* God and man) is the unique Son of God and the one mediator between God and humanity, Unification theology cannot. As we have seen, the Unification Church denies Jesus as God in the biblical sense, and states that He is but a man who has attained "the purpose of creation."[85] This means He is a "perfected man." In other words, "However great his value may be, he cannot assume a value greater than that of a man who has attained the purpose of creation."[86] In the end, this means that Jesus is not now unique,[87] and sets the stage for the coming of Sun Myung Moon.

---

[80]But see Acts 2:22-23.

[81]No author, *Divine Principle* (New York: The Holy Spirit Association for the Unification of World Christianity, 1973), 145.

[82]Ibid., 142.

[83]Ibid. See also p. 148.

[84]Ibid., 147.

[85]Ibid., 209.

[86]Ibid.

[87]Despite attempts by Unification Church theologians to counter this, it still remains that the uniqueness of Jesus is denied. One cannot have a unique Jesus who is *not* God and *not* able to complete His mission of securing full salvation, while another man can, and, as we shall see from their perspective, has!

Because Jesus as a "perfected man" failed to complete His mission (providing spiritual salvation only; not physical salvation), "Christ must come again on the earth to accomplish the purpose of the providence of the physical, as well as spiritual salvation, by redeeming the original sin which had not been liquidated even through the cross."[88] Who is this "Lord of the Second Coming"[89] that will fulfill the original mission of Jesus? Sun Myung Moon. The headlines of the September 1992 *Unification News,* a monthly newspaper of the Unification Church, read, "Rev. and Mrs. Moon Initiate Messianic Reign as the True Parents: World Peace is at Hand." In a speech by Moon contained therein, he proclaimed, "I have fulfilled my mission as the Lord of the Second Advent, Savior and the True Parent.[90] I am proclaiming this in this place because the time has come to do so."[91] The *Divine Principle* also states that this Lord of the Second advent "is to be born on the earth as the King of Kings."[92]

Jesus' Resurrection and Ascension

If Jesus failed to fulfill God's plan of physical salvation, there is no theological reason to expect that He Himself rose physically from the dead. Instead, Jesus presently lives in the spirit world "as a spirit

---

[88] *Divine Principle*, 148.

[89] See (no author) *The Divine Principle Home Study Course,* 6 vols. (New York: The Holy Spirit Association for the Unification of World Christianity, 1980), 3:39.

[90] Both Moon and his wife are considered the "True Parents," Moon the perfected Adam and Mrs. Moon the perfected Eve. Their marriage is considered the "Marriage of the Lamb" of the Book of Revelation (19:7). Through this Moon has fulfilled what Jesus did not accomplish (producing offspring and starting the kingdom of God physically on earth).

[91] "Reappearance of True Parents and the Ideal Family," *Unification News,* Sept. 1992, p. 5, col. 2. The *Divine Principle* points to Moon as the coming Christ. On pp. 516 and 520, respectively, we read, "**Where will Christ Come Again?** If Christ is to be born as a man in the flesh on this earth, and not to come again in a spiritual body, he will surely be born in a certain nation of God's elect in some place of God's predestination. Where, then, would the place of predestination be, and which nation would be God's elect?" "Therefore, the nation of the East where Christ will come again would be none other than Korea" (emphases original). Moon was born in Korea.

[92] Pg. 509.

person"[93] or "spirit man."[94] One Unification theologian illustrates how one can affirm Jesus' resurrection, but in the end *redefine* it:

> How does the Unificationist understand the resurrection of Jesus?.... Because of the resurrection, Jewish Christians could preach to their countrymen: "This Jesus God has raised up..." [quoting Acts 2:32, 36].... Like most liberal Protestants, Unificationists believe that Jesus' resurrection was spiritual and not physical.[95]

United Pentecostal Church

Though the United Pentecostal Church declares the deity of Christ, it does so in a way that makes Him the only person in the godhead, thus reducing His actual personal existence before the incarnation to an abstract thought in the Father's mind.[96] Its view of Christ as it relates to the Godhead therefore has some negative theological implications for the work of Christ.[97]

---

[93] *Outline of the Principle: Level 4*, 142.

[94] *Divine Principle*, 212.

[95] Young Oon Kim, *Unification Theology* (New York: The Holy Spirit Association for the Unification of World Christianity, 1980), 171, 172.

[96] See under United Pentecostal Church in chap. 1.

[97] Another form of modern modalism is found in Swedenborgianism. Emanuel Swedenborg (1688-1772) is said to be the messenger of a restored Christianity. The full name of this restored church was the "New Church Signified by the New Jerusalem in the Revelation." Several groups follow Swedenborg's teachings, one of which is the Church of the New Jerusalem. Regarding his doctrine of God, he taught that the Father, Son, and Holy Spirit are the three "essentials" of one God, and that "this Divine Trinity is in the Lord God the Redeemer and Saviour, Jesus Christ" (Emanuel Swedenborg, *The True Christian Religion*, 3 vols. [Boston and New York: Houghton Mifflin Co., 1907], 1:275). This greatly affects Swedenborg's view of Christ's vicarious atonement paid *to the Father* on behalf of sinners. Writing of Swedenborg's denial of the Christian doctrine of the Trinity, and his consequent "restoration" of it in its "true" fashion, one of his followers astutely observed, "The restitution of the true doctrine of the Trinity in Unity necessitated a restatement of the doctrine of the Atonement; since, if there are not three persons in the Trinity, it is impossible for one of these to offer Himself as a sacrifice to the claimant justice of another.... In this view of the Atonement, there is no substitution of the innocent for the guilty" (G. Trobridge, *Swedenborg: Life and Teaching* [New York: Swedenborg Foundation, Inc., 1938], 131, 132).

The Atonement

The teaching that there is only one person in the Godhead, and that this one person is the Father at certain times, the Son at other times, and Holy Spirit at other times, is known as modalism.[98] For United Pentecostalism, the only person in the Godhead is Jesus (thus their designation "Jesus only"). Jesus therefore has three different modes or roles. Consequently Jesus is also the Father and the Holy Spirit. *The three persons never exist simultaneously.* For example, when Jesus on the cross cried, "My God, My God, why hast Thou forsaken Me?" we learn, "This verse (Matthew 27:46) cannot describe an actual separation between the Father and Son because Jesus is the Father."[99]

Who, then, was appeased at the atonement of Christ? Was there an atonement made by Jesus on behalf of sinners in order to provide the way for the Father to remove His wrath from sinners? Put another way, the logical result of modalism is that Christ's substitutionary death on the cross is not paid *to the Father* on behalf of sinners (see Rom. 3:25; 5:9; 1 Thess. 5:9-10; 2 Cor. 5:18-19[100]). As Harold O. J. Brown states, if modalism is true, "then the later Christian concept of substitutionary satisfaction, which holds that Christ takes our place and pays our debt to the Father, becomes at best a symbol, not a reality."[101]

Further, modalism, carried to its logical conclusion,[102] leads to *patripassionism,* the doctrine that it was the Father who suffered on the

---

[98]Again, see chap. 1.

[99]David K. Bernard, *The Oneness of God* (Hazelwood, Mo.: Word Aflame Press, 1983), 178.

[100]See ibid., where Bernard writes, "The Bible states that 'God was in Christ, reconciling the world unto himself' (2 Corinthians 5:19). Jesus was God the Father made manifest in flesh to reconcile the world to Himself." Though this interpretation acknowledges that "God" is synonymous with the Father (see 2 Cor. 1: 2-3), it fails to see two *persons* in v.18: "Now all these things are from God [the Father], who reconciled us to *himself* through *Christ,* and gave us the ministry of reconciliation." It also fails to see that the preposition *en* ("in") does not designate Jesus as the Father, but means that Christ and the Father are in perfect fellowship and union.

[101]Harold O. J. Brown, *Heresies: The Image of Christ in the Mirror of Heresy from the Apostles to the Present* (Grand Rapids, Mich.: Baker Book House, 1984), 100.

[102]United Pentecostal Christology tries to escape this charge, and falls into error on yet another front, that of severing Christ's two natures. In the end,

cross.[103] When United Pentecostals state that "Jesus was God the Father manifest in flesh to reconcile the world to Himself,"[104] it provides ground for this charge. United Pentecostal theologians, however, attempt to avoid this by splitting the two natures of Christ (the severing of His two natures is erroneous, since in Scripture every act of Jesus is performed by His *whole* person, as both God and man[105]): "So the human nature of Jesus cried out on the cross as Jesus took on the sin of the whole world and felt the eternal punishment of separation for that sin."[106] In other words, "it was the human nature feeling the wrath and judgment of God [His other nature!] upon the sins of mankind."[107] This not only splits His natures, but has as well one of Christ's natures suffering to appease the wrath of His other nature.

The Mediatorship of Christ

Biblically speaking, there is an inseparable link between Christ's atonement is His mediatorship (see 1 Tim. 2:5; 1 John 2:1). As was the

---

however, patripassionism must result, even though United Pentecostal theologians deny it. Natures do not communicate with each other, persons do. This being true, and taking at face value their statements that Jesus is the Father incarnate, patripassionism implicitly and logically follows. Statements made by Bernard evidence his severing of the two natures of Christ (see also above in the body text). He holds that "the human nature of Jesus cried out on the cross," and "the human nature [felt] the wrath and judgment of God [the Father, His other nature]." But what of the fact that in Scripture, what should be true of one nature is given to the other, as is found in 1 Cor. 2:8b: "They would not have crucified the Lord of Glory"? Here crucifixion and death, if Bernard is consistent, would be true only of Christ's human nature. Paul, however, states this in the context of His nature as deity (they crucified *the Lord of Glory*)! See chap. 9, n. 11 for more details. Additionally, Bernard fails to recognize that whenever Christ says something or does something, the scriptural witness is that He does it as a *whole* person.

[103] As ancient modalists taught. Exemplars of this heresy were Praxeas and Noetus (both ca. late second to early third centuries).

[104] Bernard, *The Oneness of God,* 178.

[105] More on this in detail in the next chapter. Further statements by Bernard imply the severing of the two natures of Christ: "Jesus prayed in His humanity, not in His deity.... [W]e say the human nature of Jesus prayed to the divine Spirit of Jesus that dwelt in the man" (ibid., 176, 178).

[106] Bernard, *The Oneness of God,* 180.

[107] Ibid., 178.

case with His atonement, which was made on our behalf *to the Father,* His mediatorial role as well must occur on our behalf *to the Father.*

United Pentecostalism, however, is forced to admit (because of its insistence of one person in the Godhead, and because Scripture is clear that the Son offers atonement for sin *to* the Father) that Christ's mediation for believers takes place between His human nature and His God nature. This renders nonexistent Christ's mediation between believers and the *person*[108] of the Father. Speaking of 1 Timothy 2:5 ("For there is one God, and one mediator also between God and men, the man Christ Jesus"), United Pentecostal theologian David Bernard states, "There are *not* two personalities in God; the duality is in Jesus as God and Jesus as man."[109]

Unitarian Universalism

Unitarian Universalism denies the deity of Jesus Christ, but affirms His humanity. This results in Jesus being *merely* a man and in turn has tremendous negative christological implications regarding His work.

The Atonement

In a book titled *Religions of America,*[110] spokespeople from various religious movements were asked a series of pertinent doctrinal questions. Speaking for Unitarianism were Karl M. Chworowsky and Christopher Gist Raible. "Dr. Chworowsky was, at the time of his death, minister emeritus of the First Unitarian Church of Fairfield County, Westport, Connecticut," and "Christopher Gist Raible, a life-long Unitarian, is Director of Extension of the Unitarian Universalist Association."[111]

Of the atonement we read, "Unitarian Universalists reject the idea that God sacrificed Jesus, 'His Son,' to 'atone' for human sin."[112] One other Unitarian theologian, James Freeman Clarke, stated, "The parable of the prodigal son teaches us plainly that when we repent and return to

---

[108]Since *natures* are not *persons.*

[109]*The Oneness of God,* 110, emphasis original.

[110]Leo Rosten, *Religions of America* (New York: Simon and Schuster, 1975).

[111]Ibid., 263.

[112]Ibid., 268.

God, we shall be received, and that without any reference to belief in the atonement."[113]

The Virgin Birth and the Resurrection of Jesus

Following are some statements by Unitarians regarding these two doctrines:

> Jesus is God's son and so is of divine origin, but his birth was not supernatural. The New testament account of his birth is a beautiful and useful, even helpful, myth.[114]

> **How Do Unitarian Universalists View the Virgin Birth? The Resurrection?** The modern Unitarian Universalist finds much of the old terminology no longer pertinent to the religious needs of people today. Concepts such as the virgin birth and the resurrection are of this nature. Unitarian Universalists emphatically reject them as contrary to both scientific and historical evidence.[115]

Salvation

Obvious in Unitarian theology is the rejection of salvation by grace through faith in Jesus Christ alone. Following are two brief examples.

> But there is no vicarious salvation; each man is responsible for his own salvation.[116]

> Salvation is universal. Man is capable of infinite improvement, liberalism asserts... [H]e is achieving his own salvation.[117]

---

[113]Quoted in Prescott B. Wintersteen, *Christology in American Unitarianism* (Boston: The Unitarian Universalist Christian Fellowship, 1977), 65.

[114]Ibid., 137.

[115]Rosten, *Religions of America,* 267.

[116]Wintersteen, *Christology in American Unitarianism,* 140.

[117]John Nicholls Booth, *Introducing Unitarian Universalism* (Boston: Unitarian Universalist Association, 1963), 16.

Baha'i

The Baha'i Faith is no exception to the plethora of religious groups that refuse to acknowledge Christ as God the Son. Therefore it cannot acknowledge Jesus' work on behalf of sinners.

The Virgin Birth

Because the Baha'i Faith has its roots in Islam, its adherents acknowledge the virgin birth.[118] But, as is the case with Islam, since to them Jesus is not God the Son, and the virgin birth by biblical necessity must include this acknowledgment (see Matt. 1:23), the doctrine in the biblical sense is denied.[119]

The Atonement

Baha'i theology states,

> But the mass of Christians believe that, as Adam ate of the forbidden tree, he sinned in that He disobeyed, and that the disastrous consequences of this disobedience have been transmitted as a heritage and have remained among His descendants.... This explanation is unreasonable and evidently wrong, for it means that all men, even the Prophets and the Messengers of God... have become guilty sinners, and until the day of the sacrifice of Christ were held captive in hell in painful torment.... But Christ Who is the Word of God,[120] sacrificed Himself.... *Christ's intention was to represent and promote a Cause which was to educate the human world.*[121]

---

[118]See Richard Backwell, *The Christianity of Jesus* (Wellington Place, Peterhead, Scotland: Volturna Press, 1972), 27, and Laura Clifford Barney, coll. and trans., *Some Answered Questions: Abdul-Baha* (Wilmette, Ill.: Baha'i Publishing Trust, 1981), 90. Backwell, however, seems at times to doubt it (pp. 22-23, 27).

[119]See this chap. under Islam.

[120]"Word of God" in Baha'i theology is the impersonal collection of the divine perfections of Christ. See chap. 1.

[121]Barney, *Some Answered Questions: Abdul-Baha*, 120, emphases added.

Christ's Mediatorship

The Baha'i Faith's denial of the unique deity of Jesus leads to a denial of His unique mediatorial role in two ways. *First,* if Christ is merely one of Nine Great Manifestations of God,[122] then there is *not* one mediator between God and humanity. *Second,* in Baha'i Christology, if Christ's work on the cross on behalf of sinners *did* carry the meaning it does in the Bible (i.e., sacrifice of the perfect and innocent victim fundamentally required by God for the reconciliation of sinners to Himself), it would require the same of the other eight Manifestations. Christ, then, would not be unique, for they admit that "the fundamental basis of the revealed religion of God is immutable, unchanging throughout the centuries, not subject to the varying conditions of the human world," and that "every one of them [the Nine Great Manifestations] is the Way of God that connecteth this world to the realms above."[123]

Resurrection and Ascension of Christ

"We do not believe that there was a bodily resurrection after the Crucifixion of Christ."[124] "His resurrection from the interior of the earth is also symbolical; it is a spiritual and divine fact, and not material; and likewise His ascension to heaven is a spiritual and not material ascension."[125]

The Word-Faith Movement

Understanding the systematic theological structure of the Word-Faith Movement greatly aids in comprehending how it finally arrives at the heresies documented in this section.

---

[122]See chaps. 1, 3.

[123]Shoghi Effendi, trans., *Gleanings from the Writings of Baha'u'llah* (Wilmette, Ill.: Baha'i Publishing Trust, 1976), 50.

[124]Helen Hornby, comp., *Lights of Guidance* (New Delhi: Baha'i Publishing Trust, 1988), 492, "from a letter written on behalf of the Guardian to an individual believer, October 9, 1947."

[125]Barney, *Some Answered Questions: Abdul-Baha,* 104.

Its Systematic Theological Grid

According to teachers within the movement, God used His faith (which is a cosmic force) to speak the creation into being. He created Adam as a god to rule over the creation. Adam, however, committed "high treason" and as a result took on the nature of Satan. He then lost his capacity to act as a god. Thus the human race, the children of Adam, necessarily shares the consequences of Adam's act of treason. But Christ came and identified with us, paid the price on the cross *and* in hell, and became the first person to be born again. Those, then, who believe on Him can have the curse reversed, changing them and elevating them to the status of being gods. Believers now can call things into being by using the force of faith, as God did when creating all things.

There is in the above some truth mixed with error. It is true, for example, that Jesus identified with humanity, in that He became as we are. But by virtue of His person there must be parameters set to the Christian doctrinal concept of Christ's identification. Was He a sinner? No, for according to Hebrews 4:15 He was without sin. Was He born again? Only sinners have to be born again. Are we willing to carry the doctrine of the identification of Christ with humanity to that extent?

Jesus on the Cross Taking the Nature of Satan

Because of the unbiblical view of the fall of humanity taught in Word-Faith circles, which has Adam (and consequently humanity) actually taking on Satan's nature, Benny Hinn, noted televangelist from Orlando, Florida, once stated, "He [Jesus] became one with the nature of *Satan,* so all those who had the nature of *Satan* can partake of the nature of God."[126] In the following, Kenneth E. Hagin strongly implies that Jesus on the cross took on Satan's nature: "**Spiritual death also means having Satan's nature**.... Jesus tasted death— spiritual death— for every man."[127] Lastly, Kenneth Copeland states, "The righteousness of God was made to be sin. He accepted the nature of Satan in His own

---

[126]"Benny Hinn" television program on TBN (December 15, 1990), emphasis original. Taken from Hank Hanegraaff, *Christianity in Crisis* (Eugene, Oreg.: Harvest House Publishers, 1993), 155-56.

[127]Kenneth E. Hagin, *The Name of Jesus* (Tulsa, Okla.: Kenneth Hagin Ministries, 1979), 31, bold original.

spirit."[128] This logically leads to the next heresy, that of the born again Jesus.

Jesus was Born Again

The "born again Jesus" doctrine of Word-Faith teachers expresses that Jesus became an actual sinner on the cross (Satan's nature entered Jesus), died, went into hell, and became the first person to be born again out of the pit of hell. Kenneth E. Hagin states that "Jesus was the first person ever to be born again."[129] Kenneth Copeland declares that "He [Jesus] was the first man to be reborn under the new covenant,"[130] and that "you have to realize that He went into the pit of hell as a mortal man made sin! But He didn't stay there, thank God. He was reborn in the pit of hell."[131]

Redemption and Atonement

Because Christian doctrines are closely linked, error in one area creates error in others. Since teachers in the Word-Faith Movement believe that Jesus went into hell and was reborn, another error surfaces. There was a portion of His work on behalf of humanity that remained *unfinished* on the cross.

This begs the question, "When Jesus cried 'It is finished,' what did He mean?":

> When Jesus cried, *It is finished!*, He was not speaking of the plan of redemption. There were still three days and nights to go through before He went to the throne.... Jesus' death on the cross was only the beginning of the complete work of redemption.[132]

---

[128]Kenneth Copeland, (audiotape) *What Happened from the Cross to the Throne* (Fort Worth, Tex.: Kenneth Copeland Ministries, 1990).

[129]Hagin, *The Name of Jesus*, 29.

[130]Kenneth Copeland, "Jesus Our Lord of Glory," *Believer's Voice of Victory* 10, 4 (April 1982): 3.

[131]Kenneth Copeland, (audiotape) *What Happened from the Cross to the Throne*.

[132]Kenneth Copeland, "Jesus Our Lord of Glory," 3, emphases and bold original.

Do you think that the punishment for our sin was to die on a cross? If that were the case, the two thieves could have paid your price. No, the punishment was to go to hell itself and serve time in hell separated from God.[133]

Conclusion

As previously stated, error begets error. In this chapter we have seen that heresies regarding the work of Christ arise from denials of His deity and/or His full humanity, and from error in other areas of doctrine (exemplified by the Word-Faith Movement: what happened to the *nature* of humanity after the fall gives rise to what happened to Jesus on the cross, which in turn results in a born again Jesus who did not finish his work on the cross). A Jesus that is not fully God and not real humanity cannot save. Precisely, and as we shall see in detail in the next chapter, it is who He is (both God and man) that makes His work infinitely efficacious on behalf of sinners, and evidences the theological necessity of both His humanity and His deity if the Christian message of salvation is to be faithful to the text. We turn now to the biblical witness of Christ's humanity and work.

---

[133]Frederick K. C. Price, *Ever Increasing Faith Messenger* magazine (June 1980): 7.

Chapter 9

The Humanity and Work of Christ

"A Christianity without a theology of the atonement according to the Scriptures is not the authentic message of the gospel."—H. D. McDonald, The Atonement of the Death of Christ

"Vicarious atonement has no place in the philosophy of Spiritualism."—Joseph Whitwell, Spiritualist Manual

Christian theology presents the awe-inspiring truth of God in the history of redemption. It rightly places God in the center, along with what He has done by His grace to save sinners. Most central to this is the work of Jesus Christ. In Christ we have all we need for eternal life. And there is no other way to eternal life. It is therefore the greatest and most precious message the world will ever hear.

Interestingly, the God who acts for the salvation of sinners has acted *His* way, not ours. That is to say, God has purposed that His plan of salvation would involve humanity paying for sin, and at the same time involve Himself as the one who *does it all,* thus justifying the ungodly. How *could* this be done? The answer lies in the historic person of Jesus Christ. The purpose of this chapter is to probe the mystery of the incarnation and its relation to the saving work of Christ, and how that work applies to His people.

The Humanity of Christ

Because denials of the humanity of Christ occur less frequently than those concerning His deity, we may be less prone to search Scripture regarding His humanity. After all, once Christ is accepted as a historical figure, and today there is no denial of that among thinking persons, the natural conclusion would of course be that He was a man.

But how important *is it* to believe that Jesus was and is truly a man? Is it necessary? It is both important and necessary. The great promise of salvation to all who believe in Christ is given by virtue of the fact that He was a man. If He were not a true human being, that is to say, fully human as we are, there would have been no reason for His work to apply to us. For this reason we should make the humanity of Christ a focus of study.

At the same time, it is important to remember that although this section focuses largely on the humanity of Christ, His work cannot hold the infinite value it does if He is not fully God. Therefore we must strive for a balanced view of the Savior, one that holds up equally His humanity *and* His deity. The former because He was *the* human being who took upon Himself the sins of God's people, thus satisfying the justice of Almighty God, who requires that humanity pay for sin. The latter because His deity renders His work of infinite worth. Thus, although many believe Jesus was a man, it is not enough to believe He was *merely* a man. In the one person of Christ, *who is both God and man*, there exists the intrinsic worth capable of graciously giving salvation to whomever should call upon His name.

Heresy as regards the person of Christ is not limited to those who deny the deity of Jesus. At the opposite end of the spectrum exist those who deny His true humanity. Today, as in the days of the early Church, gnostic denials[1] of Christ's true humanity abound. They challenge the

---

[1] It is not difficult for those who have not thought out the negative implications of denying Jesus' *full* humanity to slip into error. For example, a person confronted with the issue of *how* the two natures of Christ relate to each other could easily echo Apollinarianism, which is named after its founder, Apollinaris (fourth century). He taught that the *logos,* or Christ's divine nature, took the place of the human soul of Jesus. Thus, to Apollinaris, the meaning of

fundamental doctrine of His humanity and render His substitutionary atonement null and void. We saw this demonstrated in the previous chapter with Christian Science.

Truly Human?

The Scripture is clear on Jesus' humanity. He was born of a woman (Gal. 4:4), who was a virgin (Matt. 1:18-23). Though He had no human father as we do in the biological sense, we nonetheless infer His full humanity by virtue of the fact that Jesus developed from conception in the womb of a human mother just as all human beings do. Witness as well the genealogies in Matthew and Luke. Here Jesus' human ancestry is mentioned. Further, His full, complete humanity is emphasized by the writer of Hebrews, where it is stated that Christ "likewise"[2] shared in our flesh and blood (2:14) and was made like His brethren "in all things"[3] (2:17).

In the prologue to the Gospel of John "the Word became flesh" (1:14; see also 1 Tim. 3:16). His flesh, His humanity, "became" at a certain point in time[4] at the conception, just as other full human beings experience. Further, in his first epistle, John evidently battled a type of Docetism (the belief that Jesus merely "seemed" to be a man) that threatened the real and true humanity of Christ. He instructed the Church with words that not only waged war on this heresy, but at the

---

John 1:14, where "the Word became *flesh,*" was that only Jesus' outer shell (his body) was human. This, of course, posed problems for Church theologians, who recognized the error. If Christ was not fully human, they countered, then His work could not be applied to humanity fully. In short, if Christ did not possess a human soul, there was no reason for believers' souls to be redeemed. Apollinaris failed to take into account the human emotions of Christ that arose from His human soul (He was deeply moved in spirit and wept [John 11:33, 35]). This should have influenced his exegesis of "flesh" in John 1:14. As we shall see in the exegesis of Heb. 2:14, 17, Scripture pronounces Christ fully human.

[2]Implying real human conception and birth (see F. F. Bruce, *The Epistle to the Hebrews* [Grand Rapids, Mich.: Wm. B. Eerdmans Publishing Co., 1964), 48.

[3]Gr. *kata panta,* κατὰ πάντα; may also be translated "in every respect."

[4]The meaning of the aorist tense for the verb *ginomai,* γίνομαι. See Leon Morris, *The Gospel According to John* (Grand Rapids, Mich.: Wm. B. Eerdmans Publishing Co., 1971), 102.

same time affirmed Christ's true humanity: "Every spirit that confesses that Jesus Christ has come in the flesh is from God" (1 John 4:2). In his second epistle he wrote, "For many deceivers have gone out into the world, those who do not acknowledge Jesus Christ as coming in the flesh. This is the deceiver and the antichrist" (2 John 7). From all these texts we gather that Jesus was truly a human being. Jesus also referred to Himself as a man (John 8:40), and others refer to Him as a man (John 1:30; Acts 2:22; Rom. 5:15; 1 Tim. 2:5).

We also conclude that Jesus is truly and fully human from what Jesus *did*. Luke 2:42 tells us that Jesus, as humans do, "became twelve." As a boy of twelve He also was in subjection to His parents (Luke 2:51). After this we are told that Jesus increased in wisdom and age (Luke 2:52). The Lord also experienced the physical wants of the body: He thirsted (John 19:28), was hungry (Matt. 4:2), and craved rest because He grew tired (John 4:6). He experienced the emotions that characterize humanity. Reacting to the death of Lazarus, Jesus was "deeply moved in spirit" and "Jesus wept" (John 11:33, 35). And, of course, He died. He died just as all human beings do (John 19:33).

The Christian Church also affirms, due to the testimony of Scripture, that the resurrected, ascended, and soon coming Jesus is fully human. After the resurrection He appeared to His disciples, and on one occasion comforted them by His humanity, for they thought they saw a spirit. Jesus said, "See My hands and My feet, that it is I Myself; touch me and see, for a spirit does not have flesh and bones as you see that I have" (Luke 24:39). On another occasion He invited Thomas to touch His hands and side (John 20:27) which had been wounded at His crucifixion. This strongly suggests the continuance of His humanity even through the resurrection. Then, before His ascension to the right hand of the Father, Jesus appeared to His disciples bodily, instructed them, and "was lifted up while they were looking on" (Acts 1:9). Presently, in His resurrected and ascended state, Jesus is a man (1 Tim. 2:5). Finally, immediately after His ascension, "two men in white clothing stood beside [the apostles]; and they also said, 'Men of Galilee,...this Jesus...will come in just the same way as you have watched Him go into heaven'" (Acts 1:10-11).

Perhaps some question Christ's true humanity in light of the fact that He did not sin (Heb. 4:15). How could Jesus be *truly* human if He did not sin? The answer lies in recognizing the unbiblical presupposition in the question. It is assumed that true humans *must* sin.

Should we make this assumption? Adam, when he was created in the garden was fully a human being. He was before the fall[5] sinless, and still a man. Moreover, a second presupposition exists in the question, namely that we *must* measure Christ's humanness in light of what *we* are. This is faulty as well. Rather, we should measure what humanity should be *by Christ.*

The Glorious Implications

By the grace of the true and living God, Christ became truly human. Because Jesus is truly human His atonement on the cross has taken place on behalf of His people, saving them from the eternal torment that would be theirs had He not come for them. Because He is truly human He is now the Christian's great mediator and high priest, able to intercede for His people. Because of His true humanity we Christians not only see what true humanity should be, but rejoice in the blessed truth that we at the resurrection will be that true humanity.

Two Natures, One Person

From the Scripture we learn that Jesus is both God and man. By the third and fourth centuries the Church increasingly became aware that *specifics* concerning this affirmation needed to be outlined. In this time period challenges to the Church's understanding of Christ began with denials of His deity. After answering these denials with precise statements, the Church then faced the challenge of *exactly how* Christ's two natures related to each other. In other words, *further questions* naturally arose. Are these two natures in Jesus mixed? Separated? United? And what is so important about the way these early Christians answered these questions? At the end of this period of controversy, the Church was to confess that Jesus Christ possesses two natures, deity and humanity, in their fullest capacities: He is fully God and fully man; two natures in the one person of Christ.

---

[5]The theological and soteriological implications of Christ being *perfectly* fully human are immeasurable. Christ is the second Adam. As such He has done what Adam could not do, and therefore can represent us before the Father as perfect humanity, reconciling us to God by His life, death and resurrection. *By, in* and *through* Christ all believers will be restored to the humanity they were created to be!

Nicaea and Chalcedon

Though the historic creeds of the early Church are not Scripture, they nonetheless elaborate upon Christian doctrine in such a way as to guard against heresy, and this by careful exegesis and contemplation of Scripture. Simply put, the creeds do not create orthodoxy, they pronounce the orthodoxy taught in Scripture to answer the question of the day. Two examples, the Nicene (325) and Chalcedonian (451) creeds, served specifically to safeguard the Church against heresy that arose from attempts to answer specific theological questions. The council of Nicaea was called to settle whether or not the Scripture confesses Jesus as God the Son, and then how Christ as God related to God the Father. The council of Chalcedon was convened to once and for all settle the issue of how Christ's two natures related to each other.[6] The council of Nicaea pronounced that Christ is of the same nature (Gr. *homoousios*) as the Father, yet they are two separate persons. By doing so the council pronounced heretical the Arian position that Christ is of a different nature (*heteroousios*) than the Father, a being who was created by the Father in time. For the Arians, *once the Son of God was not.*

What led to Chalcedon were a number of suggestions from theologians as to the relationship of the two natures of Christ. For example, Apollinaris (d. ca. 390) held that Jesus did not have a human soul, and that the *logos* (the divine nature) replaced the human soul in the person of Christ. The Nestorian position[7] held that there were two distinct persons in Jesus, thus ending in a split of the God-man. At

---

[6]The general consensus is that Chalcedon does not speculate on *how* the two natures of Christ relate, but only states what should *not* be confessed, i.e., the two natures are *not* confused, changed, divided, or separated (the "four negatives"). However, I believe that *to a certain extent* Chalcedon does indeed explain how the two natures relate. For example, the creed states that Christ is "to be acknowledged in two natures,...the distinction of natures being by no means taken away by the union." Here the term "union" (Gr. *henōsin,* ἕνωσιν) is chosen in addition to the four negatives. Further, the creed states that "the property of each nature [is] preserved" in this union.

[7]I phrase it this way because it is not likely that Nestorius (patriarch of Constantinople in 428) himself actually held to the position. Many scholars feel Nestorius was not treated fairly, and that his position was orthodox. Nonetheless, I shall label the position "Nestorianism" with the understanding that whether or not Nestorius taught it, it was still pronounced heretical.

Chalcedon both these positions were rejected. In addition, both before and after Chalcedon the Monophysite[8] position claimed that Christ had a single nature, that both deity and humanity were somehow fused into one. Here the danger is a Christ that is a divinized man and thus not true humanity. One important final point to remember with these examples is that the Apollinarians, Nestorians (at least confessionally), and Monophysites, unlike the Arians and the proponents of Gnosticism, remained within the confessional boundaries of the council of Nicaea.

The Outcome

With Nicaea having settled the question of the deity of Christ in relation to the Father, it remained for Chalcedon to pronounce the scriptural view of how Christ's deity relates to His humanity. What emerged was faithful to the Scripture, the orthodox position of one person, two natures. Each nature is possessed in fullness. He is not partially God and partially man. Thus the creed states, "coessential [*homoousion;* same in nature] with the Father according to the Godhead, and coessential [*homoousion;* same in nature] with us according to the manhood." Further, the two distinct natures are "united" together, one not mixing with the other, and the two not separated. Thus the creed's statement, "one and the same Christ...to be acknowledged in two natures, without confusion (mixture), without change, without division, and without separation, the distinction of natures being by no means taken away by the union [in the one person]."

Why So Important?

Chalcedon proclaimed the union of the two natures in the one person of Christ, but more importantly set boundaries that should not be crossed. Its pronunciation that the two natures, possessed in their

---

[8]From the Gr. *monos* (μόνος, "one") and *phusis* (φύσις, "nature"). I speak here of the Monophysitism of Eutyches (ca. 380-456), who taught that the humanity of Christ was absorbed into His divinity. Though the Monophysites were not called by this specific designation until after Chalcedon, I nonetheless use the term to refer to the Eutychian doctrine of one nature. Also, note that some Monophysites rejected Eutyches' *absorption* theory, but still held to only one nature in Christ.

fullness, cannot be confused, changed, divided, nor separated specifically targeted the conclusions of Apollinarianism, Nestorianism, and Eutychian Monophysitism. With its statement that the two natures are possessed in their fullness the Apollinarian view was incorrect; Nestorianism was impeached because the two natures cannot be divided or separated; and Monophysitism lost favor with the orthodox position because the two natures cannot be changed or confused (mixed).

All this was not simply for the sake of an intellectual tug of war. There were distinct theological problems that resulted from Apollinarianism, Nestorianism, and Monophysitism. I shall mention one or two for each position.

A problem with Apollinarianism was that if Jesus did not have a human soul, he was not fully human, and therefore was *not* made like us in every respect (Heb. 2:17). As such he could not be capable of redeeming the human soul. Nestorianism's doctrine that Christ had two persons resulted in a split of the God-man. This posed problems with the doctrine of the Trinity (because there are three persons in the Trinity, not four). Additionally, two persons split in this way suggests that the *one person* of Christ did not thirst, grow weary, say "I AM," suffer on the cross, etc.[9] Lastly, Monophysitism's doctrine of one nature (as set forth by Eutyches) renders Christ a divinized man, for it espouses an absorption of the humanity into the divinity.[10] The problem here would be the same as that of Apollinarianism. Christ was not made like His brethren in every respect (Heb. 2:17). Therefore He could not, as a divinized man (thus entirely different from us), represent us on the cross.

How Do We Phrase It?

How, then, do we articulate the position of the union of two natures in the one person of Christ when faced with the sayings and actions of Jesus? How do we make sense of Him hungering, thirsting, growing

---

[9]Christians can easily fall into the error of Nestorianism, making such statements as, "Jesus' deity said 'I AM,'" or, "It was Jesus' humanity that was hungry." Scripture, however, relates that Jesus as full deity *and* full humanity in *one person*, did all the above.

[10]For this reason some do not like the term "God-man" referring to Christ. When I use the term, however, I use it in the Chalcedonian sense.

weary, stating "I AM," and dying on the cross? I suggest a way that honors both the distinction of natures *and* their union in the one person: *By virtue of His _____ (which is in perfect union without mixture, change, division or separation from the other nature), the whole (one) person of Christ could _____.* We answer the above questions by filling in the blanks. By virtue of His humanity, the whole person of Christ could hunger. By virtue of His humanity, the whole person of Christ could die on the cross. By virtue of His deity, the whole person of Christ could state, "I AM."[11]

A Final Word

Reading about the issues and struggling through them ourselves leads to a better understanding of Christ and His work on behalf of sinners. We have, in the sovereign care of God, the hindsight to avoid the errors of others, errors regarding the person of Christ that carried with them unscriptural implications regarding His work.

---

[11]See Charles Hodge, *Systematic Theology,* 3 vols. (Grand Rapids, Mich.: Wm. B. Eerdmans Publishing Co., reprinted, 1986), 2:392-93. Here Hodge lists as categories biblical passages (1) "in which the person [of Christ] is the subject, but the predicate [act or saying of Christ] is true only of the divine nature, or of the Logos. As when our Lord said, 'Before Abraham was I am'"; and (2) "in which the person [of Christ] is the subject, but the predicate is true only of the human nature. As when Christ said, 'I thirst.'" See also Louis Berkhof, *Systematic Theology* (Grand Rapids, Mich.: Wm. B. Eerdmans Publishing Co., fourth revised and enlarged edition, reprinted, 1984), 323-24. In stating this, we must take care not to speculate too far and cross over the limits set by Chalcedon.

Regarding the union of the two natures in the one person of Christ, we also have in Scripture statements concerning "that which is proper to one nature...attributed to the person [of Christ] denominated by the other nature" (*The Westminster Confession of Faith,* chap. 8, art. 7, contained in Philip Schaff, ed., *The Creeds of Christendom,* 3 vols. [Grand Rapids, Mich.: Baker Book House, sixth edition, reprinted, 1985], 3:622). For example, 1 Cor. 2:8b reads, "for if they understood it, they would not have crucified the Lord of glory." See also Rom. 9:5 (*The Westminster Confession of Faith* lists neither of these verses, but lists Acts 20:28; John 3:13; 1 John 3:16).

The Virgin Conception and Birth

The Lord Jesus Christ, the Son of God, was conceived in the womb of the virgin Mary by the Holy Spirit, and was born from the virgin Mary. Doctrinally the virgin conception and birth is indispensable because God has chosen it to be the vehicle by which the eternal Son of God became one of us. Thus through the virgin birth He has come for the salvation of His people.

Some Considerations

By stating that the virginal conception was the means by which *the eternal Son of God* became one of us necessarily eliminates the erroneous idea that Jesus became God at the virginal conception. He was, as we have seen, *always* God. Therefore it was through the virginal conception that Jesus became the *God-man*, and though "there is truth in the close connection established between the virgin birth of our Lord and His Deity," it would be "a mistake to suspend the Deity on the virgin birth as its *ultimate* source or reason."[12]

Nor should we should think that because His conception and birth occurred within and from a virgin, His sinlessness therefore came about only from the fact that He had no human father. Some have proposed the idea that original sin is transferred from the male, not the female, thus producing a sinless Christ. But there is a reason to believe that females as well transfer original sin. Mary was in need of a Savior, just as any sinner was (Luke 1:47), and David infers in his confessional Psalm that "in sin my mother conceived me" (Ps. 51:5). It would therefore be plausible to suggest that Christ was preserved from the

---

[12]Geerhardus Vos, *The Self-disclosure of Jesus* (1926; reprint, Phillipsburg, N.J.: Presbyterian and Reformed, 1978), 182, quoted in Robert L. Reymond, *Jesus, Divine Messiah* (Phillipsburg, N.J.: Presbyterian and Reformed Publishing Co., 1990), 133, emphasis added. By this statement Vos means to communicate that Jesus did not need the virgin birth to be God, since He was God from all eternity. That is why Vos states that though Christ's deity *as the God-man* is closely tied to the virgin birth, it is not the *ultimate* source of His deity.

stain of sin by the divine and supernatural intervention of God from the time of the virginal conception.[13]

Its Purpose

As mentioned before, the purpose of the virgin birth is at least twofold. First, it was the means by which the Son of God was incarnated in the womb of the virgin, the means by which God tabernacled with His people (John 1:14). Second, it provided the means by which He who is fully God and fully human could save His people from their sins (Matt. 1:21).

Scriptural Evidence

The two main references to the virgin birth in the New Testament are found in Matthew and Luke.

In both accounts Mary is called a virgin. Matthew's account begins with the statement that "before [Joseph and Mary] came together she was found to be with child by the Holy Spirit" (1:18). He follows later with a quotation from Isaiah to show that Isaiah's prophecy had been fulfilled: "Behold, the virgin shall be with child, and shall bear a Son, and they shall call His name Immanuel, which translated means, God with us" (1:23). Finally, Matthew states that Joseph "kept her a virgin until[14] she gave birth to a son; and he called His name Jesus" (1:25). In Luke the angel Gabriel was sent to a virgin named Mary (1:26-27) to announce to her that she was going to conceive and bear a son (1:25). After Mary asked the angel how this could be, since she was a virgin (1:34), the angel answered, "The Holy Spirit will come upon you, and the power of the Most High will overshadow you"[15] (1:35). The

---

[13]For all the above under this section I am once again indebted to Robert Reymond (*Jesus, Divine Messiah*, 133-35).

[14]Implying of course that Joseph and Mary had intercourse after the virgin birth.

[15]I take the first phrase ("The Holy Spirit will come upon you") as synonymous with the second ("and the power of the Most High will overshadow you"). That is to say, the Holy Spirit coming upon Mary *is* the Most High (God) overshadowing. This verse therefore proclaims the deity of the Holy Spirit. The phraseology of the power of the Most High overshadowing

emphasis on Mary's virginity at the beginning of the narrative, coupled with the angel's answer to Mary's question (that she would conceive in a way *other* than the conventional one), make it unquestionable that Jesus' conception and birth would be from a virgin.

Finally, the direct agent of the conception of Jesus was God the Holy Spirit. In Matthew 1:18, 20 we read, "she was found to be with child by the Holy Spirit," and "that which has been conceived in her is of the Holy Spirit." Here the Greek preposition translated as "by" (v. 18) and then as "of" (v. 20)[16] is *ek* (ἐκ). This denotes *the means*[17] by which the pre-existent son of God became flesh. The same may be said of Luke 1:35, for the Holy Spirit's activity (His coming upon, His overshadowing) is the cause of the conception.

The Atonement

It was necessary to *precede* this study of the crucifixion and atonement of Jesus with a study of *who* He is, because *who* He is enables Him to be the "lamb who takes away the sin of the world!" It is *who* He is that allows God through the cross event to graciously provide salvation for His people,[18] and render *what* was accomplished on the cross of Christ of utmost importance.

Preliminaries

Before any discussion of the atonement takes place, there should be a discussion of (1) who and what God is, and (2) who and what humanity is. I shall not exhaust the point, but at least a cursory knowledge in both areas is vital to understanding the atonement.[19]

---

in Luke 1:35 is reminiscent of the divine presence by the cloud that covered the tabernacle and filled the tent with the glory of God (see Exod. 40:34-38).

[16]NASB. Translations could also read "through" and "from."

[17]Grammatically an ablative (or genitive) of means.

[18]I might also state that in the study of theology, the converse is true as well. What He has done enables us to see who He is. The nature of this study, however, comes in the challenge of the heresies of the cults, and thus necessitates first to see who Christ is.

[19]Gnostic cults like Christian Science, Unity School of Christianity, and Religious Science fail to do biblical justice to both. The result is a denial of the

God is at the center of the atonement. He is the initiator. He is the giver. He is the provider. He is holy, just, and He is love. He created all things, including humanity, and it was perfect, "very good" (Gen. 1:31). In his love and by His grace He gave to man all that was needed. But man, in his rebellion against the holy and righteous God and His decrees, fell from the pure and innocent state in the Garden, and so sin entered the world and came to all (Rom. 5:12). We therefore are depraved, sinful, to the extent that there is no one that seeks the face of the righteous God apart from His grace (Rom. 3:10-12, 23). This necessitates a demand. A demand from this holy Being that justice be served, that human beings pay the debt owed to Him for the sins they have committed (Rom. 1:18-20; 3:19). God cannot simply let sin go without passing His divine judgment upon the sinner. He cannot. His holiness forbids Him. His righteousness forbids Him (Rom. 3:25).

God is at the center of the atonement in at least two ways: His holiness and His love. In His holiness He cannot pass over sin without judgment. And in His love He has provided the way by which His justice is carried out. That way is the atonement of Christ.

What Does Atonement Mean?

The word carries several nuances, such as covering of sins, reconciliation, and propitiation (removing of wrath; satisfaction). By atonement God forgives sinners, removes His wrath from them, and reconciles them to Himself. Moreover, connected with atonement is sacrifice, the actual death of a victim. This death is *substitutionary.* Here one *takes the place of* others. One suffers, dies, and sheds blood *on behalf of* others.

Old Testament[20]

God's provision of substitutionary sacrifice and atonement through the shedding of blood occurs immediately after the fall. In Genesis 3 God pronounced His judgment, but interlaced it with the promise that

---

atonement of Christ on the cross, for the atonement is the natural outgrowth of both the character of God and the sinfulness of humanity.

[20]For much of the following see W. S. Ried in Goeffrey W. Bromily, gen. ed., *The International Bible Encyclopedia,* 4 vols. (Grand Rapids, Mich.: Wm. B. Eerdmans Publishing Co., 1979), 1:353-54.

He would "put enmity between you [the serpent] and the woman, and between your seed and her seed" (v. 15). This is the great promise of the One to come, and the pronouncement is immediately followed with a type of this great promise, the sacrificing of an animal and its skin used as a covering.

In the patriarchal period and at the Exodus, atonement was substitutionary and pointed to the ultimate atonement provided by Christ. Noah built an altar of sacrifice *to God* (this must be emphasized, for the sacrifice is made *to God*, which is a type of Christ's sacrifice and atonement made *to the Father;* see Eph. 5:2), who, because of sacrifice, made the promise of never again destroying man from the face of the earth as He had done by the flood (Gen. 8:20-21). Abraham and others made sacrifices to the LORD (Gen. 12:7-8; 13:18; 22:9; 26:25; 35:6-7; see John 8:56 for evidence that Old Testament sacrifices *pointed* to Christ). And who can forget the atonement event just before the exodus of God's people from Egypt, where the shedding of blood was provided by a substitutionary victim. The blood was placed on the lintels and doorposts, and so the LORD's wrath passed over the houses that had the blood on them (Exod. 12:23-27; see also in the laws of Moses in Leviticus, chaps. 1-7, 16, 23). In all these examples was the idea of a substitute, one who suffered vicariously for the sins of the people. This theme is contained in Leviticus 1:4: "And he shall lay his hand on the head of the burnt offering, that it may be accepted for him to make atonement on his behalf." Isaiah saw in this very act its final and fullest expression in the coming Messiah: "All of us like sheep have gone astray. Each of us has turned to his own way. But the LORD has caused the iniquity of us all to fall on Him" (Isa. 53:6).

New Testament

Since the point of Old Testament sacrifices was to point to Messiah, the writer of Hebrews, in the context of proclaiming Christ, explains, "Without the shedding of blood there is no forgiveness" (Heb. 9:22). The Messiah, Jesus the Christ, has come once for all to cleanse of sin by the shedding of His blood (Heb. 7:27; 9:28; 10:10).

Substitution[21]

As was discussed, fundamental and essential to the sacrifice is the concept of substitution. Isaiah saw this, as did others (see John 8:56). This was what John the Baptist forcefully proclaimed: "Behold, the Lamb of God who takes away the sin of the world." This substitutionary atonement is the means by which Jesus saves His people from their sins (Matt. 1:21). Indeed, the reason Jesus came was to give His life as a ransom *for* many (Mark 10:45; see also John 11:49-51; 15:13). Paul tells us that "Christ died *for* us" (Rom. 5:8; see also 1 Thess. 5:9-10), and that "Christ...gave Himself up *for* us, an offering and a sacrifice to God as a fragrant aroma" (Eph. 5:2). Further, in order to take our place, Christ lived the perfect life of obedience to the Law of God on our behalf (2 Cor. 5:21; Heb. 4:15; 7:26-27).

Propitiation

The substitutionary death and atonement of Christ is propitiatory. It takes away the wrath of God (Rom. 5:9-10; 1 Thess. 5:9-10). But it is not limited to that alone. Christ as our substitute *took upon Himself* the wrath that should have been ours. The great passage of Romans 3:21-25 teaches us that the righteousness of God that was witnessed by the Law and the Prophets, the righteousness that comes through faith in Jesus, has come (vv. 21, 22). Though all have sinned and deserve God's wrath (see Rom. 1:18), there is redemption in Jesus Christ (vv. 23, 24), "whom God [the Father] displayed publicly as a propitiation in His blood through faith" (v. 25a). That Christ is the propitiatory offering is also seen in Hebrews 2:17, 1 John 2:2 and 4:10.

Reconciliation

The atonement leads to reconciliation. By it the reconciliation of man to God becomes a reality. The estrangement that once existed

---

[21]For some of the following under the subheadings *substitution, propitiation* and *reconciliation*, and for some of the material later listed under *Theological Implications of the Resurrection and Ascension*, I thank Millard J. Erickson in his *Christian Theology* (Grand Rapids, Mich.: Baker Book House, 1985), 811-15; 778-79, respectively.

between the righteous and holy God and sinners has now in Christ become a thing of the past for those who believe. The wrath of God has been turned away from us and has been put on the substitute. The blood of the cross through Jesus Christ's actual death accomplishes this (Col. 1:20; Rom. 5:9-10).

The Love of God

Many oppose the idea that we are sinners and in need of Christ's substitutionary atonement, claiming the "love" of God as a defense. I readily and without hesitation admit that God is love. But what does that phrase mean? To answer that question we must examine where it comes from. First John 4:8 reads, "The one who does not love does not know God, for God is love." First John 4:16 states, "And we have come to know and have believed the love which God has for us. God is love, and the one who abides in love abides in God, and God abides in Him."

First, do these verses appear in the context of God *not* judging? To state it another way, do these verses teach that God will not judge sinners because God is love? No, and one must not cancel out the wrath of God, which is *presently* a reality (Rom. 1:18),[22] because of the love of God. The two must be held in check and balance, for Scripture teaches both. A second point will aid in keeping this balance.

Second, in 1 John 4:8, 16 it is clear that Christians are commanded to love one another (cf. vv. 7, 11, 12, 20, 21). Further, "we love, because He first loved us" (v. 19). This begs the question, "What, then, does John mean by *love*?" The key lies in understanding that *John defines love by what God has done for sinners!*:

> By this the love of God was manifested in us, that God has sent His only begotten Son into the world so that we might live through Him. In this is love, not that we loved God, but that He loved us and sent His Son to be the propitiation for our sins (vv. 9-10).

John defines love as God sparing from His wrath those who trust in Christ. That is to say, the phrase "God is love" appears in the context of the sparing of sinners from the justified wrath of the holy God through

---

[22]The thrust of the Gr. present passive verb *apokaluptetai,* ἀποκαλύπτεται ("it is *continually* being revealed").

the substitutionary atonement of Jesus Christ.[23] This, then, is how we keep the wrath of God and the love of God in balance.

Hebrews 2:14-17

I have mentioned many times throughout this work that the doctrines of Christianity are inseparable. They have fastening them together inextricable links. Hebrews 2:14-17 serves as an example of this. The doctrine of Christ's full humanity is necessary for the fulfillment of His substitutionary atonement.

The Epistle to the Hebrews confirms the all-sufficiency of Christ. It does so by explaining that Christ is God's final word to His covenant people (1:1-2), and that He is the "once for all" sacrifice for sin (7:27; 9:28; 10:10). These claims are grounded in the fact that He is both God (1:3; 8) and man (Heb. 2:14-17):

(14) Since then the children share in flesh and blood, He Himself likewise also partook of the same, that through death He might render powerless him who had the power of death, that is, the devil; (15) and might deliver those who through fear of death were subject to slavery all their lives. (16) For assuredly He does not give help to angels, but He gives help to the descendant of Abraham. (17) Therefore, He had to be made like His brethren in all things, that He might become a merciful and faithful high priest in things pertaining to God, to make propitiation for the sins of the people.

In verse 14a the "children" spoken of are the children that God has given to Christ (v. 13). They are Christians made anew in Christ. And "since then" (or "since therefore")[24] these children are "flesh and blood," i.e. human beings, Christ "likewise" was made flesh and blood. Christ Himself is, like us, truly human.

Why did He *have* to be human? The first *reason*[25] is that through death He might render the devil powerless (v. 14b). Jesus had to be

---

[23]Further, when sinners have been redeemed by His grace through faith in Christ, they may then fulfill the purpose (note the Gr. *hina* introducing the subjunctive clause in 1 John 4:9, *hina zēsōmen di' autou,* ἵνα ζήσωμεν δι' αὐτοῦ, "*so that* we may live through Him") of living through Him, thus loving one another.

[24]Gr. *epei oun,* ἐπεὶ οὖν.

[25]Signaled by the Gr. *hina* (ἵνα) starting the second part of v. 14.

human, that through His substitutionary death and blood atonement[26] He might take away forever the devil's power. The second reason is given in verse 15. His complete humanity allows His atoning death to deliver His people from fear of death. Then, as verse 16 states in explanatory fashion,[27] Christ has not identified with angels (He has not become an angel), but with the descendant of Abraham, "the family of faith"[28] (see vv. 10-13).

All the above being so,[29] Christ "had to be made like His brethren in all things" (or "in every respect"[30]), though of course He was without sin (4:15). The point is that if He was to deliver Christians from the power and the fear of death, He would have to share in their complete humanity. As the writer continues, we learn the ultimate purpose of Christ's full humanity: *in order that*[31] He may serve as the believer's great high priest, *to make propitiation for the sins of the people.* By Christ being human He is thus capable of taking upon Himself the wrath we justly deserve. Humanity must pay the price of sin, and Christ did, in our stead.

Salvation

Jesus (1) always existed as God the Son in fellowship with the Father, (2) united with His full deity full humanity by being born of the virgin Mary by the agency of God the Holy Spirit, (3) lived a life in perfect obedience to the Father, and (4) was crucified and shed His blood to make propitiation for the sins of the people. *Salvation* occurs when the work of Christ is applied to sinners, who are then delivered (saved) from the penalty of sin, which is eternal judgment. Paul tells believers that they "have been saved" (Eph. 2:5, 8), indicating that they *presently* stand delivered by God.[32] Paul also tells believers that they

---

[26]Though the text specifically does not mention His blood, His shed blood is indeed a central theme of the whole epistle. Thus, there is every exegetical reason to believe that the writer has Christ's vicarious atonement in view.

[27]Gr. *gar* (γὰρ, "for") is explanatory.

[28]Bruce, *The Epistle to the Hebrews*, 51.

[29]Signaled by the Gr. *hothen*, ὅθεν.

[30]Gr. *kata panta*, κατὰ πάντα.

[31]Gr. *hina.*

[32]Gr. *este sesōsmenoi*, ἐστε σεσῳσμένοι, "you [pl.] are having been saved."

"*shall* be saved from the wrath of God through Him [Christ]" (Rom. 5:9).[33]

Through Christ Alone

Salvation is in Jesus alone: "I am the way, and the truth, and the life; no one comes to the Father, but through Me" (John 14:6); "And there is salvation in no one else; for there is no other name under heaven that has been given among men, by which we must be saved" (Acts 4:12). It is exegetically unsound to proclaim any other message. This is an *exclusive* claim, and must be maintained if the Church is to stay "the Church."

Is this claim of Christ universally binding upon *all* humanity at *all* times? To begin to answer, John 14:6 must be interpreted in light of what has preceded it. In the prologue of his Gospel, John writes first that Jesus is God (1:1). He then calls Jesus God's *unique* Son (3:16; cf. 1:14, 18). God the Father sent His Son into the world, that whoever believes in Him might have eternal life and not perish (3:16). Since Jesus is *God*, and since He is the Father's *unique Son* sent to the world in order that sinners might be saved, by necessity His claims and the claims of His apostles are unique and exclusive *for all time and all cultures*. This message, this kind of preaching, characterized the powerful ministries of the apostles. It remains today the only message that will be empowered by the Spirit of God.

How Is Salvation Apprehended?

By Grace through faith. Grace is the agent, faith the vehicle. Having been convinced by the Holy Spirit that we are sinners, and that without faith (trust) in God's only provision for salvation we will incur the wrath of God (cf. Eph. 2:1-3), we then place our faith in the person and work of Christ, and are saved. We are saved by the grace of God through faith in Jesus Christ (Eph. 2:8a; cf. 2:3-4). And lest we believe that we have anything to do with it, Paul is quick to add that this is "not of yourselves, it is the gift of God" (Eph. 2:8b).

---

[33]Though Christians *are* saved, they also *will be* saved. This evidences the "already, not yet" aspects of the kingdom of God.

Theologically Related Terms

Salvation includes *regeneration, justification, adoption, sanctification, and glorification.*

Regeneration is the *new birth.* This occurs when a person is spiritually reborn, born again (see John 3:3). As such the person is a new creation in Christ and sees things from a new and godly perspective (2 Cor. 5:17). If we have been regenerated our desire is to live righteously and to please God in all we do, that He might be glorified.

Paul writes that we have been justified by faith (Rom. 5:1). *Justification* is a declaration by God that we are viewed by Him in such a way that we may have fellowship with Him. We are justified in His sight on the basis of the cross of Christ. But we can only be declared righteous if the righteousness of Christ is reckoned to us by faith in Christ (Rom. 4:5, 11, 16, 24; 5:1).

Adoption reverses the alienation (see Eph. 2:12) of the individual with God due to sin, and brings the believer into the family of God in the ultimate, salvific sense. To become a child of God in the salvific sense, one must through Christ be adopted (Rom. 8:15, 23;[34] Gal. 4:5; Eph. 1:5).[35]

Sanctification is the continuing process of being set apart for God, and applies "to the church of God..., to those who have been sanctified[36] in Christ Jesus" (1 Cor. 1:2). Believers are set apart to live righteously in Christ to the glory of God. It continues what regeneration began.

Glorification is the completion of the process of sanctification. This takes place when Christ comes to establish His kingdom in all its fullness. When glorified, believers will receive new bodies, patterned,

---

[34]Adoption is used here in the sense of our bodies being redeemed at the consummation of the ages.

[35]Basing universal salvation on the fact that all are children of God fails to take into account the doctrines of God's holiness and humanity's sinfulness. Further, it fails to account for the two levels of "children" in the Bible. Though all may be children of God *by creation,* not all are children of God *by adoption.*

[36]Gr. *hēgiasmenois,* ἡγιασμένοις, the perfect passive participle indicating a completed action in the past that continues in the believer's life.

of course, after Jesus Christ's glorious body of flesh and bones (Phil. 3:20-21; 1 John 3:2; cf. Luke 24:39).

The Mediatorship/High Priesthood of Christ

Because of who He is and what He has done, Jesus is our mediator (1 Tim. 2:5-6) and great high priest (Heb. 2:17; 3:1; 4:14). These offices belong to Christ exclusively (cf. Heb. 7:24[37]), for He is God's unique Son who has made propitiation *to the Father* for the sins of the people. In this section I will discuss His mediatorial and high priestly role in the context of His crucifixion and death.

1 Timothy 2:5

"For there is one God, and one mediator also between God and men, the man Christ Jesus." Christ is called the only mediator between God and humanity. The important question is *why*.

Verse 6a immediately follows: "who gave Himself as a ransom for all." The tie between His death on the cross and His mediatorship is inescapable. This clause cannot be severed from verse 5; it is connected to it, and is the *reason* (along with the fact that He is a "man") for the title "mediator." Simply put, Jesus is the sole mediator between God and humanity *because* of His crucifixion and death on the cross.[38]

---

[37]Christ's "Melchizedek Priesthood" is "permanent" (Gr. *aparabaton*, ἀπαράβατον). Considering that Hebrews calls Christ both God (1:3, 8) and man (2:14, 17), states that He is God's final word to the people of the new covenant (1:3), and states that His sacrifice on the cross is all-sufficient and once for all (7:27), both Mormonism and the Scottish Rite of Freemasonry greatly err in their giving of the Melchizedek Priesthood to male adherents. For Mormonism, see *Doctrines of the Gospel: Student Manual* (Salt Lake City, Utah: The Church of Jesus Christ of Latter-day Saints, 1986), 67-68. For Masonry see Albert Pike, *Liturgy of the Ancient and Accepted Scottish Rite of Freemasonry for the Southern Jurisdiction of the United States,* part 4, degrees 19-30 (no other bibliographical information given, except to say that it was obtained from the Scottish Rite, Southern Jurisdiction of Washington, D.C.), 20. This is difficult to obtain. The reader may consult my *Masonic Rites and Wrongs: An Examination of Freemasonry* (Phillipsburg, N.J.: Presbyterian and Reformed Publishing Co., 1995), 182.

[38]It therefore is theologically dangerous to label anyone else mediator, "co-mediatrix" or "the mediatrix of graces." See Introduction, n. 25.

Hebrews 9:14-15

If the blood of bulls and goats once served for the cleansing of the flesh (Heb. 9:13),

> (14) how much more will the blood of Christ, who through the eternal Spirit offered Himself without blemish to God, cleanse your conscience from dead works to serve the living God? (15) And for this reason He is the mediator of a new covenant, in order that since a death has taken place for the redemption of the transgressions that were committed under the first covenant, those who have been called may receive the promise of the eternal inheritance.

Once again Christ is called the mediator. As mediator, Jesus has offered Himself "to God [the Father]." And again for this title we have as the reason (v. 15[39]) "the blood of Christ," the crucifixion and death of Christ (v. 14). The purpose is found in verse 15, "that[40] those who have been called might receive the promise of the eternal inheritance."

1 John 2:1-2a

John's first epistle opens with a declaration about the incarnate Word, Jesus Christ. The apostle emphasizes the physical nature of Jesus; He was seen with the eye, he was handled with the hand (1 John 1:1). Then comes the sobering truth that sin is very real, even in the life of the believer, and that the believer must acknowledge sin in his life and confess it. When this occurs, the blood of Christ *continues* to cleanse[41] the believer (v. 7), making fellowship with God possible on a continuing basis.

John is also careful to exhort believers that sin, although very real, is something they should resist. But when they fail, they may go to Jesus, the "Advocate." He writes, *"My little children, I am writing these things to you that you may not sin. And if anyone sins, we have an Advocate with the Father, Jesus Christ the righteous; and He Himself is the propitiation for our sins"* (1 John 2:1-2a).

---

[39]Gr. *dia touto,* διὰ τοῦτο, "therefore," "for this reason."

[40]Gr. *hopōs,* ὅπως.

[41]Gr. *katharizei,* καθαρίζει, the present tense, thus continuous action.

Jesus *intercedes* for His people. He is the Advocate in the legal sense, that believers may continue their righteous standing before God the Father. The phrase "with[42] the Father" in 1 John 2:1 does not mean that Jesus, *along with* the Father, is the Advocate. Rather, Jesus is the Advocate *in the Father's presence*. The preposition "with" refers to the *closeness* of relationship between the Father and the Son, a fact already communicated by John in the introduction: "we...proclaim to you the eternal life [Jesus], which was with[43] the Father" (1:2). This should also be considered in light of the very first verse of the Gospel of John, which states that "the Word was with[44] God [the Father]" (John 1:1). Thus, "if anyone sins, we have an Advocate with the Father" means that when Christians sin, they may call upon the Advocate, who is close to the Father and will intercede for them.

Once again (as was the case with 1 Tim. 2:5 and Heb. 9:15), Christ's mediatorial role in 1 John 2:1 arises because of His act of substitutionary atonement (propitiation) on the cross. After stating that Christ is our Advocate, John immediately and emphatically makes mention of the atonement (v. 2). Any mention of Christ's mediatorship without regard to His substitutionary atonement is incomplete; the two are linked in such a way that the former cannot exist without the latter. And because of the latter, Christ must be viewed as our *only* mediator.

The Resurrection of Christ

When the Bible speaks of the resurrection of Christ, it speaks of Christ being raised from the dead *bodily*.[45] Christ died a real death, and

---

[42]Gr. *pros*, πρὸς.

[43]Ibid.

[44]Ibid.

[45]Two biblical passages often cited by Jehovah's Witnesses to deny Christ's *bodily* resurrection and ascension are 1 Cor. 15:50 and 1 Pet. 3:18. We read in 1 Cor. 15:50 that "flesh and blood cannot inherit the kingdom of God." The Witnesses take this to mean that Jesus cannot have a body in His present state with the Father. The phrase *flesh and blood,* however, refers to the present mortal, corruptible and perishable bodies *we now possess* (see vv. 42, 50, 53, 54). These must and will be "changed" (v. 51) at the resurrection (v. 52). Christ, of course, does not possess a mortal, corruptible and perishable body. He as the resurrected and ascended Son of God possesses a glorified and immortal body. Thus, the Jehovah's Witnesses commit a category fallacy by

three days after His death His body was made alive. Made alive, however, in a new state. At His resurrection His body was made glorious and immortal. Moreover, it was a body of flesh and bones (Luke 24:39). Jesus' resurrected body is the prototype of what Christians' resurrection bodies will be (1 John 3:2; Phil. 3:21). Finally, though the *state* of Christ's human body was changed, He nonetheless remains human (in union with His deity).

Scriptural Evidence

That Christ was raised bodily from the dead is confirmed in at least three passages.[46]

John 2:19, 21

Jesus says, "Destroy this temple, and in three days I will raise it up" (v. 19). John then interprets what Jesus meant by "temple": "He was speaking of the temple of [or *which was*[47]] His body." Note the

---

applying 1 Cor. 15:50 and its phrase "flesh and blood" to the now resurrected Christ.

In 1 Pet. 3:18 we read that Christ was "put to death in the flesh [Gr. *sarki*, σαρκὶ], but made alive in the spirit [Gr. *pneumati*, πνεύματι]." They interpret this to mean that Jesus' body died, but His spirit was raised (thus He was raised a spirit creature). Rather than speaking about the *parts* of Christ that died and rose, i.e., His body and His spirit, this verse speaks of the *spheres* (or realms) in which Christ died and was made alive. In the Greek text we have two datives, *sarki* ("in the flesh") and *pneumati* ("in the spirit"). These should be viewed as datives of sphere. That is to say, Christ was put to death *in the fleshly sphere* (the fleshly realm, the physical realm where the soldiers nailed Him to the cross), but was made alive *in the spiritual sphere* (the spiritual realm). Verse 19 follows: "in which [Gr. *en hō*, ἐν ᾧ] also He went and made proclamation to the spirits now in prison." The preposition *en* with the dative relative pronoun *hō* ("in which") refers back to the spiritual sphere *"in which"* Christ was made alive (end of v. 18). Consequently He made proclamation *to the spirits in this spiritual sphere* (v. 19). Taken this way the verse makes perfect sense.

[46]In addition to the following, see Phil. 3:21.

[47]I take the Gr. *tou sōmatos*, τοῦ σώματος, as an appositive genitive (or epexegetical genitive, or genitive of definition).

pronouns, "*this* temple," "the temple of *His* body." The point is that *His* body was raised.[48]

John 20:27[49]

Eight days before one of Jesus' post-resurrection appearances, Thomas was doubting that his companions had seen the Lord (John 20:25). Jesus then appeared to Thomas and the other disciples and invited Thomas to physically touch His resurrected body (20:27). The fact that Jesus' hands still had the prints of the nails, and that His side still had the hole in it, proves that Jesus' prediction in John 2:19 was true. There He promised to raise up *His* body in three days.

Luke 24:39

"See My hands and My feet, that it is I Myself; touch Me and see, for a spirit does not have flesh and bones as you see that I have."

On yet another occasion Jesus appeared physically to His disciples. As is the case with John 20:27, based on the prediction in John 2:19 that Jesus would raise up His own body, we must take this verse to teach that the Jesus who appeared to the disciples is the *same* Jesus who died. The opening verse of the pericope states "He *Himself* stood in their midst" (24:36).

Luke 24:37 mentions that the disciples were frightened because they thought they were seeing a spirit. In the following verse Jesus Himself asked them why they were troubled and why they were doubting. As quoted above, He showed them His hands and feet, saying, "It is I Myself." He then ate with them, which further proves the physical nature of His resurrection (v. 43).

---

[48]Jehovah's Witnesses state that after His death, the body of Jesus was annihilated before His *spirit* was resurrected. They further believe that the post "resurrection" appearances were made with other "materialized" bodies made to look like Jesus' former body.

[49]When sharing with a Jehovah's Witness concerning *their* teaching that Jesus' original body was not raised, start with John 2:19-21. If not, Jehovah's Witnesses may interpret this passage and the following passage to mean that Jesus *did* appear in a body (a *materialized* and *different* body). When John 2:19-21 is mentioned first, it eliminates this option on their part.

The Ascension of Christ

Acts 1 gives an eyewitness account of the ascension. Luke states that after Christ's post-resurrection appearances (cf. v. 3), Christ ascended into heaven in the cloud (vv. 9, 11; cf. Luke 24:50-51; Eph. 4:8-10; Heb. 1:3; 4:14; 9:24). Christ ascended to the right hand of the Father in His own glorified body of flesh and bones. Therefore the significance of the incarnation continues with the ascension. Jesus is still, and forever will be, the God-man, our great high priest and mediator.

Theological Implications of the Resurrection and Ascension

First, if Christ is not resurrected we are still in our sins, our preaching is in vain, we are proven false witnesses of God, our faith is worthless, all the dead will perish, and we of all the people of the world are most to be pitied (1 Cor. 15:14-19).

Second, as noted above, the resurrection and ascension mark a continuation of Jesus' incarnation. He still remains the God-man.

Third, as the unique Son of God, and because He is both God and man, He is able to be mediator and great high priest. Because of Christ's continuing incarnation as mediator and high priest, His blood keeps on cleansing[50] as sin is confessed (1 John 1:7; cf. 2:1).

Fourth, the resurrection and ascension are necessary if Christ is going to "prepare a place" for us (John 14:2-3: "*I go* to prepare a place for you").

Fifth, because Christ is the prototype of the new humanity to come, believers have the hope of being given new resurrection bodies (Phil. 3:20-21; 1 John 3:2).

Sixth, Christ told His disciples that if He did not go away, the Holy Spirit would not come (John 16:7). Thus, Christ's resurrection and ascension are necessary for the Spirit to exercise His role in the Church.

Seventh, the atonement of Christ, which provides His people with justification and forgiveness, is brought to its conclusion in His resurrection (see Rom. 4:25). Because He lives forever, His people will live forever.

---

[50]So interpreted because of the present tense of the verb *katharizo.*

Eighth, the resurrection and ascension of Jesus precede His exaltation (He ascended to the right hand of the Father in exaltation [Acts 2:33]; by the phrase "right hand of the Father" is meant a place of absolute authority and power). If the exaltation is to take place, both the resurrection and ascension must occur.

Finally, because of His resurrection, ascension, and exaltation, He will come again as exalted and righteous judge of the world (Acts 17:31). As a result, every knee will bow and every tongue will confess that Jesus is Lord, to the glory of God the Father (Phil. 2:10-11).[51]

Conclusion

He who was eternally with the Father, the timeless Son of God, the *logos,* united to Himself full and perfect humanity. He did so to give His life as a ransom for many. Without His humanity He would not be able make atonement for the sins of the people. Without His humanity He would not be capable of being the Christian's mediator and great high priest, able to intercede on behalf of His people to the Father. Without His humanity the Christian would never have the hope of one day being given a new body in conformity with the body of His glory.

---

[51]These verses in Philippians do not mean that all will be saved, i.e., all will one day confess Christ as Lord, and God will forgive them. Universalism results from such a reading, partly because it fails to interpret the passage in light of Christ's statement in Matt. 7:21-23. Here the false prophets, at the final judgment will call Jesus "Lord" (v. 22), but will not be saved (see v. 23).

Appendix 1

On the Spirit

Common among cults is a denial of the deity and personality of the Holy Spirit. For example, the Jehovah's Witnesses believe the Holy Spirit to be God's "active force," an "it," and not God. Christian Science calls the Holy Ghost "Divine Science," and the descent of the Holy Ghost some sort of divinely derived consciousness that illumines people.

Because He is God, and because He indwells and empowers both the Church and individual Christians, we should have an understanding of who the Holy Spirit is. *The Holy Spirit is the third person of the Trinity.* From this sentence we gather (1) that the Spirit is a person and (2) that He is God.

The Personality of the Holy Spirit

A person is someone who has *will, intellect,* and *emotion.* In 1 Corinthians 12:11 we are told that the Spirit distributes His gifts "just as He wills." In 1 Corinthians 2:11 the Spirit is said to know the thoughts of God. And in Ephesians 4:30 the Spirit can be grieved.

These are, respectively, examples of the Holy Spirit exercising will, intellect and emotion.

Further evidencing the Spirit's personality are things that He does. Only a person can speak (Acts 13:2), teach (John 14:26), send out workers (Acts 13:4), be lied to and be tempted (Acts 5:3, 4, 9), be grieved (Eph. 4:30), be blasphemed (Matt. 12:31), and exercise will (1 Cor. 12:11).

Even though the personality of the Spirit is not primarily determined because of pronouns in both Greek and Hebrew, and even though the noun in Greek for *Spirit* is neuter and not masculine or feminine (the Hebrew for *Spirit* is feminine), I use the pronouns "He" and "Him" when referring to the Holy Spirit. There are two reasons for this. *First,* to use the pronoun "it" in English implies lack of personality. As we have seen, the Spirit is a person, and therefore we should avoid the use of "it." *Second,* in John 16:13, 14 John breaks a rule of Greek grammar in the effort to refer to the Spirit as "He." In Greek, pronouns must match their referents in person and gender. So, when we come to John 16:13 ("But when He [*ekeinos,* ἐκεῖνος, masculine pronoun], the Spirit [*pneuma,* πνεῦμα, neuter noun] of truth, comes"), and John 16:14 ("He [*ekeinos*] shall glorify Me"), we notice that the pronoun/noun matching is not followed. Here, *ekeinos,* which is masculine, does not match *pneuma,* a neuter noun (it should have been the neuter *ekeino,* ἐκεῖνο). My conclusion is that John (and Jesus) intends to refer to the Holy Spirit as "He."

Finally, the Spirit is referred to by Christ as the "comforter" (*parakletos,* παράκλητος) in John 14:26, 15:26, and 16:7. Jesus Himself is called the "comforter" (*parakletos;* also translated as "advocate") in 1 John 2:1. Quite interesting are Jesus' words in John 14:16. Here He states that the Father is going to send to the disciples "another comforter." This strongly implies the personality of the Holy Spirit, for just as Jesus was the comforter, and only a person can be such, so is the Spirit. The conclusion is that since Jesus is a person, the Spirit is as well.[1]

---

[1]Context supports this interpretation of John 14:16. Jesus' teaching on the Spirit contained in chaps. 14, 15 and 16 provide grounds for calling the Spirit "another (i.e., of the same kind) comforter." Note that the text uses *allos* (ἄλλος), usually denoting "another of the same kind," and not *heteros* (ἕτερος), meaning "different." This distinction between the Greek *allos* and *heteros,* however, does not always hold throughout the New Testament.

The Deity of the Holy Spirit

There are four ways by which we conclude that the Holy Spirit is God. First are Scripture passages which equate the Spirit with God, second are passages that see Him functionally as God, third are passages that place Him on equal par with the Father and the Son, and fourth are passages that assign divine attributes to Him.

An example of the first occurs in Acts 5:3-4. Here Peter is holding Ananias accountable for keeping for himself some of the money he had obtained from selling a piece of property. Peter asks, "Why has Satan filled your heart to lie to the Holy Spirit?" (v. 3). In verse 4 Peter states, "You have not lied to men, but to God." This is a synonymous parallelism. Peter equates lying to the Holy Spirit with lying to God and thus calls the Spirit "God." Some see in these verses two referents, namely the Spirit (v. 3) and the Father (v. 4). This may be, but even here the point is that the Spirit and the Father are both being lied to; the first is just as severe as the second and implies equality.

That the Spirit functions as God is evidenced by 1 Corinthians 6:19: "Do you not know that your [plural] body is a temple of the Holy Spirit who is in you [plural]." Such a statement should not be taken lightly. This temple language is without doubt reminiscent of the presence of Yahweh in His temple in the Old Testament. The Spirit is God's presence among His covenant people.[2] As Gordon Fee states, "we are indwelt by God himself. The Spirit is the fulfillment of God's promise to dwell in and among his people; the Spirit is God *present* among us."[3]

Fulfilling our third category are Matthew 28:19 and 2 Corinthians 13:14. The command in Matthew is to baptize disciples "in the name of the Father and the Son and the Holy Spirit." The doxology in 2

Context must rule. See, for example, Paul's use of *allos* for "another Jesus" in 2 Cor. 11:4, and his use of *heteros* in the same verse for "different gospel" and "different spirit." It is difficult to imagine that by "another Jesus" Paul meant another of the same kind. Therefore the fact that Jesus calls the Holy Spirit "another" (*allos*) comforter does not *necessarily* mean another of the same kind, unless context supports it, and it does.

[2]See also the synonymous parallelism in Ps. 139:7: "Where can I go from Thy Spirit? Or where can I flee from Thy presence?" Here the Spirit *is* God's presence.

[3]Gordon D. Fee, *God's Empowering Presence: The Holy Spirit in the Letters of Paul* (Peabody, Mass.: Hendrickson Publishers, 1994), 8.

Corinthians reads, "The grace of our Lord Jesus Christ, and the love of God, and the fellowship of the Holy Spirit, be with you all." In both of these the Spirit is listed together with the Father and the Son. In Matthew the Spirit shares with the Father and Son ownership of new believers, as well as sharing with both persons the "authority" (i.e. *name*) into which new believers are baptized. In 1 Corinthians the Spirit shares, with the Father and the Son, ministry to all believers. In both texts there is an implied equality of all three persons.

Finally, divine attributes are assigned to the Holy Spirit (I could have placed these in our second category as well). He is everywhere present (omnipresent, Ps. 139:7), knows all things (omniscient, 1 Cor. 2:11), exercises infinite power (sovereign omnipotence, Luke 1:35; John 16:8; 1 Cor. 12:11), is Himself eternal (Heb. 9:14), and is creator (Gen. 1:2).

Appendix 2

On the Trinity

The doctrine of the Trinity has been tried, tested, attacked, and erroneously redefined throughout the centuries. The Christian, in the face of these challenges, must give a reasoned defense of what the Scripture says regarding this basic and essential doctrine of Christianity.

Some Presuppositions

For our purpose we shall assume three things: (1) the Bible is the word of God;[1] (2) we are finite; (3) God is infinite. Therefore, although we cannot *fully comprehend how* the one God is three persons (because of presuppositions 2 and 3), we can nonetheless *fully apprehend that* the one God is three persons (because of presupposition 1).

---

[1] In calling this a presupposition I by no means suggest that it cannot be defended, or that I *blindly* believe that the Bible is the word of God. Two good introductory books on the subject are Josh McDowell, *Evidence that Demands a Verdict* (San Bernardino, Calif.: Here's Life Publishers, Inc., 1979), and Norman L. Geisler and William E. Nix, *A General Introduction to the Bible* (Chicago, Ill.: Moody Press, 1986).

The Doctrine

Three sentences provide us with a statement of the doctrine, each with Scripture to support them: There is one God (Isa. 43:10). God is the Father (2 Pet. 1:17), and the Son (John 20:28), and the Holy Spirit (Acts 5:3-4). The three distinct persons are the one God (Matt. 28:19). Following is a commentary on this statement.

There is One God

Christianity is monotheistic. It believes in the existence of only one God: "Before Me there was no God formed, and there will be none after me" (Isa. 43:10). Other "so-called" gods (cf. 1 Cor. 8:5) do not in reality exist as deity (cf. Gal. 4:8).

God is the Father

In 2 Peter 1:17 we have a person called the Father, and He is called God: "For when He received honor and glory from God the Father, such an utterance as this was made to Him by the Majestic Glory, 'This is My beloved Son with whom I am well-pleased.'"

And the Son

In John 20:28 Thomas confesses Jesus as both Lord and God. We therefore have a person called the Son, and He is called God: "Thomas answered and said to Him, 'My Lord and my God!'"

And the Holy Spirit

Peter in Acts 5:3 exclaims, "Ananias, why has Satan filled your heart to lie to the Holy Spirit?" He then states that Ananias has "not lied to men, but to God" (v. 4). Here we have a person called the Holy Spirit, and He is equated with God (see Appendix 1).

If there is only one God, and there are three persons in the New Testament that are called God, we must conclude that *somehow* the three persons are the one God (remember our presuppositions).

The Three Distinct Persons are the One God

Matthew 28:19 states, "baptizing them in the name of the Father and the Son and the Holy Spirit." The "name," the authority, into which believers are baptized (and with whom they are identified) is "the Father and the Son and the Holy Spirit." "Name" is *singular*, and consists of the three distinct persons. Why distinct? A Greek grammatical rule states that when two or more singular personal nouns (not proper names) are connected by "and" (*kai,* καὶ), and all these nouns are preceded by the definite article "the," they must be understood as separate and distinct.[2] Here we have three singular personal nouns (Father, Son, Holy Spirit) that are each preceded by the definite article "the" (*tou,* τοῦ) and are separated by "and" (*kai*):

> *eis to onoma tou patros*
> in   the name of the Father

> *kai tou huiou*
> and of the Son

> *kai tou hagiou pneumatos*[3]
> and of the Holy Spirit

For this reason the Church believes that the one God (the one name, the one authority) with whom believers are identified, and by whom

---

[2]See James A. Brooks and Carlton L. Winbery, *Syntax of New Testament Greek* (Lanham, Md.: University Press of America, 1979), 70, and F. Blass and A. Debrunner, *A Greek Grammar of the New Testament and Other Early Christian Literature,* trans. and rev. by Robert W. Funk (Chicago, Ill.: University of Chicago Press, 1961), 144-45. With proper names the article need not be repeated for distinctness (see Matt. 17:1: *ton Petron kai Iakōbon kai Iōannēn,* τὸν Πέτρον καὶ Ἰάκωβον καὶ Ἰωάννην, "Peter and James and John"). The same holds for plural nouns (see Matt. 3:7: *tōn Pharisaiōn kai Saddoukaiōn,* τῶν Φαρισαίων καὶ Σαδδουκαίων, "the Pharisees and Sadducees"), and impersonal nouns (see Eph. 3:12: *tēn parrēsian kai prosagōgēn,* τὴν παρρησίαν καὶ προσαγωγὴν, "the boldness and access").

[3]εἰς τὸ ὄνομα τοῦ πατρὸς καὶ τοῦ υἱοῦ καὶ τοῦ ἁγίου πνεύματος.

believers are owned, is the Father and the Son and the Holy Spirit. Further, the three distinct persons exist *simultaneously* as the one God.[4]

This theme of ownership by the Father, the Son, and the Holy Spirit must not go without notice. The Old Testament parallel of *Yahweh's* ownership of His covenant people is vivid. Yahweh's people are "called by My name" (Isa. 43:7). As such they are His possession and come under His authority (cf. Isa. 43:1, 10a). Simply put, covenant people belong to the Deity. It is precisely this covenantal theme that is expressed in Matthew 28:19, for newly baptized ones are those who have come into covenant relationship with, and fall under the ownership of, the Father and the Son and the Holy Spirit. It therefore is beyond doubt that the Deity, the one "name," is the Father and the Son and the Holy Spirit.

---

[4]Three persons existing simultaneously is evidenced by Christ praying to the Father (Matt. 26:42), and by the Father and the Son and the Holy Spirit being present at Jesus' baptism (Matt. 3:16-17). Another example of at least two persons of the Trinity existing at the same time is found in 2 John 3, where we read that "grace, mercy and peace will be with us, from God the Father and from Jesus Christ, the Son of the Father." Further, the fact that the Father *sends* the Son implies the Son's existence *with the Father* (see John 1:1; 17:3, 5; 1 John 1:2) in order for the Father to send Him. The simultaneous existence of the three persons is in distinct contrast to modalism, which states that there is only one person in the Godhead, and that this one person exists at any given moment only as the Father, then at another time only as the Son, and then only as the Holy Spirit. In short, "one person, three modes." Modern-day expressions of modalism are found in the United Pentecostal Church and in Swedenborgianism (see chaps. 1 and 8 under United Pentecostal Church, and chap. 8, n. 97 for Swedenborgianism). Oftentimes those who hold to the doctrine of the Trinity erroneously describe it in modalistic terms, one of the most popular analogies being, "I'm one person, and I am a Father, a husband, and an executive."

Scripture and Source Index

Note: Scripture passages listed in the Table of Contents are not listed herein.

Genesis
1:1 16
1:2 220
1:26-27 107n
1:31 201
2:9 155
2:16-17 155
3:15 202
6:2 29
8:20-21 202
12:7-8 202
13:18 202
16:11 57
17:3 82
18:19 93n
19:13 61
21:33 27
22:9 202
22:11 127
26:24 88

26:25 202
32:10 140
35:6-7 202
46:2 127

Exodus
3:4 127
4:22 29, 56, 107n
4:23 29
4:31 57
5:3 156
6:10 142
9:15 156
12:23-27 202
12:46 26
15:7 69
16:7 142
16:31-33 155n
21:6 133n
22:24 69

23:17 70
24:16 57, 72n
24:17 57, 72n
32:10 69
32:11 69
32:12 69
32:32-33 155n
33:14 57
34:5 73
34:6 73, 148
40:34 72, 142
40:34-35 24
40:34-38 200n

Leviticus
1:4 202
19:31 xvin
20:6 xvin
24:11 129

68:18 97, 98
68:28-30 97
68:31 97
69:28 155n
78:24 155n
78:31 69
78:38 69
78:49 69
78:70 88
79:6 69
82:6 133n
82:7 133n
86:12 148
89:3 88, 140
89:7 29
89:9 62
89:20 88
89:27 108n, 134n, 136
89:27a 108
89:27b 108
90:2 3, 21, 22n
94:1 113
96:3 122
102:1 135
102:12 135
102:15 135
102:16 135
102:18 135
102:19 135
102:22 135
102:25-27 23n
103:19 61
103:20 61
104:3 30n, 60
105:6 88
105:26 88
105:42 88
106:21 113
107:27-28 62
107:29 61n, 62
110:1 68, 69, 136
110:5 69
113:1 88

118:22 143
119:89 65
119:160 65
130:8 28, 56
136:1 157
136:3 157
136:22 88
139:7 219n, 220
148:2 61

Proverbs
3:11-12 156
3:12 156
24:12 156

Ecclesiastes
12:7 126n

Isaiah
5:7 60
6:1 70, 81
6:5 67, 70
6:10 80
6:10b 128n
7:14 28n
8:12b-13a 144
8:13 143n, 144, 145
8:13-14 144
8:14 143n
8:14b 144
8:15 143n
8:19-20 xvin
9:6 28n, 57, 108n, 145, 145n
10:21 57, 145, 145n
11:4 157
13:6-9 94
19:1 30n, 60, 72n, 152, 153n
20:3 88
26:17 94
26:18 94
26:19 94
26:21 94

27:1 94
27:2 94
27:12 94
27:13 94
28:11 92n
28:12 92n
28:16 143
37:35 88
40:3 58
40:8 64
40:10 158
40:28 27
41:8 140
42:8 63, 152n
43:1 122, 128
43:3 113
43:5 66
43:6 29
43:7 122, 128
43:10 xix, 31n, 56, 88, 122, 123, 128, 140, 222
43:11 113, 114, 114n
43:12 122
43:21 122, 128
43:25 59
44:6 82, 106n, 155, 158
44:8 122
45:15 113
45:21 113, 114, 114n
45:21-24 141
45:23 95n
45:23b 104
48:11 152n
48:12 155, 158
49:18 95n
49:26 113
52:13 104
52:13-14 102n
52:13-53:12 102
52:14 103

53:1 80
53:2 102n, 103
53:6 202
53:12 102, 103
53:12a 104
56:5 155n
56:7 63
56:7b 63
60:16 113
62:2 155n
62:11 158
63:8 113
65:15 155n
66:6 62

Jeremiah
2:21 60
4:31 95n
6:14 94
6:24 95
7:11 63
7:11a 63
7:25 88
8:11 94n
9:23-24 148
9:23-26 105
11:16-17 60
11:20 156
12:2 60
14:8 113
17:10 156, 158
22:23 95n
24:6 60
24:7 105
30:6 95n
31:9 29

Ezekiel
1:7 154
1:13 154n
1:24 154
1:26 153, 154
1:26-28 154
1:27 154

1:28 82, 154, 155
3:23 82
8:2 154n
9:1 61
9:5 61
9:7 61
11:5 146
11:23 72n
33:27 156
34:11 67
34:16a 67
34:17 67
34:22 67
37:12-13 76
37:26-27 57, 72
43:2 154

Daniel
2:47 151
7:9 63n, 76n, 82, 154
7:9-10 76, 154n
7:10-12 63n
7:13 30, 30n, 152, 152n, 153
7:13-14 152n
7:18 63n
7:22 63n
7:27 152n
8:18 153
9:6 88
10:6 154
10:16 67, 154
12:7 27

Hosea
6:11 60
11:1 29
13:4 113, 114, 114n

Joel
2:13 73
2:28-32 123

2:32 90, 92, 124, 125, 128
3:11-14 60

Amos
3:7 88
9:11 129n
9:12 129n

Jonah
4:2 73

Micah
5:4a 28n

Nahum
1:3 30n, 60

Zephaniah
1:3 60
1:18 60

Zechariah
1:6 88
2:5 106, 142
3:2 32
7:13 25n
9:10 25n
12:1 24
12:10 97n, 152n
14:4 72n
14:5 157
14:5b 61
14:7 72n
14:8 72n
14:9 141, 157

Malachi
2:10 12
2:17 63, 63n
3:1 58, 63, 63n
3:1a 58n
4:5 58, 58n

Matthew
1:18 xxvi, 58, 71,
199, 200
1:18-23 191
1:20 xxvi, 58, 71,
200
1:21 28, 199, 203
1:21-23 66, 112n,
142n
1:23 28, 59n, 142,
183, 199
1:25 199
2:4-6 27
2:6 27
2:8-11 27
3:4 58
3:7 223n
3:13 58
3:16-17 224n
4:2 192
4:8 102
5:18 65
6:24 140
7:15 xvi, xxiv
7:16 xxiv
7:21-23 xxiv, 63,
215n
8:18-27 62n
8:25 62
8:26 61
9:6 30n
10:40 28
11:14 58n
11:27 30n, 70n
12:8 60n
12:31 218
13:24-30 60
13:36-42 60
13:43 60
14:24 61
14:30 62
14:33 62
16:16 41n
16:24 62

16:27 95
17:1 223n
17:12-13 58n
19:28 30n, 63, 63n
19:29-30 63n
21:9 91n
21:13 64
21:14 64
21:15 64
21:16a 64
21:37-38 30n
21:42 143n
22:23-45 69n
22:31-32 69n
22:36 69n
22:42 69n
23:39 91n
24:5 xxiv, xxv
24:24 xxv
24:30 30n, 153n
24:30-31 60
24:36 30n
25:31 61, 63
25:32-46 63n
26:42 224n
26:63 60n
26:64 60n
26:64-65 60
27:9-10 26n
27:46 179
28:18 153n
28:19 30n, 219,
222, 223
28:20 142

Mark
1:4 58
1:9 58
2:5-7 xxvii, 30n
2:10 30n
2:28 60n
3:14 124n
4:35-41 62n
4:39 61

9:11-13 58n
9:37 28
10:45 203
11:9 91n
11:10 91n
11:17 64
11:32 20n
12:6 30n
12:18-37 69n
12:26 69n
12:28 69n
12:32 69n
12:35 69n
13:26 30n
13:32 30n
14:61-64 60
15:39 19n

Luke
1:17 58n
1:25 199
1:26-27 199
1:34 199
1:35 57, 199n, 200,
200n, 220
1:42 91n
1:47 198
1:68 91n
2:42 192
2:51 xxviin, 192
2:52 192
3:2 58
3:21 58
5:5 66, 67
5:6-7 66
5:24 30n
6:5 60n
8:22-25 62n
8:24 61
9:26 62n, 118n
9:48 28
10:22 30n, 70n
13:35 91n
16:15 123

4:25 214
5:1 208
5:8 203
5:9 179, 207
5:9-10 203, 204
5:12 201
5:15 192
8:3 29
8:14 29n
8:15 208
8:23 208
9:5 118, 125n, 197n
9:21-23 128
10:9 31n, 90, 111, 125
10:12 91
10:12-14 111
10:13 31n, 90
14:10 95
14:11 95n

1 Corinthians
1:2 208
1:3 111n
1:8 94n
2:8 106
2:8b 179n, 197n
2:11 217, 220
3:8 77n
4:1 88
6:19 219
8:5 222
8:6 92n
10:26 92n
11:19 xivn
12:3 125
12:3b 92n
12:11 217, 218, 220
14:21 92n
15:14-19 214
15:28 xxviin
15:42 211n
15:50 211n
15:51 211n

15:52 211n
15:53 211n
15:54 211n

2 Corinthians
1:2 111n
1:2-3 179n
1:3 91n
3:17 89
4:4 72, 106, 130
4:6 72, 106
5:11 95
5:17 106n, 208
5:18 179n
5:18-19 179
5:19 179n
5:21 203
7:1 96
8:9 29
10:17 105
11:3 xvin
11:4 xvin, xxi, xxiii, 219n
11:13-15 xvin
11:31 91n
12:8-9 111
12:9 126
13:14 74n, 219

Galatians
1:1 74n
1:3 111n
1:6-8 xvin
1:7 88
1:8 xv
1:9 xv
1:10 88
1:12 96
2:4 xv
4:4 29, 191
4:5 208
4:6 89
4:8 222

Ephesians
1:2 93n, 111n
1:3 91n, 93n
1:5 208
1:15 93n
1:17 93n
1:20-23 91
2:1-3 207
2:3-4 207
2:5 206
2:8 98, 206
2:8a 207
2:8b 207
2:12 208
2:20 143n
2:21 93n
3:11 93n
3:12 223n
3:14 93n
4:1 93n
4:5 93n
4:6 91
4:7 98
4:8-10 214
4:17 93n
4:30 217, 218
5:2 202, 203
5:8 93n
5:10 93n
5:17 93n
5:19 93n
5:20 93n
5:21 95
5:27 xxiin
6:1 93n
6:4 93n
6:6 88
6:7 93n
6:8 93n
6:10 93n
6:21 93n
6:23 93n
6:24 93n

General Index

on John 8:24 22n
on John 8:58 22n
on John 10:30 79
on John 14:28 xxviin, 3
on John 17:3 24n
on John 17:11 & 22 79
on John 20:28 82n, 83n
on Acts 1:8 121n
on 1 Corinthians 15:28 xxviin
on 1 Corinthians 15:50 211n
on Philippians 2:5-8 34n
on Colossians 1:15 2, 3, 106, 107, 109
on Colossians 2:9 110n
on Hebrews 1:6 134n, 136
on 1 Peter 3:18 211n
on Revelation 1:1 3
on Revelation 1:7 161n
on Revelation 3:14 3
on the Spirit 217
Jesus Seminar 46
Judaism xxiin
Justification
definition of 208

Kimball, Spencer W. 37n
Krishna 9, 43, 52, 52n

Ladd, G. E. 151, 154
Longenecker, Richard N. 124n, 127
LXX. *See* Septuagint

Mahāyāna Buddhism 53
Marcion xvii, xviin
Mary
as co-mediator xxin
as mediatrix xxiin
as mediatrix of graces xxiin
as Queen over all things xxiin
Masonry. *See* Freemasonry
Mayor, J. B. 141n
McConkie, Bruce R. 4, 166n
Metzger, Bruce 83n, 107n
Modalism

definition of 12, 18n, 78n, 179, 224n
Monism
definition of 38n, 50, 167
Monophysites. *See* Monophysitism
Monophysitism 195n, 196
Moon, Sun Myung 10, 11, 176, 177
Morris, Leon 25n, 64n, 74n, 75n, 78n, 81, 82, 136n
Moulton, J. H. 117n, 116n
Muhammad 9, 43

Nestorianism 194n, 196, 196n
Nestorians. *See* Nestorianism
Nestorius 194n
Nicaea
council of xiii, xxvn, 2n, 194, 195
Noetus 18n, 78n, 180n

Ontological Christology
definition of xxvi
Orthodoxy
definition of xiv

Pantheism
definition of 23. *See also* Absolute Pantheism
Patripassionism
definition of 179
Philo
logos of 16n
Polycarp xiii, xvii, xviin
Polytheism
definition of 4n
Prabhupada, Swami 52
Praxeas 18n, 180n
Price, Fred 47
Propitiation
definition of 201, 203

Raible, Christopher Gist 181
Ramanuja 50
Reconciliation
definition of 203

About the Author

Steven Tsoukalas earned the M.Div. from Gordon-Conwell Theological Seminary. He has taught courses at Gordon-Conwell in the field of cults-related Christian apologetics and evangelism, and has been researching religious movements since 1985. Steven is Executive Director of Sound Doctrine Ministries in Exeter, New Hampshire, and is the author of *Masonic Rites and Wrongs: An Examination of Freemasonry* (Phillipsburg, N.J.: Presbyterian and Reformed Publishing Company, 1995).